The Sustainable MBA

The Manager's guide to green Business

Giselle Weybrecht

A John Wiley and Sons, Ltd, Publication

Library of Congress Cataloging-in-Publication Data
A catalogue record for this book is available from the Library of Congress.

British Library Cataloguing in Publication Data
A catalogue record for this book is available from the British Library

ISBN 9780470741146 (HB/)

Typeset in 11/15 and ITC Garamond by Macmillan Publishing Solutions.
Printed and bound in Great Britain by TJ International Ltd, Padstow, Cornwall, an ISO14001
Environmental Management System Accredited Company, using vegetable-based ink and FSC paper.

FSC
Mixed Sources
Product group from well-managed
forests and other controlled sources

Cert no. TT-COC-002785
www.fsc.org
© 1996 Forest Stewardship Council

*Para mis abuelos
Elena y Antonio Paulino,
por sus vidas llenas de entusiasmo,
alegria y entrega a los demas.*

Contents

Contents

Contents

Preface

I like cows. So when I saw a book titled 'The Purple Cow' in the business section of a bookstore in Melbourne, Australia, it drew me in like a magnet. In it the author, Seth Godin says, "Don't worry about being perfect, instead be remarkable."

When I became engaged in the field of sustainable development in my teens I realized three things. First, that we as individuals can solve pretty much any problem if we want to, provided we put our minds to it and work together. Second, people want to be engaged, they want to be part of something bigger than themselves. Third, even though there is so much knowledge out there, it is so spread out and often so difficult to understand that people get scared off. So when it comes to sustainable development, most people want to get involved, want to do their part, they just don't know how to.

Sustainability has become an incredibly vast and complex field. Specialists have sprung up everywhere to help people understand what it all means. But for sustainability to truly become a reality everyone needs to understand its language. It has never been about getting things perfect, it has always been about getting people to engage, to do something, to get started.

After participating in the preparatory and follow up meetings to the World Summit on Sustainable Development (and having the chance to speak at the event in the plenary on water issues on behalf of youth), I started following the work of the business caucus led by the WBCSD and the ICC. In 2005, I started an MBA at London Business School to learn more about the business sector and the role it could play in moving the sustainable development agenda forward.

While there, many students would come up to me asking about sustainability and the UN where I had spent several years. They were interested in going into careers in this area and curious about what it all meant and how it related to them. But as the two years went by, nearly all of them went on to 'standard' post MBA jobs. Although they were driven and passionate, they were forced to make choices between the high paying typical post MBA jobs, and the often lower paying sustainability jobs that were available at the time.

This, however, wasn't the problem. Some estimates state that over 60% of today's business leaders have MBAs, not to mention those that have undergraduate business degrees or have passed through executive business training. The majority of these students have little or no exposure to sustainability in their classes. How can sustainability really be taken seriously if every year thousands of new managers are entering the ranks of business without being exposed to these issues, or taught how to recognize and evaluate the risks and take advantage of the opportunities? This also goes beyond just business students; it includes future law makers, government officials, architects and engineers. Imagine the change a whole new generation of managers and leaders could have on the business sector if they were armed with the knowledge and the tools to explore sustainability in their businesses and their jobs, whatever job that may be.

During the second year of the MBA my dear friend and fellow student Ariel Speicher agreed to explore these issues with me. We set out to understand why sustainability was not being addressed in the curriculum and what could be done to change that. We found that in order to really reach all the students, and not just those who were already interested in these issues, the information needed to be embedded into the material already being taught. If the topics weren't being introduced then how could students know their importance?

So rather than wait and hope for things to change, I starting working on a booklet that would be made available to the students and alumni that would give clear information on what sustainability was and how managers could use it. It would be organized according to the different classes taught in an MBA so that students could easily follow it and use it as part of their core courses. It would be full of tips, tools and useful advice on how to bring these ideas to whatever career they chose to enter post graduation.

The idea was well received by students and professors, in addition to alumni and young working managers, that as graduation arrived I started exploring ways to scale up the idea. Rosemary at Wiley believed in the project and provided the opportunity to think big and turn the booklet idea into a book. I then set off to interview over 100 CEOs, business leaders, sustainability experts from NGOs and international organizations, academics and students from around the world in order to make the book as relevant and useful as possible.

I hope that this book will be used by students, young managers, their bosses, green teams, and anyone who is interested to learn what sustainable business is all about, in order to get engaged and apply it to their jobs. Hopefully we will have a whole new generation of business leaders who speak the language of sustainable business and are ready to really move things forward in remarkable new ways.

Acknowledgments

So many people have been engaged and supportive of this project, too many to list here. I apologize in advance for those names I will inevitably miss. First a big thank you to Alison Clayson and Bryan Mundell who have always supported me with all my crazy ideas. Bryan, thank you for patiently reading through all my very rough drafts and giving such fantastic feedback. Ariel Speicher, thank you for believing and supporting this project from the beginning. Thanks to Mark Mullens, Debra Zupancic, Al Martine, Andrew Likierman and Michael Kelly who also supported this from day one. Thank you to Connie Giordano for her editing magic and Paul Woolfenden for his inspirational chats and fantastic illustrations.

Over the past year I have interviewed over 100 CEOs, business leaders, sustainability experts, authors, NGOs, international organizations, academic and students from around the world. Thank you to the following people for agreeing to be interviewed, for reading through drafts, for sharing your passion for these issues and for providing various bits of inspiration: Kevin Roberts, Richard Hytner, Jane Kendall, Roger Kennedy and Fleur Diston at Saatchi and Saatchi, Roger Adams at ACCA, Sean Ansett at At Stake Advisors, Anders Aspling at GRLI, Roger Bancroft at GreenEarth Cleaning, Shima Barakat and Shai Vyakarnam at University of Cambridge, Leeora Black and Gail Rehbein at ACCSR, Richard Boele at Banarra, Gib Bulloch and Peter Lacy at Accenture, Alice Chapple at Forum for the Future, David Collison at University of Dundee, Jackson Carroll at McKinsey, Peggy Cunningham at Queens' University, Kim Custard, Nancy Parker, Jeremy Lardeau and Andrew Smith at PWC, Rebecca Dixon and Susanna Jacobson at Mercer, John Elkington at Volans, Jed Emerson and Lila Preston at GenerationIM,

Neil Earnshaw at Enviroman, Stephanos Fotiou, Cornis Lugt, Peter Graham and Sonia Valdivia at UNEPTIE, Katie Fry, Maggie Brenneke and Jodie Thorpe at Sustainability, Martin Hancock at Westpac, Alan Knight and Daniel Waistell at Accountability, David Logan at Corporate Citizenship, Adam Ognall at UKSIF, Nick Robins at HSBC, Richard Peters at NAB, Simon Pickard at EABIS, Stephanie Robertson at SiPMACT, John Scott at PepsiCo, Graham Sim at GE, Laura Somoggi at Unilever, Mark Wade at Shell, Shauna Sadowski at Clif Bar, Robert Tacon at UNEPFI, John Talberth at Redefining Progress, Katherine Teh - White at Futureye, Karen Wilson and Bert Twaalfhoven at EFER, Kameel Virjee at the World Bank, Anne Wallin at Dow Chemicals, Will Oulton at FTSE, Brad Whitaker at Schlumberger, Justin Golbach at The Aspen Institute, David Roth at WPP, author Bob Willard, members of the AIESEC and OIKOS networks, Jeremy Higgs, Ramanie Kunanayagam and Scott Houston, Ila Panik, Svetlana Ignatieva, Peter Arias, Scott McCormick, Sayida Vanenburg, David Murray, Gavin Murray, Henna Jain, Jay Walljasper, Leif Holmberg, Malcolm Fox, Aleksandar Maricic, Sanne Martens, Ed Perkins, Pete Spark and Adrian Ruiz Carvajal.

A big thank you to Dave Challis, Katherine Madden and the World Business Council for Sustainable Development Future Leaders Team, to the incredible global alumni community from Bearhs Environmental Leadership Programme at Berkeley (including Bill Sonnenschein) and to the team and many of my fellow members of Net Impact around the world.

To the London Business School Community including all the students and alumni who took the time to speak and email me. Thank you to all the professors and staff who helped, especially John Mullins, Andrew Scott, Andrea Masini, Caitlin Anstee, Michael Blowfield, Dennis Oswald, Rob Goffee, Anne Sandford, Gareth Howells, Mohan Madireddi and John Stopford. A special thank you to Professor Craig Smith and Accenture.

Thanks to Claire Andrews I was introduced to Rosemary Nixon. It is because of the whole team at Wiley that you hold this book in your hands today.

A little thank you to the dolphins at the Curacao Dolphin Academy, the guide dog puppies in Cambridgeshire, the kangaroos in Oz and my mountain bike who all provided hours of inspiration and constructive distraction time.

Thank you to Howard and Joyce Mills for reading through draft after draft. The biggest thank you goes to my family, to my parents Earl and Elena Weybrecht, my brother Michael and my aunt Carmen for their patience, love and continued support. Last but not least, without you Rich I wouldn't have been able to do any of it.

It is a great time to be a manager. People want to get engaged and involved in the world around them, they just don't know how to. The world is a lot more colourful with sustainability in it and I hope this book will add even more colour to the mix.

This book is dedicated to my grandparents (the dedication is written in Spanish); To my grandparents Elena and Antonio Paulino, for their lives full of enthusiasm, joy and generosity to others.

PART 1

SETTING THE SCENE

About this book
What is sustainability?
What does this mean for business?
The sustainability journey
Getting started

1 About this Book

'Your Chinese clock radio sounds, waking you up with news from the BBC, and you slip out of your Egyptian cotton sheets and into the shower. You dry off and put on underwear from El Salvador, jeans from Lesotho, and your favourite blue shirt from Sri Lanka. A cup of Tanzanian coffee, some Brazilian orange juice, and you're off to work in your Japanese car - assembled in Kentucky, powered by gasoline from Saudi Arabia, Nigeria, and Russia. Good morning!'

WORLDCHANGING

The world we live in today is ever shrinking, and although increased communication and globalization play their part, they are not the only reasons. There is a growing realization that everything and everyone has become very interdependent. With almost 7 billion people living on the planet, regardless of who you are, where you live or what you do, you are impacted by and have an impact on the health of the planet, society and the world economy. The decisions we make as employees, as consumers and as citizens on a daily basis impact both business and the wider society.

Consider this: People are wondering what is happening to the bees. Bees play a crucial role in the supply of the world's food as they are essential for the pollination of one third of the world's crops, valued at

$ 215 billion annually worldwide. Unfortunately, no one knows exactly why bee colonies are disappearing, and few people seem particularly bothered with it . . . yet. Since we are so dependent on these little creatures for the food we eat, perhaps we should be more concerned about the worldwide loss of these bee colonies. While there appears to be no single definitive cause for this potential disaster, intervention by man and industry through the use of pesticides and stress to colonies are considered to be factors.

The world's challenges are also business challenges. Not only do environmental, economic and social issues impact the ability of a business to operate now and in the future, but they impact their employees, the communities in which they operate, their customers, the sources of their materials.

For this reason, managers and employees at all levels and in all types of organizations are placing greater emphasis on sustainability, and are increasingly interested in bringing sustainability culture and tools into their daily operations. Although many start because of a desire to make a positive impact on the world, they are finding that the results can be significant in terms of real business benefits, such as reduced costs and liabilities, greater service quality, higher customer satisfaction and improved corporate image.

Nevertheless, many managers face considerable uncertainty over what they can, or should be doing, to enhance their environmental and social practices and sustainability goals. They often believe that applying new tools to address these challenges may be good for society, but not necessarily for the business itself. A lack of understanding of the potential benefits, fear of moving in new directions, confusion over the range of tools available to address sustainability issues, overwhelming and often-contradictory amounts of information are among the reasons why many are slow to act.

This book aims to give managers and individuals the knowledge and tools to be able to apply sustainability practices to their business in a way that is both profitable to the business and to society as a whole. The book does not appoint

blame for the challenges we face, but instead focuses on how businesses and employees can take action to be part of the solution.

Imagine what you could do as a company if you had 7 billion employees all pulling in the right direction?

Who is *The Sustainable MBA* for and why should I read it?

This book is aimed at managers, both experienced and new, who are interested or curious to know more about the field of business and sustainability and how they can apply these ideas to their jobs, regardless of what they do or where in the world they do it. Because it provides an introduction to these issues, it will be of interest if you fall into one, and probably more than one, of the following groups:

- ❑ I am in a *management position* and need to better understand what sustainability is but don't have the time to spend hours researching. I understand that I can make an impact through my work and my decisions, but am not sure how to.
- ❑ I am an *entrepreneur* and am interested in starting my own business and want to incorporate some sort of sustainability elements into it, either as part of my core offering or as part of the way I do business. I understand that sustainability provides a range of exciting new opportunities that I want to understand and explore.
- ❑ I am a *CEO* or board member and want to learn more about how I can move my business to be more sustainable. I understand that this is becoming the new business reality and that business success and sustainability are linked. I understand that in order to really move forward in this area, CEO leadership is required.

❑ I run or work for a ***small business*** and am overwhelmed by the amount of information out there on sustainability. I want to do something but am not sure what to do and where to start. I understand that I can tap into sustainability opportunities even with my limited budget and time and that these tools can help strengthen my overall business.

❑ I am an ***employee*** where my day-to-day job doesn't currently have anything to do with sustainability, but I think it could, and I want to know how I can incorporate it into my job. Regardless, I understand that sustainability tools and strategies will increasingly become part of everyone's day-to-day job and I want to understand what it is all about.

❑ I work in ***sustainability*** but mostly spend my time in one area and am not as familiar with everything else happening in this vast and growing field. My job rarely involves stepping back and thinking about the big picture.

❑ I am a ***teacher*** or a ***trainer*** and want to incorporate sustainability messages into my teaching lessons. I understand that if the new generation of employees and managers are aware of these issues, this could have a huge impact.

❑ I am a ***student*** and want to know more about this issue. I hope someday to be working for a company that takes sustainability seriously. I am passionate about these issues and want to make sure I direct that passion into an area where I can really make an impact.

❑ I am a ***consumer*** and want to make the right choices on a day-to-day basis. I understand that the products I buy help to support either good business practices or bad ones. I find it difficult to sort through quickly and easily and would like some help.

❑ *I* just want to know more about sustainability, but am overwhelmed by all the information out there and not sure where to begin.

Regardless of whether or not you have the word 'sustainability' in your job description, it is increasingly important that you understand what sustainability means, both as a concept, and as a set of decisions and actions that impact your organization. Few jobs require or even provide the chance to step back and think about the big pictures. So, regardless of your job function or the industry you work in, you will find that this book has some information directly relevant to you, while also introducing you to some of the tools that other industries are exploring.

What you will find in *The Sustainable MBA?*

The Sustainable MBA equips individual employees with the tools to be able to take sustainability from talk to action; to understand what is happening in this area, sell these ideas to others on their team and implement them. For this reason the book provides a vast amount of information and resources on the topic including:

- *An overview of sustainability tools:* The book provides an overview of the work being done in sustainability. While sustainability is an interdisciplinary subject, the typical MBA, the typical business and employee expertise and training is still, for the most part, divided by functional areas. This is why the book is organized to follow the typical MBA.
- *Business case:* For every tool and idea introduced, the business case is presented to help you understand the advantages it could bring and to present a case to sell it to your team or managers.
- *How tos and guides to implementation:* The book does more than simply outline the tools and ideas involved in sustainability, it also provides information on how to implement them, with links to resources for more information and help.
- *Challenges:* The book outlines the challenges involved in pursuing different sustainability strategies in order to give managers a 'heads up' on what to expect. At the same time, the challenges presented

act as a call to the next generation of corporate leaders to build their careers around tackling these problems.

- **Knowledge from experts around the world:** The book draws on a vast amount of information and research that has been undertaken in this area by groups internationally as well as over 100 interviews with students, professors, experts, thought leaders, businesses, CEOs, entrepreneurs, NGOs and international organizations working and interested in this area.
- **Tips for sustainability champions:** Whether you are looking to be a sustainability champion at work or as a consumer, the book is filled with tips for individuals and teams who are looking to explore some of these tools including handy lists and lessons learned. They build the case that sustainability and business profit and success are inextricably linked together, rather than diametrically opposed to one another.
- **Many additional resources:** Because the field of sustainability is a complex and changing field, the book contains many links to organizations and websites where you can find up-to-date information, statistics, best practice and information. The focus is on international websites because they change less frequently, and because they often link to other national or local initiatives happening in countries around the world.
- **Trends and new ideas:** Last but not least, the book presents many exciting trends happening around the world in sustainability—things you want to keep an eye out for.

How *The Sustainable MBA* is organized

The **Introduction** sets the scene with the basics on what sustainability is, what this means for business, what the sustainability journey looks like and how to get started. It also provides tips on how to recognize leading companies, how to sell sustainability to your team and how to get past excuses.

The **Core Topics** present information on sustainability as it relates to the main topics introduced in a typical MBA programme and the core functional areas of a business; *Accounting, Economics, Ethics, Entrepreneurship, Finance, Marketing, Operations, Organizational Behaviour* and *Strategy*.

The **Tools** provide information on how to conduct audits and assessments, as well as a guide on how to *green the office and buildings* you work in. Other tools are spread out through the book, and all present guidelines, techniques and concepts that a business can use to incorporate sustainability into their operations.

The **Wrapping It Up** section provides ideas on how *you as an individual* can make a difference, as an employee, a consumer and a citizen, and how your actions in each of these spheres has an impact on sustainable business. The section also provides a look at what *the future* may bring as well as some *tips for moving forward*.

Finally the **Who, What, Where, How** section provides some additional resources for individuals looking to learn more about who has a role to play in sustainability, how different industries are involved, and links to organizations working in sustainability business in different regions around the world.

Ideas on how to use this book

There are many different ways an individual or a business can use this book to explore sustainable business options.

- ❑ Take this book and read it from cover to cover or dip in and out to learn more about the issues that interest you.
- ❑ Provide copies to members of your team to raise the general awareness in your office on these issues.
- ❑ Start a brainstorming session around the areas that your business could explore.

❏ Use it as a reference guide when you are interested in finding out more.

❏ Organize a short or long course around this information.

❏ Use it as a way to learn more about what business is doing to make smarter choices as a consumer.

Planet Earth fact sheet

- There are over 6 700 000 000 people in the world. The world's population is predicted to reach 7 billion early in 2012 and top 9 billion in 2050, with the majority of the increase taking place in developing countries. Median age: total: 28.4 years.
- These people live in 195 countries in the world (192 of them are members of the UN). Much of this population is concentrated in coastal cities with several hundred million living within 1 metre elevation of mean sea level.
- They speak 6 000 to 7 000 different languages, half of which are at risk of disappearing. There are 878 properties on the UNESCO World Heritage list, a list of sites around the world considered to have outstanding universal value.
- The earth is 70.8 % Water and 29.2 % Land. Of all water, 97 % is salt water and only 3 % is freshwater. Of the 3 % only 5 % is readily available, mostly in underground aquifers. Nearly 20 % of the population lacks access to safe drinking water and 40 % are without adequate sanitation. By 2025, 40 % of the world will live in water-scarce regions.
- If the GDP of countries is compared to the annual revenue of companies, then in 2008 38 companies would have been in the top 100 countries.
- Over two-thirds of the world's 785 million illiterate adults are women.
- One million people become new mobile subscribers everyday. Some 85 % of them live in emerging markets.[1] More than 2 billion mobile phones are in use around the world. Over 1 581 571 589 people use the Internet.

- Ten largest urban agglomerations: Tokyo (Japan)-35 676 000; New York-Newark (US)-19 040 000; Ciudad de Mexico (Mexico)-19 028 000; Mumbai (India)-18 978 000; Sao Paulo (Brazil)-18 845 000; Delhi (India)-15 926 000; Shanghai (China)-14 987 000; Kolkata (India)-14 787 000; Dhaka (Bangladesh)-13 458 000; Buenos Aires (Argentina)-12 795 000 (2007).
- The world's population drives 600 million cars, while more than 1 billion bicycles are in use.
- Forests cover 30 % of the planet's total land area, the ten most forest rich countries are Russia, Brazil, Canada, the US, China, Australia, Congo, Indonesia, Peru and India.
- There are at least 15 million other species on the planet. Nearly 30 % of all medicines found in pharmacies were developed from wild plants and animals.

2 What Is Sustainability?

'You can resist an invading army; you cannot resist an idea whose time has come'

VICTOR HUGO

The basics

In 1983, the World Commission on Environment and Development (also referred to as the Brundtland Commission named after its chair Gro Harlem Brundtland), was convened by the United Nations to address growing concern 'about the accelerating deterioration of the human environment and natural resources and the consequences of that deterioration for economic and social development'. In 1987, the Commission's report, known as the Brundtland Report or Our Common Future, alerted the world to the urgency of making progress towards economic development that could be sustained without depleting natural resources or harming the environment.The report provides the world with the most widely quoted definition of sustainable development:

> 'development that meets the needs of the present without compromising the ability of future generations to meet their own needs. It contains within it two key concepts:
>
> the concept of needs, in particular the essential needs of the world's poor, to which overriding priority should be given;

and the idea of limitations imposed by the state of technology and social organization on the environment's ability to meet present and future needs.'

As the International Institute for Sustainable Development put it, 'Sustainable development focuses on improving the quality of life for all of the Earth's citizens without increasing the use of natural resources beyond the capacity of the environment to supply them indefinitely. It requires an understanding that inaction has consequences and that we must find innovative ways to change institutional structures and influence individual behaviour. It is about taking action, changing policy and practice at all levels, from the individual to the international.'[2] They provided a variation of the Brundtland definition aimed at business:

'For the business enterprise, sustainable development means adopting business strategies and activities that meet the needs of the enterprise and its stakeholders today while protecting, sustaining and enhancing the human and natural resources that will be needed in the future'.

The idea of sustainable development is nothing new. Societies over time have had to learn to balance social, environmental and economic concerns in order to prosper and to continue for generations. At its core, sustainable development is about creating the appropriate balance and interaction between:

- *Social Equity*, which refers to issues such as human rights, peace, security, justice, gender equality and cultural diversity among others. (Also referred to as People.)
- *Environmental Protection*, which refers to the natural environment including water, energy, agriculture, biodiversity, fish, forests and air. (Also referred to as Planet.)
- *Economic Development*, which refers to an understanding of the limits and potential of economic growth and includes issues such as poverty reduction, responsible consumption, corporate responsibility,

energy efficiency and conservation, waste management, employment and education. (Also referred to as Profit.)

Two other elements tie social, environmental and economics issues together. These are:

- *Governance*, which acts as an overarching principle that provides the context for sustainable development to occur by promoting structures at the local, national and international levels that are transparent and effective.
- *Culture*, including our shared attitudes, values, goals and practices provides the framework for sustainability as it guides and shapes our day-to-day behaviour.

All three issues are intertwined and affect each other. As outdoor gear and apparel retailer REI's CSR Manager put it, 'We don't distinguish between environmental and social challenges around sustainability for business. In fact, all these issues intermingle. Eventually, someplace along the way, there's really no such thing as an environmental problem that doesn't have social consequences, and there's really no such thing as a social problem that doesn't really fold into or have dimensions that are environmental.'[3] Sustainability therefore involves seeing the world as a system and looks at how things interact within that system.

Other definitions

Many models have been developed around the world by business, NGOs and international organizations to provide other ways of understanding sustainability, based on the balancing of social, environmental and economics:

The Five Capital Model looks at different kinds of capital from which we derive the goods and services we need to improve the quality of our lives:

- *Natural Capital* is any stock or flow of energy and material that produces goods and services.

- *Human Capital* consists of people's health, knowledge, skills and motivation.
- *Social Capital* concerns the institutions that help us maintain and develop human capital in partnership with others; e.g. families, communities, businesses, trade unions, schools and voluntary organizations.
- *Manufactured Capital* comprises material goods or fixed assets which contribute to the production process rather than being the output itself; e.g. tools, machines and buildings.
- *Financial Capital* plays an important role in our economy, enabling the other types of Capital to be owned and traded. However, unlike the other types, it has no real value itself but is representative of natural, human, social or manufactured capital; e.g. shares, bonds or banknotes. (www.forumforthefuture.org)

The Natural Step framework derives from systems thinking; recognizing that what happens in one part of a system affects every other part. It takes an upstream approach to sustainability and addresses problems at the source. The framework begins by understanding the broader system within which problems occur and developing effective, durable solutions to the environmental and social issues of the new century. According to The Natural Step, 'Creating a sustainable world means creating new ways for people to live and thrive—while keeping the planet's ecosystems and the global social tissue healthy and able to sustain us and future generations.' (www.naturalstep.org)

The Earth Charter (2000) initiated by Maurice Strong (Chairman of the Rio Summit) and Mikhail Gorbachev was the result of a call from the World Commission on Environment and Development for a 'universal declaration' to guide the transition to sustainable development. It is the product of a decade long, worldwide, cross-cultural conversation about common goals and shared values. It looks at respecting and caring for the earth's community through ecological integrity, social and economic justice, democracy non-violence and peace, among other things. (www.earthcharter.org)

The Ecological Footprint is a resource management tool that measures how much land and water area a human population requires to produce the resources it consumes and to absorb its wastes using prevailing technology. It can be used by a country, a region, a city, a business or an individual. It now takes more than one year and four months for the Earth to regenerate what is used in a single year. As long as our governments and business leaders do not know how much of nature's capacity is being used or how resource use compares to existing stocks, overshoot may go undetected—increasing the ecological deficit and reducing nature's capacity to meet society's needs. (www.footprintnetwork.org)

Underlying many of these models for defining sustainability are several principles that guide accountability and responsibility:

- *The Precautionary principle* states that 'In order to protect the environment, the precautionary approach shall be widely applied by States according to their capabilities. Where there are threats of serious or irreversible damage, lack of full scientific certainty shall not be used as a reason for postponing cost effective measures to prevent environmental damage.' (www.pprinciple.net)
- *The Proximity principle* says that the treatment and disposal of waste should take place as near as possible to the point of production as is technically and environmentally possible.
- *The Polluter-pays principle* says that the cost of pollution should be covered by those who cause it. It is generally recognized as a principle of International Environmental Law and a fundamental part of the environmental policy of both the OECD and the EC. (www.eoearth.org/article/Polluter_pays_principle)

The number of terms used to better understand and communicate what sustainability means to business and society and how to take action seems to grow by the day. The 'sustainability glossary' includes concepts such as corporate social responsibility, corporate citizenship, tools such as eco-design and anything starting with the word green. The choice of terms is usually made by the individual, the company or the country, based on the strategy they are implementing, the issues that are most important to them, the tools they decide to use or simply on what they believe speaks most to their people. **Although the myriad of terms represent a variety of concepts, principles, distinct tools and ways of understanding the issues, they all come together in a field that in this book we call Sustainability.**

Sustainable development: a global effort

'Earth provides enough to satisfy every man's need, but not every man's greed'

Mahatma Gandhi

The actions that the business sector are taking in sustainability are part of global efforts to move the sustainable development agenda forward in conjunction with national governments, NGOs and other major groups recognized by the UN. Several major international conferences over the past three decades have focused on sustainable development.

The first conference to focus the world's attention on the environment was the UN Stockholm Conference on the Human Environment in 1972. This led to the creation of national agencies for the environment, as well as the UN Environment Program (www.unep.org) which today has many programmes focused on business and industry (www.uneptie.org).

1972–1992: During this time, several major international conferences and agreements started taking shape including the Convention on International Trade in Endangered Species of Flora and Fauna, Convention on the Law of the Sea, and the first global meeting to link environment and human settlements (Habitat).

1992–2000: Twenty years after the initial international conference, the world reconvened in 1992 for the UN Conference on Environment and Development, more popularly known as the Earth Summit, which took place in Rio di Janeiro, Brazil. One its major accomplishments was the development of Agenda 21, a comprehensive plan of action towards sustainable development to be executed globally, nationally and locally which still today is a good reference of the issues (www.un.org/esa/sustdev/documents/agenda21). In the eight years that followed several international conferences were organized to focus on different aspects of sustainable development. This included the creation of new organizations such as the World Trade Organization, and events such as the World

Conference on Human Rights, The World Summit for Social Development and the signing of the Kyoto Protocol on Climate Change.

2002: Ten years after the Earth Summit, the world came together again in Johannesburg, South Africa for the World Summit on Sustainable Development which aimed at adopting concrete steps and identifying quantifiable targets for better implementation of Agenda 21. Attendees placed important focus on partnerships (in particular between the private and public sectors) and their role in development (www.johannesburgsummit.org).

2000–2015: In 2000, the United Nations Millennium Summit brought together world leaders who committed their nations to a new global partnership to reduce extreme poverty and set out a series of time-bound targets, with a deadline of 2015, which have become known as the Millennium Development Goals. The eight goals (www.un.org/millenniumgoals) are:

Goal 1: Eradicate extreme poverty and hunger
Goal 2: Achieve universal primary education
Goal 3: Promote gender equality and empower women
Goal 4: Reduce child mortality
Goal 5: Improve maternal health
Goal 6: Combat HIV/AIDS, malaria and other diseases
Goal 7: Ensure environmental sustainability
Goal 8: Develop a global partnership for development.

The Millennium Project was commissioned by the United Nations Secretary-General in 2002 to develop a concrete action plan for the world to achieve the Millennium Development Goals. (www.unmillenniumproject.org)

2000–today: The UN Global Compact was launched in 2000 as both a policy platform and a practical framework for companies that are committed to sustainability and responsible business practices. It is the largest corporate citizenship and sustainability initiative in the world with over 4700 corporate participants and stakeholders from over 130 countries. Compact members support broader UN goals, such as the Millennium Development goals, and also on mainstreaming its ten principles in business activities around the world:

1. *Human rights*
   Businesses should support and respect the protection of internationally proclaimed human rights;

(continued)

And make sure that they are not complicit in human rights abuses.

2. *Labour standards*

Businesses should uphold the freedom of association and the effective recognition of the right to collective bargaining;

the elimination of all forms of forced and compulsory labour;

the effective abolition of child labour; and

the elimination of discrimination in respect of employment and occupation.

3. *Environment*

Businesses should support a precautionary approach to environmental challenges;

undertake initiatives to promote greater environmental responsibility; and

encourage the development and diffusion of environmentally friendly technologies.

4. *Anti-corruption*

Businesses should work against corruption in all its forms, including extortion and bribery. (www.unglobalcompact.org)

For a full timeline of Sustainable Development Conferences and events see (sdgateway.net/introsd/timeline.htm)

3 What does this Mean for Business?

'We are launching Ecomagination not because it is trendy or moral, but because it will accelerate our growth and make us more competitive'
GENERAL ELECTRIC CEO JEFF IMMELT[4]

You are certainly not alone if you are wondering, 'What does this have to do with my business?' However, the answer is simple: everything. In 1970, Milton Freidman said 'There is one and only one social responsibility of business—to use its resources and engage in activities designed to increase its profits so long as it stays within the rules of the game'. Nearly 40 years on, it is the way companies create those profits and the rules of the game that have changed as we realize both the necessity of adopting sustainability into everyday business practices, as well as the business opportunities this brings.

Today employees in organizations of all sizes and in all sectors are applying sustainability strategies to their work and are increasingly outspoken about the benefits. Those who are successful are building a business case for sustainability that suits the unique needs of their project, their initiative, their division or even their whole company. While the details of the sustainability strategy adopted by each business will vary, here are some compelling reasons why businesses are incorporating sustainability concepts into their day to day operations:

1.	Reduce Costs	6.	Attract Quality Employees
2.	Preserve Resources	7.	Satisfy Customer Needs
3.	Comply with Legislation	8.	Meet Stakeholder Expectations
4.	Enhance Reputation	9.	Attract Capital Investment
5.	Differentiate	10.	Capitalize on New Opportunities

Reduce costs: All companies have an interest in keeping costs in check. Sustainability provides a mechanism to reduce costs by focusing on using less resources (e.g. raw materials, energy, hazardous materials, people and water), making processes more efficient and minimizing or eliminating waste. Often these kinds of changes are referred to as 'low hanging fruit' or 'easy wins' because, at least initially, small changes can have a big impact. However, larger structural changes that can be more complicated and take a longer time to implement can also have the greatest impact in the long run. Procter & Gamble's programme to 'Design manufacturing waste out', for example, has saved the company over $ 500 million, and eliminated 2 million tonnes of waste.

Preserve resources: A key element of sustainable business practices is the preservation of the resource base. Companies are realizing that the raw materials that they depend on to produce their products are being threatened. For example, Brazil based Natura has a programme to sustainably use locally available raw materials that form the basis of its range of cosmetic products. Natura works closely with certifiers to guarantee the proper sourcing of its resources and to promote conservation through compliance with environmental and social guidelines.

Keep up with legislation: There are an increasing number of control mechanisms, regulations and standards being put in place that companies must follow. These cover a wide range of areas, including discharge of pollution, worker safety, product content, technical performance, labelling, requirements for reusing and recycling and ecosystem protection. Some of these, such as the Global Reporting Initiative, are currently voluntary but will increasingly be considered industry standards. Others are mandatory such as the European WEEE initiative or 'take back' laws, which require manufactures to take back all vehicles and electronics equipment sold in a particular country and recycle or dispose of them safely after use. It is likely that regulations and 'voluntary' standards will increase, both in number and stringency. In addition, the costs or consequences of not conforming, or leaving it to the last minute to conform, need to be considered in a business case.

Enhance reputation: As Warren Buffet puts it, 'it takes twenty years to build a reputation and five minutes to ruin it.' Today, those five minutes may feel more like 30 seconds. Petrobras, Brazil's national energy company, stunned by a series of catastrophic oil spills and other accidents around the turn of the century realized it would have to fundamentally change to protect its business and reputation. The company launched the biggest environmental and operational safety programme in Brazil's history, overhauled its operations and pushed cultural change from the top down. Environmental and social performance is now central to the firm's strategy and Petrobras is now recognized as a global leader in the oil and gas sector, led actively by its CEO.[5]

Differentiate: Being seen as sustainable can help differentiate your business. This can increase income by securing the loyalty of current customers and attract new ones resulting in increased market share. Businesses can grow revenue from new markets for sustainable products and services, and they can also grow market share through better quality products that benefit the customer. One example of this is MAS, a Sri Lankan apparel manufacturer with customers including Victoria's Secret, Gap, Marks & Spencer and Nike. In a market replete with low-cost rivals, MAS differentiated itself based on its exemplary employment practices (called 'Women Go Beyond'), its green plant and organic and fair trade products. This persuaded several western firms to choose it as a strategic partner.

Attract and retain quality employees: The CEO of IKEA Anders Dahlvig said that the pressure to be 'green' is 'now coming from underneath, from our co-workers themselves who expect us as a company to do more, faster'. Employees are more likely to feel proud of working for employers who take their responsibilities to society seriously. More businesses are realizing this, and are prioritizing these issues in order to maximize their capacity to attract and retain skilled and talented employees, which in turn increases their ability to innovate and compete.

Satisfy customer needs: Public expectations of what is possible are ever increasing. The eco-conscious consumer is a growing population who expects the brands they buy to meet their green standards while also meeting their product needs. Many organizations are getting involved in sustainability because their customers, clients or business partners are asking them to. People are increasingly looking to do business with companies that share their level of commitment.

Meet stakeholder expectations: In 2005 the then CEO of Wal-Mart, Lee Scott, recognized that the time when CEOs could sit in their towers and make decisions without consulting stakeholders was over. 'We thought we could sit in Bentonville, take care of customers, take care of associates—and the world would leave us alone. It doesn't work that way any more'.[6] Companies need to earn their 'license to operate'. They kicked-off an environmental initiative to improve their environmental stewardship reputation and increase their bottom line. Conversely, constant failure to address the concerns and expectations of these groups will reduce investor confidence in the firm's stock, impacting the cost of financing and thus profit making opportunities.

Attract capital investment: Just as consumers are becoming more aware of the importance of sustainability issues, so are investors. There is growth in socially responsible investment and ethically screened funds as well as industry standards such as the Dow Jones Index, FTSE4Good, London principles for financial institutions and the Equator Principles for project finance. As environmental and social criteria are becoming a standard part of lending risk assessments, sustainable businesses are more likely to be able to attract capital from banks and investors.

Capitalize on new opportunities: Mexican cement company, Cemex, considered ways to create a whole new business around improving the living standards of the 20 million people with inadequate shelter in Mexico. As a result, they now provide housing for poor people at a profit through a special programme that enables low-earners to pay weekly installments of $ 11.50 for 70 weeks to gradually buy the building materials they need to build a home. The programme, called Patrimonio Hoy, provides quality products on low-cost credit at fixed prices, as well as technical building advice. So far 83 million US dollars have been granted with an on-time payment rate of more than 99%. The programme has expanded to over 100 centres across Mexico and South America.

While the previous list shows some of the reasons you *should* consider adopting a sustainability strategy for your business, the *actual* reasons why managers are getting involved in the sustainability debate can vary widely. For some, involvement occurs as part of a personal journey, a realization that what they do today will affect their children and families, and the desire to contribute in a meaningful way. Others are forced into reacting as a result of a public relations scandal or accident, or because customers, regulations or other employees are asking for action on these issues. Regardless of how it starts, there are some points to keep in mind:

- *Sustainability is already a part of how you do business:* For most businesses this does not mean starting from scratch. Sustainability is about making the business more efficient and can be built into the way that companies already operate.
- *It doesn't matter how or why you begin . . .* Exploring sustainability in a company can begin in the smallest way, such as through a recycling programme or offering employees a subsidy for taking public transportation to work. Simple small things can make an impact over time.
- *. . . what matters is how you continue:* The benefits you get from particular decisions or choices to start exploring these issues, or the reasons that you continue to develop them further might be quite different from the original reasons you choose to get involved.
- *The potentially high cost of inaction for both the business and society:* Even if an organization can find no obvious

opportunities to cut costs or increase revenues through sustainability initiatives, inaction in this area can lead to increased costs and loss of revenue.

- *Multiple benefits*: A positive change in one area can also result in positive changes in the others. For example applying eco-design principles to a product can not only result in a superior product but it can also save money, give access to new markets, to new customers and inspire and engage employees and stakeholders.
- *The impact is strongest when it is embedded into strategy and culture:* Virtually every sustainability expert will tell you the same thing; a company will experience some benefits of sustainability, but will not maximize these until it is mainstreamed into the way that companies do business. Look for truly sustainable solutions that make sense for both business and for society.
- *The CEO must be on board:* The leading companies in this area all have programmes that were started by, or actively driven and pushed by their upper management, in particular their CEOs.

These are some of the primary reasons why adopting sustainable business practices make good business sense. You will find more details on the business case as it applies to each core discipline throughout the book.

Want more?

Other work on the business case has been done by consulting firms, and companies themselves. A few to start with include the work done by UNEP and Sustainability (www.sustainability.com), To Whose Profit? Building a Business case for sustainability by the WWF (www.wwf.org.uk) and WBCSD Business Case (www.wbcsd.org). Also take a look at many excellent books that explore the business case including *The Sustainability Advantage* by Bob Willard, and *Green to Gold* by Daniel C. Esty and Andrew S. Winston.

The sustainability sales pitch

Author Bob Willard tells the story in his book, *The Sustainability Advantage*, of when he worked at IBM. He writes that he spent six months drafting a letter to then CEO, Lou Gerstner, asking him to embed sustainability into IBM's business strategy. His letter included phrases such as 'business will play a vital role in the health of our planet' and 'funding research on causes of environmental issues'. When written in 1997, the letter was treated as a philanthropic request and directed to the corporate community affairs director. Thinking back, Bob says that his original letter should have said 'Dear Lou: I have some thoughts on how IBM could increase its profit by 38%. Interested? Yours truly ... '[7]

'That all sounds nice but ...' is a familiar phrase to sustainability champions. In fact, it seems to be much easier for people to come up with excuses and reasons for why not, than to try new things, even if they think that it may make sense. Proper presentation of sustainability related projects and strategies is crucial in gathering initial and continued support. To do so, consider the following advice:

1. *Be informed:* Collect all the information you can about what is happening in your own company, in other companies (not just your competitors), work being done by NGOs and current issues relating to the work you want to do. If you know what you are talking about, it will make answering questions and getting people on board a lot easier.
2. *Create a coalition:* Engage other people who share your viewpoint or who are also interested. Focus on getting key people on board who can really help move these issues forward.
3. *Pick your moment carefully:* Different individuals, teams, departments or whole companies will be ready at different times to put some of these tools into action. Focus on doing things right the first time, rather than finding a quick fix.
4. *Package that information appropriately:* People react to information in different ways, so knowing what kind of information to present to a specific decision-making person is key. An HR manager will be interested in employee motivation and hiring better people, while a CEO will be interested in reputation, brand and financial impact.

(continued)

5. *Choose who will give the information:* Whether rightly or wrongly, people tend to believe information when it comes from certain sources. For example, many are sceptical when NGOs tell business what they should do, as they are seen as outsiders. Find the right people to present the information, people who are well respected in the organization, even the converted sceptic and you can make your case more compelling.

6. *Think of the reasons why not:* In bringing these issues to your team or your organization, make sure you think carefully about the objections your company might raise to doing this. Consider the different perspectives around the table; the roles they play in the organization, their backgrounds and their personalities, and you can gain critical understanding of why people may be unwilling to move on certain issues, as well as ideas on how your interests could converge.

7. *Make a strong case:* Have a strong case for why people should be interested in moving forward on these ideas. Make sure you outline all the potential benefits, both the direct ones and the indirect benefits. Just as important, describe what would happen if the organization doesn't move forward, such as missed opportunities or negative PR.

8. *Offer a vision:* Offer a vision of where you want to go in the short, medium and long-term, and concrete ideas on how to get there. Use stories, pictures and videos along with hard facts to make your case. Build excitement about being part of something bigger. Think big.

9. *Present the underlying problem rather than your solution:* Don't just show up at your team meeting proposing your solution. Instead, discuss the original problem that needs solving. This helps an organization or team gather around an issue and work together to solve it.

10. *If calling it Sustainability or CSR won't work, then don't:* In marketing, a product is often more successful if it's marketed as high-performing rather than solely as an environmentally or socially friendly product. In this same way, if a business is sceptical of sustainability, present it as what it is, good business sense, as ways to cut costs, generate revenue, make production more efficient.

11. *Make it straightforward:* Where possible integrate new thinking and requirement into existing processes which enables others to more easily revise their thinking about existing company resources.

Make it easy and straightforward for people to start. Link projects to the company's ambitions, values, culture and history.

12. ***Be patient:*** Even though you may be ready, for others this may represent a change in mindset and it will take them longer to come on board.

4 The Sustainability Journey

*'It is not the strongest of the species that survives, or the
most intelligent, but the one most responsive to change'*
CHARLES DARWIN

Sustainability is a journey rather than a destination in itself. It starts with
the decision to explore these issues. The obvious issues are usually vis-
ited first, energy consumption, recycling, finding ways to minimize risk.
Some companies move past these to the less obvious opportunities
such as product innovations. Other leading companies will take the less
travelled routes and make discoveries, which will put them ahead of
the pack. Sustainability for business is always changing and evolving.
Managers often think that once they have put a strategy in place, they
have reached their destination. But there is no final destination, it is the
journey that counts.

To take your sustainability journey, it is important to understand
where you currently stand and where you want to go. Whether you are
just starting out, or you have already begun to explore sustainability
issues, your journey will be different depending on the needs of your
company. However, there are some common stages that companies
might find themselves at along the way.

Not yet on board...

1. ***Reject sustainability:*** Rejection may occur because a company is
   unaware of sustainability, or believes it has nothing to do with their

business. In some cases, it may be because a company is involved in illegal activities either through ignorance or inaction, or deliberate actions. Others will see what they can get away with, and think that even if they get caught they can still get around it.

2. ***Bare minimum:*** Companies are compliant, but barely so, and not necessarily on everything. They have no sustainability strategy, and at this level, a company is doing the absolute minimum required to stay in business. Typically, they only act when a situation occurs that forces them to react. If they do anything beyond the bare minimum, they often expect to be rewarded for it.

3. ***Seen as a cost:*** Some companies see sustainability as a philanthropic activity that is just a cost. There may be other smaller initiatives, or individuals across the company who are interested in sustainability, but nothing is coordinated. In some cases they will communicate things that they haven't actually done, or exaggerate claims for things they have done.

Jump on board . . .

4. ***Cutting costs:*** Companies begin exploring the opportunity to cut costs by reducing consumption. This usually starts with office greening projects coordinated by inspired employees. It can then progress into finding ways to save costs across the operations.

5. ***Risk management:*** At this stage, companies begin to see that governance structures, including policies, performance standards, management systems, reporting, assurance processes and sustainability tools allow them to better manage their risks.

6. ***Indirect benefits:*** Companies now begin looking beyond just saving costs and managing risks, to identify the opportunities that sustainability can present. They are also beginning to recognize how it can have a benefit across the business, such as internal benefits of recruiting better employees and suppliers.

7. ***Opportunities:*** Companies are now actively engaged on multiple fronts exploring opportunities across the business in the form of new products, exploring new markets, partnerships with outside organizations.

8. ***Strategic approach:*** Beyond significant levels of activity on new opportunities, companies begin to look at these individual activities across the organization with the goal of bringing them together as part of an overall strategy. Upper management is fully involved and reinforces these messages in communications internally and externally. Sustainability reporting is adopted throughout the organization. Efforts have become cohesive, moving the whole company in a common direction.

9. ***Integrating:*** Sustainability begins to be really integrated into the way that everyone at every level does business. It is part of people's job descriptions and is incorporated into compensation, rewards and performance evaluations. All departments are involved in doing their part to move the agenda forward.

10. ***Continuous improvement:*** A company works with other businesses to really push these issues forward, raising the bar throughout the areas in which they operate. At this stage, companies continually revisit their processes to make them stronger and to acknowledge and work on their weak spots.

Some points to keep in mind when trying to assess where you currently stand:

- ***Different initiatives will be at different points along this journey:*** The inherent complexity of organizations means that a company or an organization will have many different departments, projects, activities that are at different signposts on the sustainability journey. Use the above model to see where different parts of the business stand, and also for the company as a whole.
- ***Sustainability is a complex area that is continually changing and growing:*** Everyone is still learning and the bar is constantly being raised. Therefore it is not just about whether or not you are involved in the debate, but at what level. Are you:
  - Saying you are when you aren't really? (Greenwashing)
  - Doing just enough?

- Doing the same as other companies in your industry? In other industries? In your country?
- Doing better than other companies in your industry? In other industries? In your country?
- Doing the same as other companies internationally?
- Doing better than other companies internationally?
- A leader in this area?

- *How to move from one level to the next:* There are many drivers that push companies to move from one level to the next. Most often this will be a passionate CEO or manager, or engaged employees. A negative event that forces a company to react. Anything in the business case can be a driver to change. Ultimately, a company can only reach the higher levels with senior management involvement, and where sustainability is part of a cohesive strategy.
- *Remember, this all takes time:* Sustainability isn't a light switch that you turn on and off. Implementing a sustainability strategy takes time, energy, resources, a real commitment and often a cultural change within your company. However, done properly, the paybacks more than justify the investment.

What does a leading company look like?

Companies getting involved in sustainability are providing more and more information on their activities through their websites, their annual reports, and other communication means. However, even with all this information, many consumers are not convinced. So how can you distinguish a leading company from a laggard? Unfortunately this is not easy. We often judge organizations as single entities, but they are made up of many separate parts, some good and some not so good. Here are some things you can look at to help you decide whether a company is serious about these issues:

- *Look at whether or not it makes sense:* Can you understand their sustainability strategies? Do their products and messages make sense? Is their sustainability strategy consistent? Are they seeing themselves within a larger system of the world? Are they focusing on the issues that you think are most important, or that their stakeholders think are important?

- *Look at their approach to sustainability:* Is the company proactive or reactive when it comes to sustainability? Is the company going beyond minimizing risk to exploring new opportunities? When a problem occurs or the company is criticized for their actions/inactions, how does the company react? Do they take proactive measures to make sure it doesn't happen again?

- *Look at how they engage:* How do they engage with business and non-business partners, their suppliers, their peers, the community, their employees? Are they actively involved in sustainability networks at the local, national or international level? Are they fulfilling their membership requirements of these networks?

- *Look at the future:* Although the past will tell you where the company has come from and what their record is, it is not necessarily a good guide to future activities. Look at their current performance and published policies and future commitments. How quickly are they moving? How does this compare to their peers? Are they focused on continuous improvements? Leading companies set goals that challenge and inspire. They also have clear steps that show how they will attain those goals.

- *Look at who is driving the change:* The commitment of the board and the CEO is a good indicator of how seriously a company is taking these issues. Speak to employees working for a company. Do they know about the company's sustainability strategy? Are they involved? Is it part of their jobs? If sustainability strategy is part of the way that they speak about business then this is a good sign that management is committed.

- *Look at the resources allocated to sustainability:* How many people are responsible for implementing sustainability strategies within a company? How much power and influence do they have? What kind of budget do these activities have? How much time do people have to work on these issues?

- *Look at how they communicate:* Do they make claims in their promotional materials? Are these backed up? Are they credible, or are they greenwashing? Do they seem to be genuinely engaged in these issues? Don't just base your opinion on what you hear. Just because a company is not vocal about its sustainability commitment, in no way means it is inactive. Some companies are very active in this

(continued)

area but just don't have the budgets or choose not to communicate these efforts widely.

- *Look at how they report:* Look at the quality, quantity and transparency in the information they put in their annual reports. Do they truly understand the issues affecting themselves and their stakeholders? Do they follow certain reporting guidelines such as the Global Reporting Initiative?
- *Look at the whole as well as the parts:* It is often difficult to say whether a whole company is good or bad. All companies will have examples of successful projects in this area and parts of the business that need more work. Leading companies are those that are proud of their successes and who acknowledge and are working on their weak spots.
- *Look at what gets cut:* When times get tough, are the sustainability policies the first to go?

Where to find leading sustainable companies

One way to identify which companies are doing interesting work is by looking at the annual awards and rankings. There are now countless awards given at the local, national and international levels, many of which are mentioned throughout this book. Companies take their position on some of these lists very seriously and will often use this in their communication material if they are ranked highly, and respond by making changes in their organization when lower down on the lists. A few examples of international rankings include:

- The Global 100 Most Sustainable Corporations in the World are announced each year at the World Economic Forum in Davos (www. global100.org).
- The Sustainability Yearbook is an initiative with SAM and PwC of the world's 2500 largest companies based on the Dow Jones Global Index (www.sam-group.com/yearbook).
- Business Ethics magazine and KLD Research and Analytics list of '100 Best Corporate Citizens' (www.thecro.com).

Some tips for navigating the different rankings and awards lists:

- *Look at the scope of the award:* Is the award being given to companies who are part of a particular industry? Is it about one particular element of their strategy such as their approach to supply chain management or does it cover the full company and all its activities?

- *Look at which companies are up for the awards:* Awards don't always invite all companies to enter a given award or ranking. More often than not rankings and lists focus on larger, international companies, or only those who choose to nominate themselves. Does it include both public and private companies? Is it looking at both big and small ones?
- *Look at who is giving the award:* Is the ranking or award being given by a consulting firm, the media, consumers, international organizations, an NGO? Is it being given by a recognized organization?
- *Look at what kind of data they are measuring:* Companies often tend to use data that are readily and inexpensively available. Do companies submit the information themselves? Is it collected through questionnaires, media and stakeholder reports, publicly available information, interviews directly with the company? Is the awarding organization doing its own independent research?
- *Look at the criteria and weightings:* What are the criteria for the award? Every ranking or award will have a different set of criteria to determine the winners. These criteria should be transparent and easily accessible in order to give some insight on how the awardees are being chosen.

5 Getting Started

'Many companies have already done much to improve the social and environmental consequences of their activities, yet these efforts have not been nearly as productive as they could be—for two reasons. First, they put business against society when clearly the two are interdependent. Second, they pressure companies to think of corporate social responsibility in generic ways instead of in the way most appropriate to each firm's strategy'

MICHAEL PORTER[8]

In the same way that there are no simple checklists on what to do to create a successful business, there is also no single way for a company to incorporate sustainability into its operations. But the good news is that employees and managers can get involved in sustainability without becoming experts in this area (in fact the information in this book is more than enough to get anyone started.) Employees at all levels are coming up with an incredible variety of very different ways to bring sustainability into their employer's strategy and operations. For instance, some test out sustainability tools on a small scale, with a particular product, site or service, while others choose to embed it across the whole business.

Every organization will develop these issues in widely different ways and need to find the way that works best for their particular situation, location, client base or strategy. The following list provides a guideline for getting started.

1. Understanding where you are now	4. Engage others and gather support
2. Find out what is happening around you	5. Put in place your plan
3. Decide where you want to go and why	6. Keep it going

1. **Understand where you are now.** Start by taking some time to think about what kind of company you work for. How is your organization impacted by society? How does it impact society? What are the issues that are important to you? Explore what is currently happening and whether you could build on from initiatives already taking place in the company or whether to start a new one.

   ❑ *Where do you currently stand:* Does your company reject sustainability, is it non-responsive because of lack of awareness? Is it interested but not sure where to start? Has it already started? What kind of expertise is currently in the company in this area? Are there any projects that already exist to build on?

   ❑ *How is your organization impacted by society and the environment?* What issues affect your company's operations. Climate change? Water? Human rights? What issues do your stakeholders think are important for you to consider? What issues affect your competitors?

   ❑ *What impact does your organization have on society and the environment?* How do your operations impact society in positive ways? What about negative ways? Are you releasing pollutants? Generating waste?

   ❑ *What issues are important to you?* What about to your employees, your customers, your business partners?

❑ *What kind of a culture does your company have:* Is your company open to exploring new opportunities? Is it fast or slow to respond? Is it innovative? Does it have employees who would be keen to explore these issues?

2. **Find out what is happening around you.** Once you understand what is happening inside your organization and the issues that affect you, take a look at what is happening around you in terms of regulations, best practices and interesting initiatives that others are doing.

❑ *What regulations affect you:* Understand which regulations and industry standards affect you and your operations now and how they could impact you in the future. Above all make sure you are compliant with the regulations that affect you.

❑ *What voluntary mechanisms are out there:* Which standards, certification systems and eco-labels are relevant to your business? Are your competitors using them? Are your customers and stakeholders asking for them? Are they becoming widely accepted industry standards?

❑ *What is the rest of the industry doing?* What are your competitors doing? What about the organizations in your supply chain, your customers, your suppliers? What about other industries?

❑ *Look at the 'best practices':* What are the leaders doing in this area in your sector? What about in other sectors? What challenges have they encountered and what lessons have they learned that you can apply?

3. **Decide where you want to go and why.** Once you understand what is happening around you and how that affects you now and

may affect you in the future. Determine how you are going to proceed:

- ❏ *What are your drivers?* Why are you looking at these issues? Is it because of a passionate CEO? Are your employees asking for it? Your customers? What pressures are pushing you to do this? Are you looking to strengthen your brand, grow revenue or market share?
- ❏ *What is the business case?* Translate the drivers into business reasons. What is the business case? What are the costs? What are the benefits? Will it increase employee retention? Will it serve to build better products or increase market share? What impact could it have on your reputation and brand? With your relationship with your stakeholders?
- ❏ *What frameworks and tools work for you?* An organization can choose a sustainability framework (or create a hybrid) to develop a vision for sustainability. Is it one offered by an NGO (such as the Natural Step)? Is it the Triple Bottom Line? Is it a framework offered in a book or through a consulting firm? Is it your own? Use these as a starting point.
- ❏ *What is your baseline?* Conduct audits and assessment in order to identify where your strengths and weaknesses lie, to create a baseline to better understand your business and products and to use to track progress towards your goals.
- ❏ *What is the best point of entry:* Does your organization want to focus on a particular issue such as water or climate change? Create new or improved products and services? Does it want to start small with a particular product or process, or does it want to start big? Are you looking to enter new markets? Do you have any 'unsustainable' products that you want to remove from the marketplace?
- ❏ *At what scale?* Look at individual processes or groups of processes (i.e. production line), a system (lighting or packaging),

a product or product line, a facility, department or location, by regional or geographical groups of departments or facilities, or for the entire company.

❑ *What is the budget?* What resources are you willing to put towards your plan? How many employees, how much of their time? Will you have a whole team looking at these issues or just a few people?

4. **Engage others and gather support.** Experience shows that in order for sustainability to be successfully mainstreamed into an operation or business, employees, the CEO and other stakeholders must be fully engaged. Engagement requires building active relationships not only with customers and suppliers but also with local communities, social groups, governments, citizens and employees. Each has power to welcome the company with open arms and to help it achieve its goals, or to block, disrupt and make its life difficult.

❑ *Confirm CEO/management commitment:* If the CEO or management is not on board, sustainability activities will remain of secondary importance. CEOs must assign clear responsibility, resources and authority and communicate these messages consistently.

❑ *Build cooperation internally:* Involve people from across departments and from all levels of the company. Employees are also a valuable sounding board, they often sense a problem before management acknowledges it.

❑ *Engage business partners:* Involve suppliers, joint venture partners, contractors, shareholders and customers in carrying out sustainability strategy. Begin implementing sustainability screens in purchasing decisions.

❑ *Identify and engage stakeholders:* This includes all groups that are directly affected by your operations including shareholders, investors, employees, client companies, consumers, local community groups, supplier companies. Although this can be a challenging and time-consuming exercise, stakeholder engagement can help identify potential problems before they arise and help a company to understand the wider context in which it operates, and where opportunities and threats might come from.

❑ *Outside Networks:* A business can choose to take part in any number of different business and sustainability networks available locally, national, regionally and internationally, which share best practices. This includes creating alliances with other companies, NGOs, business industry sector organizations and industry specific networks.

❑ *Engage your customers:* Leverage the unprecedented power of consumers to share information about companies, products and services to promote sustainable products, usage, consumption and lifestyles.

5. **Put your plan in place and make it happen.** Develop a roadmap, revisit it regularly, and build it with clear objectives and goals to help the company go where it wants to go. Consider short, medium and long-term perspectives when putting together a strategy.

❑ *Create realistic targets and objectives:* Define actions and set targets that are SMART (Specific, Measurable, Achievable, Realistic and Time Specific). Break down sustainability targets and objectives in order to make them meaningful for individuals, subsidiaries, divisions and departments. Select appropriate indicators and metrics to help you keep track of your progress.

❑ *Prioritize:* Determine what the most important issues are. Be selective and look at prioritizing based on both importance and difficulty. Where do you want to be in 1, 5, 20 years? What do you have to do to get there?

❑ *Create a structure:* Choose a structure that will enable your strategy to be a success. Will you have a sustainability coordinator? Task forces? A chief sustainability officer? Will it be incorporated into individual jobs? Who will have overall responsibility?

❑ *Create pilot projects:* Pilot projects and prototypes are a good opportunity to test ideas and show others the impact they can have and learn some important lessons.

❑ *Align business systems:* Look at ways to embed sustainability goals across all functions of a business; whether it is re-visiting incentive systems to align them with sustainability goals in the HR department or exploring eco-efficiency and waste minimization opportunities in the production lines. Also look at budgeting and training. Depending on the strategy you choose, certain systems and processes may need to be modified to ensure that day-to-day activities are performed in a manner consistent with these objectives.

❑ *Give people the tools:* Including sustainability targets and objectives in performance appraisal so they have the right incentives. Run workshops to train staff ensuring that sustainability is the responsibility of everyone in the organization and not just of a specific department.

6. **Keep it going.** It doesn't stop once you have started implementing your sustainability plan. With a strategy in place that engages internal and external groups, and activities starting up, continue to monitor the progress of your strategies and the impacts it has on your business both directly and indirectly, and revise as needed. Successful strategies take time and effort to implement and should be continually revisited.

- ❏ *Communicate internally:* Do other employees know what the sustainability strategy is? Do they know what their role is? Communicate continually internally about status, the successes, what needs more work and so on.

- ❏ *Communicate externally:* Publish reports at least annually that detail your sustainability impacts, goals and progress, and disseminate information to your stakeholders. Use websites and other communication mediums to tell others about what you are doing.

- ❏ *Monitor:* Use status checks and regular audits to monitor how you are doing and communicate that to all relevant parties.

- ❏ *Scaling up:* Review what has worked and what hasn't before increasing the scale of the effort. What lessons have been learnt? Can they be applied to other parts of the business?

- ❏ *Look for Continuous improvement:* Put the plan into action with a focus on achieving continuous improvement rather than trying to reach a goal and then stop. Keep revisiting the process. A sustainability strategy should complement and build on existing programmes and initiatives.

Want more?

International Chamber of Commerce (ICC): Founded in 1919, the ICC 'serves the world business community by promoting trade and investment, opening markets, services and the free flow of capital.' The Business Charter for Sustainable Development has 16 principles, which provide business with a basis for sound environmental management. (www.iccwbo.org)

Guidelines for Multinational Enterprises of the Organization for Economic Cooperation and Development (OECD) are recommendations addressed by governments to multinational enterprises operating in or from adhering countries. They provide voluntary principles and standards for responsible business conduct in a variety of areas. (www.oecd.org/daf/investment/guidelines)

Getting past internal excuses

This book should be approached with an open mind. Some parts of it will be directly relevant to you, others won't. For sustainability to work for you and the organizations that you are involved in, you should take a moment to think about the reasons why, and what this could mean for your organization, rather than thinking of the reasons why not. The majority of people have built up a list of internal excuses not to take the plunge into something new. The following will help you, and those around you, to get past the most common excuses.

- *'I have no time':* Do an audit of your time. This often shows that you spend a lot of time on tasks that do not actually benefit your work. At the same time, the audit can reveal that many of the things you currently do are already related to sustainability issues.
- *'It's not my job':* Imagine if everybody said this—nothing would ever get done! If your job is to help your business be or continue to be successful, then yes, some of the ideas introduced in this book are and increasingly will be part of your job.
- *'I want to make money, not give it away':* Look at sustainability as being a tool to reduce costs and increase revenue. Revenue minus costs equals profit. Even if you don't make money by doing the right thing, you can certainly lose money if you do the wrong thing.
- *'I'm not important enough':* If you were hired then it is because you play a role. There is always something you can do regardless of what position you have within your organization.
- *'It's all too complicated':* There are a growing number of resources out there to help individuals and companies explore these issues, (e.g. this book!). Find those things that make sense to you and start with those first.
- *'No one else around me is doing it':* If no one else is doing it, then you have an even better opportunity, in addition to the business benefits to your organization, it will give you a way to differentiate yourself and get ahead of the pack.
- *'My company isn't interested':* Your company is made up of many different individuals, some will be interested, some may not. Your company may not be interested, but other employees might be. By connecting with them and creating a group you may be able to influence your company.

(continued)

- *'My company really isn't interested':* You may find the rare instance where these issues are important to you but not to the company you work for. Remember how many companies there are, and how many of them can use your skills—it may be time to move onto one of those.
- *'It costs too much':* This all depends on how you approach it. Pursuing sustainability strategies that make sense to your business can involve upfront costs with less than hoped for short-term results. Find the 'low hanging fruit' where simple changes to sourcing or processes can make a big difference.And remember, middle and long-term results consistently show both business and societal benefits.
- *'All this sustainability stuff will pass':* Whether you like it or not, this represents the new business reality.
- *'I'm not creative':* Getting involved in sustainability requires commitment more than creativity. If you really have no ideas at all, even after reading this book, then support other people who do have good ideas.
- *'It isn't important in our industry':* All industries are getting involved in these issues. If yours isn't yet, then it will be soon. Make sure you're not left behind.Take the opportunity to be an industry leader.
- *'We don't really impact the environment':* Although the impacts may not always be obvious, every company and every individual impacts the natural and social environment around them in some way.
- *'We can't make a difference':* Companies of all sizes and individuals in all sectors are making a difference. Some of the leaders are individuals and small companies.

PART 2

THE CORE TOPICS

Bringing the pieces together:
The sustainability puzzle
Accounting
Economics
Entrepreneurship
Ethics and General
Management
Finance
Marketing
Operations and Technology
Management
Organizational Behaviour
Strategy

Bringing the pieces together:
The sustainability puzzle

Sustainability ideas are increasingly being explored across all industries around the world. Within each company, sustainability can be seen as a giant jigsaw puzzle. The chosen sustainability strategy sits at the middle of the puzzle and provides the basis for other areas of the business to get involved in exploring these issues. Entrepreneurship, Economics, Ethics and Organizational Behaviour provide the corner pieces of the puzzle, with Accounting, Finance, Marketing and Operations tying everything together.

Entrepreneurship Identifying and exploring new business solutions both inside and outside an organization.	**Accounting** Building systems, establishing sustainability targets and objectives and providing sustainability information to influence decision-making.	**Economics** Helps to understand the larger environment in which business works and which business influences. Explores mechanisms to allow companies to internalize costs to society and optimize contributions to economic and social development.
Finance Plays a key role in sending signals to companies that can enable them to invest in longer term opportunities; and requires them to responsibly and effectively manage their economic, environmental and social impacts.	**Strategy** Ensures the right approach is taken for a particular company, and that it is implemented as a real organized effort that mobilizes the whole company.	**Marketing** In designing and promoting more sustainable options and inspiring change.
Ethics Without good management, strong corporate governance, ethical behaviour and open and transparent relationships with stakeholders, sustainability issues policies and goals can go nowhere.	**Operations** Taking responsibility for all the impacts, both social and environmental, across the life-cycle of a company's products and services.	**Organizational Behaviour** Translating sustainability policy into action and creating a work environment where sustainability is embedded in the culture of the company and every aspect of the employees' life-cycle from recruitment to retirement.

The following part of the book introduces a range of tools that can be used to understand how sustainability affects different core areas of a business. Each core topic provides the following information:

- an *introduction* of the role the topic plays in sustainability
- an introduction to the *business case* for why sustainability is important to that topic
- an introduction to the different *key concepts* and *tools* relevant in that topic
- an overview of some of the *challenges* faced with moving the agenda forward in this area
- a list of some of the *trends and new ideas* being explored in this topic
- some *tips* for how you can explore these issues as an employee or as a consumer
- *additional resources* where you can get more information on everything introduced in the chapter.

6 Accounting

> *'One ton of carbon dioxide is presently trading on European markets at about £10. A hectare of rainforest stores about 500 tons and therefore has a potential value of £5,000; but, as the New York Times recently pointed out, millions of hectares of rainforest are being cut down to create agricultural land worth £100 a hectare. Why are we allowing people to be deprived of their natural habitats, biodiversity to be diminished and climatic catastrophe to be hastened, and all at a loss of £4,900 a hectare? There are no easy answers, but I am sure that part of the blame, and more importantly of the solution, is down to us accountants.'*
>
> SIR MICHAEL PEAT[9]

At the 2007 launch of the Carbon Disclosure Project, Bill Clinton referred to the need for more 'scorekeepers' in sustainability, 'we don't have the systems in place to know what the problem is, to know what the progress is to maximize the likelihood of the best outcome'. This is a vast uncharted area which is under organized, where consumers have imperfect levels of knowledge about what their options are and what impact they are having.[10] Accountants certainly can play a crucial role as 'scorekeepers' in building these systems, helping to establish sustainability targets and objectives and providing this information so it can influence decisions.

Accounting may not seem like the logical place to start efforts to green a company, but in fact, without the involvement of the accounting sector, many initiatives simply never take off. 'Although the accounting sector itself might be considered a relatively low-impact sector in terms of direct environmental and social impacts, it is the accountant's involvement in the twin issues of organizational decision-making and external reporting that imposes on the accounting profession the responsibility for understanding, absorbing and articulating the implications of the sustainable development debate'[11] according to the Association of Chartered Certified Accountants (ACCA). It is this that makes accountants well placed to influence the processes that would make sustainability part of day-to-day management.

Why is it important?

- *More people are asking for sustainability information:* Stakeholders are increasingly asking for better, more consistent information to understand how a company is performing. Governments and the business sector are increasingly putting forward voluntary and mandatory disclosure and reporting standards that can significantly impact business. And accountants need to be able to understand this information in order to report on and comply with requirements.
- *What gets measured gets managed . . . and what gets managed gets done,* as the saying goes. One decisive element of any sustainability strategy is the development of measurable objectives and targets. Accounting has an important role in collecting data to support the decision-making process and to measure the results and improvements.
- *Better decision-making:* Accounting for environmental and social costs and allocating them to the appropriate processes, products or

systems allows a company to make better decisions in relation to strategic planning, to projects, material choices, product pricing and product mix. The accounting perspective not only enables better understanding of the business but also helps to understand possible cost reductions or elimination and exploration of potential revenue opportunities.

- *Recognizing opportunities:* Identifying and gathering the right kinds of information also permits an organization to anticipate and adapt to a rapidly changing world, including identifying new business opportunities and managing risks.
- *Getting ahead of the game:* Companies will fall behind if they do not stay up to date and active in this area, in particular in the current debates for example around climate change. The efforts in climate change will eventually lead to disclosure requirements in other areas such as water, energy usage and emissions.
- *Economic instruments:* Accountants need to understand how business may be affected by the increasing number of economic and market-based instruments associated with sustainability issues such as permits, liabilities, charges and taxes.

The key concepts

The role of the accountant in sustainability is primarily to collect information to assist internal decision makers (management accounting) and to prepare financial and sustainability information for external stakeholders (financial accounting).

• Identifying the full costs of products and services	→ *Full or True Cost Accounting*
• Determining which issues are important to the business	→ *Materiality*
• Measuring progress towards goals	→ *Key Performance Indicators*

- Measuring the impact of a   → *Measuring social impact*
  company's activities in society
- Incorporating sustainability   → *Sustainability in Financial*
  into Financial Statements   *Statements*
- Verifying the accuracy of sustain- → *Assurance*
  able information and claims
- Reporting on sustainability   → *Box: Sustainability*
  programs and progress   *Reporting*

Full or true cost accounting

One of the roles of the management accountant is to measure the full costs of a firm's products and services and to correctly assign them to the appropriate parts of the business. This is important in order to better understand the profitability of their products, product lines, departments and customers and to make more informed decisions. Many would argue that clearer identification of those environmental issues which actually drive costs (i.e. activity based costing) will reduce costs, squeeze out inefficiencies and improve margins. However, many environmental and social costs that could affect these decisions are currently not being identified or measured. Thus, the typical management accountant has an incomplete, inaccurate understanding of the true costs the business faces. This can lead to inaccurate understanding of the true costs associated with a particular product or process, and can lead managers to miss opportunities to make their products and processes better and more efficient.

Understanding the true cost is not only important for strategic decision-making but also in determining how a product should be priced. While consumers buy a product based on a price (among other factors), the price often does not fully reflect the real cost of that product to society. Better incorporation of true costs into products can result in better pricing that allows customers to make purchasing decisions based on information regarding the costs to society of a product and letting them know that these costs have been paid for.

Typically accounting systems classify costs as direct materials and labour, manufacturing or factory overhead, general overhead and research and development. Environmental expenses may be classified in any or all of these categories. Several tools aim at trying to take the environmental expense out of these categories so that they can be understood independently. For example a particular product may need certain chemicals in its production. The product price may only include the cost of buying those chemicals but may not include other costs connected with their use, such as training employees to handle them safely, storing them, and insuring against damage caused by possible spills. Even if the product price includes all the costs paid by the business, it often does not include the social and environmental costs associated with use of those chemicals, such as eventual damage of a spill on the health of local people, animals and plants. Legislation so far has been working to internalize these costs through use of taxes and fines to ensure that environmental costs are being adequately passed on to the firm and thereby effectively affecting product and process costs.

Conventional operating costs such as the use of raw materials, utilities, waste and suppliers can be identified and quantified. However, other costs can be much more difficult to identify and quantify. These include:

- *Hidden and overhead costs:* Certain types of environmental costs may be hidden from managers because they are buried in overhead accounts, rather than being allocated to a particular project or process to which they relate. This affects the actual and perceived viability of such activities, and can include:
  - Initial costs relating to R&D, eco-design, qualification of suppliers, and evaluation of alternative pollution control.
  - Regulatory and voluntary environmental costs such as monitoring.
  - Back-end environmental costs that will occur at some point in the future; for example, the costs of decommissioning an old laboratory, waste disposal costs, closing a landfill or complying with future regulations.
  - Costs incurred because of past pollution, including clean up of closed or existing sites, in order to mitigate current pollution and prevent future health and environmental risks.

- **_Contingent or liability costs:_** These are costs that might be incurred at some point in the future. These are usually estimated based on the probability of occurrence. Examples include the costs of remedying and compensating for future accidental releases of contaminants into the environment (e.g. an oil spill), or fines, and penalties for future regulatory infraction.

- **_Intangible costs:_** The costs themselves are not intangible but the direct benefits often related to reputation and image that result from them often are, such as the costs of supporting the brand or improving the intellectual capital of the business. For example, a company with a strong environmental reputation may have more motivated staff, thereby increasing productivity and reducing costly worker absenteeism.

- **_Societal costs:_** These represent the costs of business' impacts on the environment and society for which business is not legally accountable (also known as externalities; see economics chapter for more). For example the cost of delivering goods includes petrol, but not the emissions of air particulates which in built up areas has an impact on human health.

> Tools such as Activity Based Costing are used to assign general overhead costs to particular products or services. For more information on this search for Full Cost Accounting and Environmental Accounting. US EPA Introduction to Environmental Accounting as a business management tool (www.epa.gov). Full Cost Accounting: An Agenda for Action ACCA (www.accaglobal.com)

According to the US Environmental Protection Agency (EPA), 'the success of environmental accounting does not depend on 'correctly' classifying all the costs a firm incurs. Rather, its goal is to ensure that relevant information is made available to those who need or can use it.'[12]

Materiality

There are a growing number of sustainability related issues, from water to climate change. No organization can be expected to respond to all of them, especially when the issues are not all seen as important to them. In the world of finance, any issue that has (very) roughly a 5 % impact on the net income has traditionally been considered to be material. However, when it comes to sustainability, it is not always so easy to tell because it isn't as easy to put a price tag on the potential impacts. So organizations need to determine which issues are material—meaning which issues could make a major difference to an organization's performance both in the short and long-term. According to NGO Accountability, 'Materiality is determining the relevance and significance of an issue to an organization and its stakeholders. A material issue is an issue that will influence the decisions, actions and performance of an organization or its stakeholders.'[13]

The first step in determining which issues are material is to make a list of all the issues that are, or could be, relevant to the business and its stakeholder, and collect the information needed to assess their significance. NGO Accountability proposes a five-point framework to help identify these issues:

1. *Issues that have a direct short-term financial impact:* These are resulting from aspects of social and environmental performance that have short-term financial impacts. For example, carbon emissions have become material for many companies over the past few years.

2. *Issues where the company has made policy-related statements or commitments:* Issues are material where a company has agreed to policy commitments of a strategic nature including regulatory or voluntary requirements for non-financial disclosure. Tesco in the UK for example has publicly set out the significance of its treatment of people to its core business strategy.

3. *Issues which other comparable organizations consider to be material:* To understand the materiality of a specific issue or aspect of performance, look at whether a company's peers consider it material. For example in the pharmaceutical sector access to medicine in developing countries is an increasingly important issue to all companies.

4. *Issues which stakeholders consider important:* It might sound obvious, but a company should take into account the concerns of stakeholders including employees and customers. If certain issues are important to your stakeholders, then they should be taken seriously.
5. *Issues that are considered social norms:* Areas that are covered by regulations or could be in the future, best practices and emerging norms should all be evaluated to determine which ones are material to a business. This includes international initiatives such as the Global Reporting Initiative and the Global Compact.[14]

Companies differ dramatically, so what is material for one company may not be for another. Not all the issues a company identifies will end up being significant to its long-term success. Therefore, once all the sustainability issues that could be material to an organization are identified and assessed, they should then be prioritized according to criteria determined by its management, such as whether they are of high, medium or low materiality. NGO Accountability explains that, once mapped, and the level of materiality determined for each issue, this information can be used:

- To determine the scope of corporate reports and other communication so that they are more strategically aligned and useful to external stakeholders.
- To promote internal understanding of the link between sustainable development issues and business strategy.
- To feed into ongoing strategy development by highlighting rapidly emerging issues and enabling them to be factored into strategy development.

Accountability work on materiality including The Materiality Report (www.accountability21.net) Global Reporting Initiative has guidance on Materiality (www.globalreporting.org) Several companies such as BP, BT, Ford and Nike have begun developing rigorous practices for determining and communicating their approach to materiality.

Key performance indicators

Having the right kind of information at the right time, and in the hands of the right people, ultimately allows for more effective decision-making. Once environmental, social and economic goals and targets are identified, key performance indicators (KPIs) are used by organizations to measure their progress against these goals. Before choosing KPIs, many organizations think they know how they are doing, however they're often surprised when they start collecting real numbers. Metrics and KPIs cannot simply be picked off the shelf. In order to be meaningful and effective, a company should select KPIs in context with the organization and its industry, so that they make sense for their business and its stakeholders.

While there is no agreement on which indicators to use or how to construct them, there is plenty of guidance. The Global Reporting Initiative is one of the primary sources of guidance in this area and is used by more than 1500 companies including many of the world's leading brands. It provides guidance for indicators on economic performance, environmental, human rights, labour, product responsibility and society. It also provides certain sector specific guidance (www.globalreporting.org).

KPIs can be used to measure progress on anything from how an office greening programme is going (i.e. % of paper recycled) to something much larger such as measuring the impact of certification programmes. For example, according to the Global Compact and the Rainforest Alliance 'Many companies engaged in certification make the investment for reasons such as increased market access, corporate social responsibility targets or reduced risk. However, they are beginning to find additional financial benefits – both direct and indirect – of participation. Regardless, only a few have made attempts to systematically analyze how the adoption of certification has affected their financial performance.' Chiquita has been tracking data, using selected KPIs, about its sustainability efforts since it first started working with the Rainforest Alliance. It found that from 1995 through 2005 while making key sustainability investments and achieving large scale Rainforest Alliance certification, Chiquita increased productivity by 27% and decreased costs by 12%.[15]

Whatever KPIs are chosen, care must be taken to present them clearly. Many indicators start out as absolute numbers of whatever is easiest to measure. Since these metrics measure basic data (such as total energy use), it becomes all too easy to draw false conclusions from this information. For example a fall in emissions could be due to a downturn in business rather than efficiency gains. Therefore, relative/normalized measures such as ratios can be more useful in understanding a company's performance (e.g. energy use per unit of output). Some pointers to keep in mind when choosing metrics:

- *Make sure metrics are related to the goals and objectives of the company:* As simple as it may sound, it is important to make sure that indicators are providing information that is useful to the company and provide data on progress towards the company's goals.
- *Choose driving metrics:* Metrics should drive performance rather than just measure outputs. For example, a company trying to improve its compliance record with regulators should develop metrics that identify and measure the root causes of non-compliance, rather than simply track the number of occurrences of non-compliance.
- *Choose leading metrics:* Metrics should not just measure things that occurred in the past such as energy use, but also capture a vision for the future (i.e. size and quantity of clean tech investments).
- *Leaders are using not just quantitative measures but qualitative as well:* Explore using KPIs to measure areas that may not be as simple to quantify, such as intangibles like reputation with customers.
- *Who is the audience for your metrics:* Is it management, government, voluntary business initiatives, investors, employees, consumers? The indicators selected should be relevant to the audience, give the information needed by or of interest to these parties, and be easy to understand and use.
- *It doesn't have to be perfect:* A certain level of inaccuracy is inevitable. The key point is to collect information that is useful in moving forward. Indicators should allow you to understand and

measure progress. It is better to estimate what you can't measure, rather than leave it out altogether.

- *It doesn't have to be overly complex:* Avoid using too many indicators. Limit the number of metrics that need attention at any one time. A lot of the data needed may already be available within the company.

Other than GRI, more guidance on indicators can be found at ISO's Environmental Performance Valuation (ISO 14031). This gives guidance on the design and use of environmental performance evaluation, and on identification and selection of environmental performance indicators, for use by all organizations, regardless of type, size, location and complexity (www.iso.org). The International Sustainability Indicators Network (www.sustainabilityindicators. org) and The WBCSD (www.wbcsd.org) report on measuring eco-efficiency, and also provide some guidance. The UN Conference on Trade and Development (UNCTAD) have also produced a guide for users and preparers of eco-efficiency indicators (www.unctad. org/en/docs/iteipc20037_en.pdf).

Measuring social impact

Organizations are often trying to positively influence the communities in which they operate. In order to do this they must be able to define the social proposition they are offering and measure the impacts of their activities on the local environment. This is important in order to improve the effectiveness of programmes, to increase the understanding of the impact of their work and to communicate the value of that work to their stakeholder. Indicators are used to measure the impact of businesses' activities on society. According to the Foundation of Social Return on Investment there are four main elements needed to measure social value creation:

- *Inputs* are the resources you need in order to make something happen. They are measured as a cost (i.e. cost of programme, value of time contributed).
- *Outputs* are the direct result of your business objectives or programme goals (i.e. the number of people trained or trees planted).
- *Outcomes* are changes that occur over the longer term as a result of the activity (i.e. new jobs, increased incomes, improved stability of life as a result of programmes).
- *Impacts* are the outcome less an estimate of what would have happened in the absence of your programme.

Tools such as Social Return on Investment are used in order to explain social value in monetary terms. Return on Investment (ROI) is a tool used to understand financial value creation. If you invest one dollar in a project and more than a dollar is returned then the project is probably worth further consideration. Social Return on Investment (SROI) works in the same way. It is a tool used to understand the environmental, social and economic value being created by organizations. Value is something that cannot always be measured specifically, but SROI tries to provide an approximate value. 'The essential rationale for calculating SROI separately from financial returns is because the market's valuation of social benefits is imperfect. In cases where it is perfect, there would be no need for an SROI analysis.'

SROI analysis should include both positive and negative impacts in the assessment and should only include impacts that are clearly and directly attributable to the company's activities. SROI analysis takes organizational time and resources. However, when done properly it can be an effective tool to improve your programmes and to communicate the value of the work you are doing whether you are a commercial company or a not for profit.

Several organizations have developed systems to better understand social impact. Anglo American created the Socio-Economic Assessment Toolbox in order to better understand whether its operations were living up to the company's stated goal of making a contribution to the economic, social and educational wellbeing of the communities associated with its operations (www.angloamerican.co.uk). The International Finance Corporation uses a Development Outcome Tracking System in order to track the development results of its activities to assess whether or not it is achieving its mission (www.ifc.org/results). The WBCSD also developed a tool for its members to aid in measuring impact (www. wbcsd.org/web/measuringimpact.htm).

There are many resources available in this area, in particular for social entrepreneurs whose whole business model rests on their social impact. The Global Social Venture Competition have resources on their website that aid in measuring social value (www.gsvc.org). Other social entrepreneurship organizations such as Skoll Social Edge (www.socialedge.org/resources/edge-wiki/ ImpactAssessment) and The SROI primer sroi.london.edu also provide many links and resources. REDF in the US has done a lot of work on SROI (www.redf.org/learn-from-redf/publications/119). The London Benchmarking Groups is a group of over 100 companies working together to measure Corporate Community Investment (www.lbg-online.net).

Sustainability in financial statements

Although much of the emphasis regarding sustainability concerns disclosing information in separate sustainability reports (explored in detail further in this section), there is increased work being done on how to include sustainability information in annual financial reports. Companies prepare their annual reports in accordance with national, and international, accounting standards: either the Generally Accepted Accounting Practice (GAAP) in that country or the International Financial Reporting Standards issued by the International Accounting Standards Board (www.iasb.org). These standards are currently being reviewed to provide more guidance for accountants to facilitate the disclosure of environmental and social issues and impacts into their annual reports. These changes will give stakeholders a better view of how sustainability issues are influencing business performance and profitability, and a more complete view of the company.

Today, the majority of annual financial reports are still issued with little or no environmental or social information. However, more organizations themselves have been exploring ways to incorporate sustainability and financial information into their annual reports. The Sigma Project proposes a framework for moving from financial to sustainability accounting, by:

- Restating the Profit and Loss Account to show how sustainability related costs and benefits can directly impact on the bottom line.
- Extending the Profit and Loss Account to encompass the external costs and benefits to the environment, society and the economy which are not traditionally taken into account.
- Extending the Balance Sheet to take a fuller account of the range of assets (including intangible assets such as brand, human capital or reputation as they relate to sustainability); and 'shadow' liabilities (including liabilities relating to sustainability risks) of the organization.[16]

Within current standards, environmental issues are treated in more depth than social issues. Some examples of environmental issues currently covered by financial reports include:

- *Liabilities:* These can include having to pay fines for non-compliance with laws, legal fees from court cases by stakeholders against the company, or costs for cleaning up a polluted site. Liabilities can either be from events that happened in the past, or provision for events that may happen in the future.
- *Intangible assets:* Those elements of a business that do not have a specific financial value, but which increasingly represent the majority of the value of a company such as brand, intellectual property and reputation.

Sustainability issues that impact a company's financials can also be included in the narrative sections of the report. This provides management with an opportunity to provide contextual and non-financial information about how sustainability issues have impacted, or may impact financial conditions and results (also referred to as operating and financial review, business review, management discussion and analysis depending on the country). Gap Inc for example summarized its commitments to social responsibility and its importance in attracting employees and delivering long-term shareholder value in the narrative of its report. Narratives often focus on a smaller set of material issues.

According to a survey by KPMG in 2008, 4 % of the world's largest companies were integrating their sustainability (corporate responsibility) and annual reports with Brazil (22 %), Switzerland (21 %) and South Africa (19 %) leading the way, and the number has been consistently growing over the years.[17] The level of integration varies, ranging from including information on sustainability in the annual report, combining the two reports one after the other, or fully integrating the two reports together. For example, Baxter Healthcare produces a separate environmental financial statement that provides a better picture of environmental performance than the balance sheet or income statement can (www.sustainability.baxter.com). Novo Nordisk combines their financial and environmental/social reporting into one document through a consolidated financial and non-financial statement (www.novonordisk.com).

Other resources include IFAC Financial Reporting Supply Chain Survey (www.ifac.org/frsc/). IASB has different resources on management commentary (www.iasb.org). PwC consulting firm also did a survey of the Fortune Global 500 companies' narrative reporting (www.pwc.com), as well as on narrative reporting among the FTSE 350 companies (corporatereporting.com/joining_the_dots.html). IAS Plus, run by Deloitte, has different resources as well (www.iasplus.com). KPMG 2008 Reporting survey has lots of information on trends in integrated reporting (www.kpmg.com). Also see some of the resources in the sustainability reporting section.

Assurance

Annual financial statements are subject to an audit or assurance process, which is done by an accounting firm to ensure accuracy and enhance credibility. This assurance statement is usually found within the first few pages of the report. Although no such regulatory requirements exist for sustainability reports, readers are increasingly looking for voluntary assurance that covers two areas:

- Assurance on management and reporting systems and associated performance, which assesses the strengths and weaknesses of the company's sustainability programmes and initiatives.
- Report content assurance that looks at the accuracy, completeness, reliability, balance and fairness of the report, similar to the verification of financial reports.

Companies that report on their environmental and social performance rely on accounting firms, environmental and engineering consultancies, certification bodies and CSR specialists for assurance of these reports to ensure credibility. Some, such as Shell, GE and Nike, have panels of independent advisers who provide expert views that are an alternative avenue to provide credibility.

Although companies are increasingly commissioning assurance statements (more than 40 % of the Global 250 have some sort of assurance), there is no single international set of principles or standard for assurance of non-financial reports. The two leading international standards for assurance are the multi-stakeholder created AA1000AS, which looks at both the verification of data and the underlying management and reporting systems; and the accounting standard ISAE 3000, which focuses more heavily on verification style assurance and data accuracy. Even with these emerging international standards, there are still inconsistencies and wide variations in the approach taken for sustainability assurance, in part due to the relative immaturity of the area.

An assurance statement typically looks at the following:

- *Specific declarations* in terms of what kind of audience the statement is aimed at, and whether or not it was made independently from the company, outlining the respective responsibilities in the audit process of the auditor and the company. Reference any standardized approaches and levels of assurance used such as AA1000AS and ISAE3000.

- *An outline of the methodology*, how the assurance provider undertook the audit, such as conducting internal interviews, scrutinizing internal data systems, reviewing external documents, interviewing external stakeholders.
- In the case of AA1000AS, assurors can provide high assurance or moderate assurance based on the amount of evidence obtained and assuror access to that evidence to support statements regarding the following three principles:
  - *Inclusivity:* Has the organization been inclusive in how they engage stakeholders in achieving an accountable and strategic response to sustainability?
  - *Materiality:* Have they identified what the material (most important) sustainability issues are to the organization and to its stakeholders?
  - *Responsiveness:* Have they responded to these and communicated appropriately? (i.e. establishing policies, objectives and targets, management systems, action plans.)
- *Recommendations and opinions* which offer insight in terms of performance, strengths and weaknesses, challenges, etc.

In some instances, the reporting organization will also provide a report to management. Such additional reports should not communicate different conclusions than are found in the publicly available assurance statement, but rather include any limitations in the scope of the disclosures on sustainability, the assurance engagement or the evidence gathering.

The AA1000 Assurance Standard developed to ensure the credibility and quality of sustainability performance and reporting (www.accountability21.net). The International Auditing and Assurance Standards Board (IAASB) standards dealing with auditing, review, other assurance, quality control and related services. It is the organization responsible for the ISAE3000 Standard (www.ifac.org/ IAASB). CorporateRegister also has some guidance on Assurance, trends and examples (www.corporateregister.com/pdf/AssureView. pdf). KPMG's annual survey on reporting also has information on trends in assurance (www.kpmg.com).

Challenges?

Despite all the work that is happening in the area of sustainability and accounting, there are still several challenges.

- *Moving from costs to revenues:* Few have moved beyond seeing environmental initiatives and values as just costs to be suffered through (legislative imperative) or costs to be reduced at the first possible opportunity. Companies are not identifying the business benefits, and ultimately profits, that correspond with the costs that must be incurred for better environmental performance.
- *Consumers:* Responsible companies have competitors who are more than happy to price their goods below their true cost, discounting the social and environmental costs. In some cases managers who do price their goods and services based on full social and environmental costs will suffer until consumers make purchasing decisions based on this.
- *Traditional accounting systems* were not designed to enable environmental data to be separately identified or evaluated such as data on waste management, compliance with laws, insurance. Several initiatives are happening at the international level relating to Accounting education, for example with the Federation of European Accountants (www.fee.be).
- *Estimating costs:* There are many difficulties in estimating the costs of environmental and social damage across the full life-cycle of a product or process. This includes problems with consistency

between companies, as well as how to translate these costs into prices.

- *Communication between departments:* In many companies, sustainability knowledge is held by a small specialist group that has no direct communication with the accountants and vice versa. They will often have different goals, perspectives and even language with regard to sustainability and inconsistencies may arise in how information is communicated.

- *Assets versus costs:* Using traditional accounting methods, end-of-pipe technologies to reduce environmental impacts are accounted for as assets, while attempts to eliminate sources of pollution at the source appear as costs. Similarly, investments in training and development are recorded as costs, while the collective knowledge and experience this creates is not recorded as an asset.

- *Short-term versus long-term:* There is a need to shift the mentality and accounting practices to look more at the long-term effects, as opposed to simply short-term implications of decisions. The challenge is to incorporate longer-term, less tangible environmental and social costs into the balance sheet rather than just measuring short-term tangible metrics.

- *Information not tracked adequately or not available:* Available information is often not sufficiently accurate or detailed for decision-making purposes. Sometimes the information is collected, but stays within different divisions of the company, where the accountants may never even become aware of its existence.

- *Quantifying the qualitative:* A major challenge in mainstreaming sustainability issues into accounting will be the ability to quantify biodiversity and so-called 'natural capital'. (See tool on valuation later in the book for more).

- *Comparability of data:* Company disclosures on sustainability issues are often inconsistent and difficult to compare across a single industry. However, several sustainability threads are common to all sectors—e.g. energy and water consumption, greenhouse gas emissions—and should be reported consistently across industries.

Trends and new ideas

> – Bringing it all together
> – Increased Disclosure
>
> – Recognizing unrecognized assets

Bringing it all together Until now the accounting profession has dealt with economic, environmental and social issues in relative isolation from each other. However, increasing attempts are being made to bring these together in recognition that conventional accounting numbers do not always tell the 'full story' of how businesses impact the environment in which they work. At the same time, within the financial reporting sector, we are seeing a growth in the number of organizations that integrate their environmental, social and financial reports. Blended Value is another tool being explored in this area. The Blended Value concept argues that though society sees companies as creating economic value and NGOs as creating social value, the reality is that all value is a combination or a 'blend' of economic, environmental and social factors. Thus maximizing value requires taking all three elements into account (www.blendedvalue.org).

Increased disclosure The key role of accountants is in measuring and communicating information used both internally and externally in decision-making. One of the key requirements for moving sustainability forward at the organizational and societal levels is better and more complete information. Several international initiatives are underway to increase the level of information available and make it comparable across or between industries. The Carbon Disclosure Project is one example, which collects data and disseminates information on climate change and greenhouse gas emissions from the world's largest companies (3000 in 2008) and makes it available to a group of institutional investors with a combined $ 57 trillion of assets under management. It holds a database on corporate climate change information on companies around the world (www.cdproject.net).

Recognizing unrecognized assets Accountants are in an ideal position to uncover where potential revenue generation opportunities lie and how to take advantage of them. One example discussed later on in this book is selling waste for profit, thereby transforming it from a cost into an asset. The protection of natural resources can provide in some instances a credit in market based regulatory systems that can be sold or traded. It also gives a company a 'license to operate' in a given community. International Paper in the US turned more than 5000 acres of unused land into a conservation bank for the endangered red-cockaded woodpecker. This resulted in public goodwill. In addition, the company is legally allowed to expand operations into other forests and sells its credits for endangered species protection, currently valued at $250 000. The Elgin Air Force Base in Florida has 400 000 acres of longleaf pine forests. Because of its fire resistance, slow growth, long lifespan and high value for lumber and resin, longleaf pine has been logged almost to extinction. In fact 72% of all remaining old growth populations in the world are at the base. The US Air Force performed studies in 2004 to assess the potential value of the forest for environment, economy and surrounding communities. Today timber sales generate $ 1.2 million a year, and 280 000 acres are open to the public for recreational opportunities that could be worth an additional $ 8–12 million a year in usage fee revenues.[18]

What you can do . . .

❑ Provide and organize information and present it in a way that leads managers to make the right decisions by making it very obvious to them where the opportunities associated with going green and the risks and costs associated with going green are.

(continued)

❑ Stay informed: Stay on top of the carbon and other sustainability debates insofar as it affects your business. Many of these discussions will affect accounting directly.

❑ Work to show the link between sustainability and profitability.

❑ Get involved with the design, operation and monitoring of purchasing policies, standards and management systems relating to the supply chain.

❑ Support stakeholder engagement processes with readily accessible and reliable information, and assist with the collation and analysis of stakeholder feedback.

❑ Identify those voluntary environmental or social codes appropriate to business or integrate operation of the codes with an existing management information system.

❑ Support benchmarking by providing relevant and reliable information in accessible, meaningful and comparable ways.[19]

Want more?

• The major **accountancy firms** are getting more involved in providing guidance on this issue to their clients and to the public via their international and country-specific websites including KPMG (www.kpmg.com), Ernst and Young (www.ey.com), PwC (www.pwc.com) and Deloitte and Touche (www.deloitte.com).

• The major **international accountancy bodies** also have increased resources on this topic for members and the public, including The Association of Chartered Certified Accountants (www.accaglobal.com), The Chartered Institute of Management Accountants (www.cimaglobal.com) and The International Federation of Accountants (ww.ifac.org).

• Some other **international initiatives** to take a look at include the UN Intergovernmental Working Group on Experts on International Standards of Accounting and Reporting (www.unctad.org/isar) and the report 'Environmental Management

Accounting Procedures and Principles' (www.un.org/esa/sustdev/publications/proceduresandprinciples.pdf).

- Many interesting resources are also coming out of national accounting bodies for example the ICAEW publication 'Sustainability: The role of accountants' (www.icaew.org).
- The Environmental and Sustainability Management Accounting Network www.eman-eu.net and The Centre for Social and Environmental Accounting Research (www.st-andrews.ac.uk/management/csear) also provide several resources on the topic.The Accounting for Sustainability Group was established byThe Prince of Wales and has resources including a forum that brings together the work being done in sustainability by different accountancy groups around the world (www.accountingforsustainability.org).
- For an excellent overview of accounting and sustainability see the IFAC Sustainability-framework (web.ifac.org/sustainability-framework)

Sustainability reporting

'Sustainability reporting is a process for publicly disclosing an organization's economic, environmental, and social performance. Many organizations find that financial reporting alone no longer satisfies the needs of shareholders, customers, communities, and other stakeholders for information about overall organizational performance.'

Global Reporting Initiative

Many organizations are incorporating environmental and social information into their public reports in response to demands from shareholders and other stakeholders for more information so that they may make better informed decisions about a companies' performance in this area. Although Sustainability Reporting remains a largely voluntary exercise in most countries, it is increasing in popularity.

Organizations of all sizes (including commercial companies, organizations, NGOs, schools and small companies) are choosing to report on their sustainability strategies for several reasons.

(continued)

- *Manage and improve their sustainability performance:* 'Reporting is a fundamental aspect of our global citizenship activities and an important form of communication with many stakeholders. The process of producing the report, the report itself and feedback from readers all help to increase awareness of global citizenship issues and promote continual improvement within HP.' Hewlett Packard Global Citizenship Report 2007.

- *Hold themselves accountable for their sustainability performance:* 'We report openly on our governance, environmental and social performance because they affect our business performance today and our ability to win societal acceptance and achieve our strategy in the future. Reporting also helps build trust and motivates staff and business partners to improve their performance.' Shell Social Responsibility Report 2005.

- *Communicate and promote awareness with external and internal stakeholders:* 'Although this is the first sustainability report which we have produced, we believe that based on the knowledge we have gained through the reporting process thus far we will produce annual updates to further improve our communication to stakeholders: particularly our key clients.' Suzi Products Sustainability Report 2007 (a supplier in South Africa to Puma shoe company).

Defining report content

Organizations around the world can take one of many different approaches, based on local cultures and regulatory differences, and on availability of the different mandatory and voluntary initiatives. The most commonly accepted framework has been created by the Global Reporting Initiative (GRI). The vision of the GRI is 'that disclosure on economic, environmental, and social performance is as commonplace and comparable as financial reporting, as important to organizational success'. The GRI guidelines present four principles for defining report content:

- *Materiality:* The report should cover topics and indicators that reflect the organization's significant economic, environmental and social impacts, or that would substantively influence the assessment and decisions of stakeholders.

- *Stakeholder inclusiveness:* The reporting organization should identify its stakeholders and explain in the report how it has responded to their reasonable expectations and interests.
- *Context:* The report should present the organization's performance in the wider context of sustainability.
- *Completeness:* The information presented in the report should be sufficient to reflect significant economic, environmental and social impacts and enable stakeholders to assess the reporting organization's performance in the reporting period.

The guidelines also have six principles defining report quality

- *Reliability:* Information and processes used in the preparation of a report should be gathered, recorded, compiled, analyzed and disclosed in a way that could be subject to examination and that establishes the quality and materiality of the information.
- *Clarity:* Information should be made available in a manner that is understandable and accessible to stakeholders using the report. A stakeholder should be able to find desired information without unreasonable effort.
- *Balance:* The report should reflect positive and negative aspects of the organization's performance to enable a reasoned assessment of overall performance.
- *Comparability:* Issues and information should be selected, compiled and reported consistently. Reported information should be presented in a manner that enables stakeholders to analyze changes in the organization's performance over time, and could support analysis relative to other organizations.
- *Accuracy:* The reported information should be sufficiently accurate and detailed for stakeholders to assess the reporting organization's performance.
- *Timeliness:* Reporting occurs on a regular schedule and information is available in time for stakeholders to make informed decisions.

Finally the guidelines have an extensive set of indicators which give details on the kind of data that should be included in reports. The indicators

(*continued*)

cover several areas including Economics, Environment, Human Rights, Labour, product Responsibility and Society. There is also guidance on unique indicators for particular industry sectors (sector supplements), country-level information (national Annexes). GRI provides special guidance for SMEs and microbusinesses and has several examples of reports produced by these.

Best practices

Organizations are compiling best practices in international and national level sustainability reporting through the use of award programs. ACCA's Sustainability Reporting Awards are given annually around the world including in Pakistan and Malaysia (www.accaglobal.org). The ACCA also includes various reports from the judges for the national awards which offer some interesting insights into sustainability reporting in those different areas. The GRI also has a Readers Choice Award, which surveys readers to find out which reports they prefer and why (www.globalreporting.org/NewsEventsPress/ReadersChoice Awards/).

In addition, Sustainability, UNEP and Standard & Poor produce an international benchmark of corporate sustainability reporting every two years (www.sustainability.com/insight/global_reporters.asp).

Companies themselves are also raising the bar by instituting their own new practices. Some trends include:

- *Growth in assurance:* An increasing number of reports begin with an assurance statement (explained earlier in this chapter).
- *Materiality:* Companies are increasingly choosing to focus their sustainability reports on the most material issues leading to generally shorter reports with greater links to business strategy. Information on less material issues is still available, usually through the companies' websites.
- *From risk to opportunity:* We are seeing a slow but steady shift towards a more progressive reporting approach, one that seeks to identify opportunities for strategic innovation and market building rather than focusing solely on risk.
- *Interaction with investors:* Many reports still lack the hard targets and forward-looking information typically sought by

investors, but this is slowly changing with development of appropriate KPIs.

- *Disclosures on public policy initiatives:* Most reports currently fail to sufficiently discuss and link their sustainability initiatives and commitments to the lobbying activities they undertake, either directly or indirectly. A small group of companies are becoming more transparent in this area.
- *Combined reports:* Companies are choosing to report on their sustainability activities in their financial reports, in separate dedicated reports, or by combining the two.
- *Mandatory:* Although still mostly a voluntary exercise, sustainability reporting has already become mandatory in some countries including France and Denmark, and as a condition of membership to certain networks such as the Global Compact.
- *Around the world:* The continued growth in sustainability reporting is primarily driven by its spread to smaller companies and emerging markets. Europe is leading in terms of number of organizations reporting, but other geographic areas are catching up fast.

Want more?

The GRI's Sustainability Reporting guidelines are free for public use (www.globalreporting.org). There are several other initiatives aimed at providing guidance in this area. The Accounting for Sustainability project developed a Connected Reporting Framework (www.sustainabilityatwork.org.uk/strategy/report). Many governments have also created national guidelines, for example the Government of Canada (www.sustainabilityreporting.ca).

For more resources on the topic, and to read different sustainability reports see The European Sustainability Reporting Association (www.sustainabilityreporting.eu), Corporate Register (www.corporateregister.com) and One Report (www.one-report.com). For regular news on sustainability reporting, see (www.enviroreporting.com/).

7 Economics

'The Earth as a whole is approximately in a steady-state. Neither the surface nor the mass of the earth is growing or shrinking ... None of this means that the earth is static—a great deal of qualitative change can happen inside a steady-state, and certainly has happened on Earth. The most important change in recent times has been the enormous growth of one subsystem of the Earth, namely the economy, relative to the total system, the ecosphere.'

HERMAN DALY[20]

In 2005 South Korea passed a law requiring all retailers to charge customers for items that are 'one-use' disposable items, such as paper cups and plastic bags. The results were significant: the use of paper bags decreased by 24 % as many Koreans now bring their own shopping bags to stores and their own cups to cafés to avoid the charges. By putting a price on waste the South Korean government created economic incentives for environmentally-friendly behaviour.[21] These regulations impact sustainability through the channel of economics.

Although economics is often blamed for creating the unsustainable world we live in, it plays an important role in sustainability. Economics is a tool that helps us to understand how we got to where we are now, and more importantly, how to move forward. It helps to explain the unintended incentives present in society that increase unsustainable behaviour, and can help us change these to incentives that support the desired, more sustainable behaviour.

Economics is also the study of how people choose to use resources. Scientists agree that drastic action is needed to save the planet and that if we are serious about doing that, we need to reshape the way that we use these resources. The good news is that economists are starting to explore opportunities to do just that by creating mechanisms that assist organizations in internalizing these costs so that buyers and sellers can make decisions based on complete information about products and services, as well as understanding the broader social and environmental consequences of the consumption of these products and services.

Why is it important?

- *Because the world is changing:* The context in which organizations are doing business is rapidly changing. Where before the US, Europe and Japan were the leading economies, today there are many other players in the world including developing and emerging markets. This is creating a more complex business environment with increased risks, but also increased opportunities for business.
- *Ecosystem services:* Nature provides many freely available benefits such as erosion control, climate regulation and pollination, not to mention freshwater, forests and wetlands. Ignoring the environmental impacts associated with economic growth will result in these resources becoming more costly for business.
- *Understanding regulatory and market based instruments:* Many problems in sustainability, such as externalities, represent market failure where the production or use of a good or service by the free market is not efficient. The mechanisms being put into place to address these market failures will directly affect businesses.
- *Better understanding of the full cost of our decisions:* The costs of activities are not always borne by the parties directly

involved which often results in consumers demanding more of a particular good or service than they would if they had to pay a price that included the full costs.

- **Increased regulations and standards:** Organizations will be faced with an increase in regulations and standards that they will have to comply with from the local to the global level.

The key concepts

Economics is about understanding the incentives in place to pursue unsustainable behaviour and in particular how to change these to support more sustainable behaviour. It is also about understanding the wider environment in which business operates and how this is changing.

- The rise of consumer societies   → **Sustainable Consumption**
- The way we manage shared   → **The Commons**
  resources
- Understanding the costs a com-   → **Externalities**
  pany's activities have on people
  and planet
- The range of policy instruments   → **Regulations and Compliance**
  that governments use
- Using market forces as a way to   → **Market Based Incentives**
  protect the planet
- Re-evaluating the way we meas-   → **Re-evaluating GDP**
  ure progress
- The impact of emerging mar-   → **Emerging markets**
  kets on global sustainability
- Attempting to understand the   → **Box: Environmental Valuation**
  value of biodiversity
- Working at the bottom of the   → **Box: Business and the**
  pyramid   **World's poor**

Sustainable consumption

Consumption patterns have been growing rapidly because of rapid population growth combined with the rise of a culture of consumerism. It is estimated that there will be 9 billion people in 2050, which represents a huge increase in the number of consumers. Globalization and increasing economic power are giving more and more of these consumers access to an increasing number of products and services. On average, around 60 % of GDP is accounted for by consumer spending on goods and services. However, the resources needed to support these global consumption patterns are putting unsustainable pressures on the earth's ecosystems and on human social systems and wellbeing.

Several tools and indices have emerged to measure and track the state of the world's ecosystems. The Ecological Footprint, for example, measures how much land and water area a human population requires to produce the resources it consumes and to absorb its wastes, using available technology. This technique can be used to calculate the footprint of an individual, a city, a business, a nation or the whole planet. Today humanity uses the equivalent of 1.3 planet Earths to provide the resources we use and to absorb our waste. Since the mid 1980s, humanity has been in ecological overshoot with annual demand on resources exceeding what Earth can regenerate each year. It now takes the Earth one year and four months to regenerate what we use in a year. If we continue with business as usual, by the early 2030s it is estimated that we will need two planet Earths to keep up with humanity's annual demand for goods and services.

The problem obviously is that we don't have two planet Earths, we only have one. But with that one planet, if we change our lifestyles and consumption patterns we can free up the resources needed to support humanity. As the WWF Living Planet Index Report states, 'there are many effective ways to change course. While technological developments will continue to play an important role in addressing the sustainability challenge, much of what needs to be done is already known, and solutions are available today.' Consumers are increasingly concerned with the negative effects the products they consume have on their health and on the environment, as well as the impact of the production

The Ecological Footprint provides resources for calculating and understanding an individual, a business, a city or even a country's footprint (www.footprintnetwork.org). The WWF Living Planet Index Report is a periodic update on the state of the world's ecosystems (www.panda.org/news_facts/publications/living_planet_report/). The Marrakech Process is a global multi-stakeholder process to promote sustainable consumption and production (www.unep.fr/scp/marrakech).

process on the environment. As a result, sustainable consumption policies and initiatives are broadening to take into account the effects of processes as well as products and the provision of services as well as goods. The need for policies that foster sustainable consumption has been recognized as a priority at the international level, for example through the development of a ten-year framework on sustainable consumption and production led by United Nations Environment Programme, United Nations Department of Economic and Social Affairs through the Marrakech Process.

The commons

UNEP says that 25% of the world's fisheries are in jeopardy of collapse due to over fishing. Restrictions are not working because fish are accessible to everyone, and it is difficult to prevent fishermen from taking all the fish they want. In this situation everyone races to catch as many fish as possible, reaping all the benefits of this natural resource but paying none of the costs. In the long run, when fish are caught faster than they can reproduce, this will result in no more fish for anyone. A 'commons' is a geographical area not owned by any private person or legal entity, and any natural resources contained in a commons thereby belong to everyone. These natural resources include the things that we inherited such as nature, air and water. Often people will misuse or overuse resources that are freely available, making them increasingly scarce. This is referred to as the 'Tragedy of the commons'.

How to manage the commons has always been an issue of much debate. Some say a Chamber of Commons is needed to regulate and protect the commons. Others try to put a financial value on the commons (see Valuation). Some of the debates raise the question of whether these common assets which are already being bought and sold in the market such as trees, water and fish are being responsibly managed on behalf of the general public who are the 'owners' of these assets.

Tradable permits are one option for protecting the commons. The European Union defines these as 'an economic policy instrument under which rights to discharge pollution or exploit resources can be exchanged through either a free or a controlled permit-market'. For example, in the case of fisheries, New Zealand put in place a quota management system to manage its fisheries in a sustainable way. Once it was determined how many fish could be caught without depleting the fish population, this number was divided up into quotas and given to companies. Companies own the quotas, and are allowed to sell or trade them. The result is they are treated with the same respect as any other valuable asset. Today approximately 80% of fish stocks are at or near target levels of sustainable harvest and the total allowable catch for some fish has even increased.

Another example is from the island of Bali in Indonesia. Rice farmers have been coordinating their use of scarce water for centuries through social networks built around 'water temples' where they meet to discuss water allocation issues. Modern analysis showed that the way they allocate water was close to ideal. However, in the 1960s the government decided to intervene, bypassing the temples and hiring hydrologists to install modern water systems and introduce heavy pesticides. The result was a disaster, so much so that in the end the government let the farmers return to their original system.

Creative commons provides tools to let creatives mark their work with the freedoms they want it to carry (www.creativecommons.org). On the commons is dedicated to exploring the ideas and action about the commons (www.onthecommons.org).

Read *The Gridlock Economy* by Michael Heller, which explores how too much private ownership can create a gridlock rather than wealth. The Eco-Patent Commons is an initiative to create a collection of patents on technology that directly or indirectly protects the environment. The patents will be pledged by companies and other intellectual property rights holders and made available to anyone free of charge. Several companies including IBM, Nokia and Sony are already members (www.wbcsd.org/web/epc). For an interesting video explaining the commons see YouTube (search The Commons, video nation) (www.youtube.com/watch?v5L7jaSjkd0jM)

The commons does not just refer to environmental systems. Knowledge and culture created by society are also part of the commons. Some companies are exploiting traditional knowledge, for example in relation to medicinal and agricultural plants, and creating products for which they are awarded exclusive rights under patent laws (this practice is known as bio-piracy). In response to this, databases and archives such as the Traditional Knowledge Digital Library in South Asia have been constructed to try to stop bio-piracy by establishing 'prior art' which disallows patents on anything that has been disclosed to the public in some form.

Externalities

A company deals with costs and services that have a value set by the market in the normal course of business. For example, if a company needs to clean up a polluted site, the cost is processed through the traditional accounting system. However, the company's activities also give rise to external costs, known as externalities, which relate to the effects that the company's activities have on the environment and on people. For example, if a company releases untreated water into a nearby river this has a detrimental effect on both the ecosystem of the river and those communities that rely on the river to survive. In most cases, these costs (cleaning up the river, helping the people) are currently absorbed by society as a whole, instead of by the company that damaged the environment. On the other hand, an externality can also be positive. For example, if a landowner chooses not to develop her or his land and in doing so preserves a local water source for an aquifer, the landowner usually won't get an economic benefit for the decision, but society does.

Externalities are important to consider because the costs or benefits to the company are often different from the costs or benefits to society as a whole. For example, if the cost of polluting is not borne by the polluters, then they will feel no economic motivation to reduce their discharge of waste. If the price of water is set below the true cost to society of using this resource, this will produce incentives to use excessive amounts of water. Because these costs and benefits are paid by society, as a whole, private economic actors (individuals and corporations) cannot make appropriate and correct calculations about whether it makes economic sense to go ahead with an activity. In this sense, externalities are often considered a form of market failure since the amount of the activity carried out by private parties in a free market will result in an inefficient use of resources.

Economists are interested in externalities as a market failure for theoretical reasons (e.g. because they can help us to understand how markets work in different societies) and practical reasons (e.g. because market failures justify the intervention of government through legislation, regulations and other tools that work through the market). Accounting for externalities is not an easy task because in many cases the extent of the impact is either unknown or difficult to measure. Even when it can be identified, there are significant challenges related to measuring and quantifying the impact to society and the environment. The most efficient solutions

> The Coase Theorem is about the economic efficiency of an economic allocation in the presence of externalities (www.econlib.org/library.Enc/bios/Coase.html) ExternE is a project by the EU on externalities (www.externe.info)

have been to work with the private companies and individuals to internalize externalities through mechanisms such as taxes and compliance costs.

Regulatory Instruments

The regulatory framework within which companies operate is extensive and complex. As governments become increasingly conscious of environmental concerns and the public demand action, companies are faced with a growing number of regulations that they must comply with. The situation becomes even more complex for companies that conduct business across borders where regulations can differ from one jurisdiction to the next, often significantly. For example, the EU operates a cap and trade system to control greenhouse gas emissions that is unique for entities operating within member states. A similar regulatory system does not exist, at least at the present time, in North America.

Companies face a range of challenges not just in understanding the different regulatory regimes that exist but in ensuring that their processes, products and services are in compliance with these requirements. Unlike voluntary standards or codes of conduct that companies may adopt to meet certain sustainability objectives on their own, regulations are enforceable by law.

Enforcement of these different mechanisms varies depending on the nature and location of the regulation. Many have their own dispute settlement mechanisms. The European Commission is exploring plans to take environmental offences to criminal courts. People could face jail time for dumping toxic waste or illegally trading endangered species for example. The US EPA has also launched an environmental crimes fugitive website to assist law enforcement agencies and the general public in finding fugitives who have violated environmental laws. At the international level the International Court of Justice is one mechanism that can be used. However, often the most effective is public and political pressure.

Ecolex is a database of information on environmental law at the international and national levels (www.ecolex.org). Centre for Environmental Law (www.ciel.org) and the Centre for International Sustainable Development Law (www.cisdl.org). Guidance for compliance with multinational environmental agreements can be found at www.unep.org/DPDL/law and www.inece.org. International Court of Justice (www.icj-cij.org). NetRegs is an online service run by the Environmental Agency to help smaller businesses navigate some of the laws affecting their activities. An increasing number of voluntary standards have been developed to fill the gaps which currently exist in regulations. Many of these are explored in the different relevant sections of this book.

Market based instruments

There is a growing realization that one way to reverse the trend of environmental decline and protect many of our common resources on earth is to use market forces. The idea is that certain unsustainable behaviours of firms or individuals are caused by a lack of economic incentives to pursue sustainable behaviour. For example, a landowner who has a wetland or an endangered species on their land may be providing a service to society by choosing not to develop his or her land, but in the process is losing the financial opportunity associated with developing that land. In response to this, market-based instruments are being created to provide financial incentives aimed at protecting the environment by altering market prices, setting limits on resource use, improving the way a market works and creating a new market where one previously didn't exist. In the case of the landowners, they can collect payments or 'credits' from the conservation of the land, and can then sell these credits to developers who are looking to offset harm they have caused to the environment. About $ 3.4 billion of regulated biodiversity offset transactions currently occur per year, a number which could grow to $10 billion by 2020.[22]

There are three broad types of MBIs: price based, quantity based and market friction.

1. **Price based instruments** work by changing the prices of goods and services to reflect their relative impact on the environment by either adding or removing a tax or fee. The advantage of these mechanisms is that a company knows how much it will cost to comply, but the overall environmental outcome can be uncertain. These can take the form of:

   - *Taxes* not only generate the revenue needed to mitigate the negative impacts, but they also raise the price of the good or service in question, thereby decreasing the demand.

   - *Subsidies* in the form of a payment or tax concession can help encourage changes in behaviour that reduce pollution. For example, a subsidy could be offered for the purchase of clean technology in order to achieve a reduction in overall pollution levels.

   - *Charges* can be imposed to encourage companies or individuals to change behaviour. For example by charging a fee to dispose of garbage, companies can be encouraged to minimize the waste they produce.

   - *Deposit-refund systems* include schemes where a buyer pays an up front charge in addition to the price of the product, which is then refunded when the product is returned. One common example of this is the beverage container deposit scheme, which is usually introduced to encourage the return of drink containers for recycling.

2. **Quantity based instruments** involve creating markets for the right to undertake an activity that has a negative environmental impact such as discharging pollutants into a river or the air, or for the right to have access to a scarce resource such as water. These are used when there is a measurable target that needs to be achieved. As opposed to the price based instruments, these provide certainty regarding the environmental outcome, but not of the cost to industry of achieving that outcome.

- *Tradable permits* involve the amount of pollution that can be released, or how much of a resource can be sustainably used, being determined and then the provision of permits for that amount. Organizations can only pollute as much as the permits they own allow. If they put in place mechanisms that allow them to cut their pollution significantly, they can sell unused credits to other companies that perhaps have not been able to cut their pollution.

- *Quota management* is a way to protect natural resources such as fisheries. Once the total amount of fish available to catch is determined, quotas are then given to fishers. One fisherman from the Alaskan Halibut fishing industry said about the quotas put in place in that industry, 'Most fishermen will now support cuts in quotas because they feel guaranteed that in the future, when the stocks recover, they would be the ones to benefit.'[23]

- *Offsets* are conservation actions designed to compensate for unavoidable impacts on the environment. For example, clearing native vegetation for a development can be offset by protecting another ecologically equivalent area of vegetation. These are usually only appropriate when the participant has first used best practices to avoid and minimize harm.

3. **Market friction instruments** aim to influence how existing markets work in order to improve environmental outcomes. One example of this is through *product differentiation* in the form of certification schemes and eco-labels. Putting these on products enables consumer preferences to be expressed through markets. For example the FSC label allows customers to choose products that are made of wood from sustainable forests, thus increasing the incentives for companies to produce such products. (More on this in the marketing chapter.)

There are many potential advantages of MBIs. They can be more cost-effective for delivering environmental outcomes than regulations or other traditional methods, and often give better results. They provide flexibility for participants to choose how they will

Biodiversity Economics sponsored by IUCN and WWF has a wide range of resources including a beginners guide (www. biodiversityeconomics.org). Conservation Finance (www.world-wildlife.org/conservationfinance). The Conservation Finance Alliance has an online guide to conservation finance (www.con-servationfinance.org). The WBCSD and IUCN have developed a free role playing game called 'Buy, Trade, Sell' which shows how ecosystem markets work (www.wbcsd.org). www.ecosystemmar-ketplace.com and www.ecosystemservicesproject.org have infor-mation on markets and payment schemes for ecosystem services. The Australian government (www.marketbasedinstruments.gov.au) also has a useful resource describing MBIs.

reach goals and to reduce pollution beyond targets. In that way they can act as a more positive influencer leading to more long-term and self-sustaining solutions. However, markets themselves do not allow us to solve all problems. Markets are very complex and it can be difficult to predict the outcomes of certain initiatives. For this reason different types of MBIs are currently being tested around the world, especially around carbon and increasingly around biodiversity and conservation.

Re-evaluating metrics

Economic progress is usually measured by gross domestic product (GDP). This represents the total dollar value of all goods and services produced over a specific time period. Although this can give a pretty good indication of the size of the economy, it does not include a number of factors that determine the wellbeing of people. As author Paul Hawken puts it, 'We have an economy where we steal the future, sell it in the present, and call it GDP'. There are also several problems with how GDP itself is measured. For example, GDP focuses on short-term economic activities rather than on developments in the assets of natural, economic and social capital, which are more important in a long-term, sustainability perspective. Both the 'beneficial' activities that cause pollution and the costly activities necessary to clean up the pollution are counted towards a country's GDP. Cutting down trees and selling lumber boost GDP, but loss of forests does nothing to decrease it.

Studies often show that as GDP goes up, other measures are levelling off and even declining. For example, the New Economic Foundation's Happy Planet Index which ranks a nation's progress based on the amount of the Earth's resources its inhabitants use and the length and happiness of people's lives found that high levels of consumption do not necessarily guarantee happiness. As Herman Daly, one of the founders of ecological economics, puts it, 'economic growth may already be making us poorer rather than richer'.[24] In response, several alternatives have been presented which look at economic, environmental and social wellbeing. These include:

- *Green Net National Product (GNP):* GDP less the costs of degradation and depletion of natural resources.
- *Genuine Progress Indicator/Index of Sustainable Economic Welfare:* Personal consumption expenditures plus the value of 'unpaid' work (e.g. volunteering), capital services and education less the costs of inequality, crime, pollution, loss of leisure, unemployment and natural capital depletion.
- *Wellbeing Index (WBI):* Going beyond GPI, this index also incorporates measures of civil freedom, security, biodiversity, health, justice and self sufficiency.
- *Human Development Index (HDI):* averages three indices reflecting a country's achievements in health and longevity (life expectancy at birth), education (adult literacy and school enrolment) and living standard (GDP per capita in PPP terms) (hdr.undp.org/en/statistics).

One country has actually moved to exploring these alternatives to GDP. According to the Centre of Bhutan Studies, 'GDP is heavily biased towards increased production and consumption, regardless of the necessity or desirability of such outputs, at the expense of other more holistic criterion ... Indicators determine policies. The almost universal use of GDP-based indicators to measure progress has helped justify policies around the world that are based on rapid material progress at the expense of environmental preservation, cultures, and community cohesion.' Bhutan came up with Gross National Happiness (GNH). The idea is that a country should not sacrifice elements important to peoples' happiness to gain material development, so GNH focuses on not just flows of money but also access to healthcare, free time with family, conservation of natural resources and other non-economic factors (www.grossnationalhappiness.com).

The Beyond GDP project looks at improving measures of progress, wealth and wellbeing and has a long list of potential alternatives (www.beyond-gdp.eu). Redefining Progress is a think-tank based in the US that is looking at sustainability indicators at the national, regional and community level (www.rprogress.org). Happy Planet Index (www.happyplanetindex.org).

Emerging markets

The global economy is changing from one that was dominated primarily by a few countries, to one where there are a larger number of global economic powers coming from developing economies. Developing world economies today account for 49% of global GDP, up from 39% in 1990. The big emerging markets include Brazil, China, Egypt, India, Indonesia, Mexico, Poland, Philippines, Russia, South Africa, South Korea and Turkey. This is pushed on by increasing power of information and communication technologies, government policies to increase economic openness and the increasing size and geographic reach of multinational enterprises.

Where traditionally it was a one-way street, with help in the form of aid going from developed to developing countries, and developed countries holding the power in terms of business relations with developing nations, it is increasingly much more complex than that. 'Globalization, a force that has been shaping the political and commercial world for most of our working lives, is entering a new and more complex phase. It is no longer a concept exported to the emerging world by traditionally-dominant economies of the West. Emerging economies have grasped globalization, packaged it up, and are, every day, sending new versions of it back to the West' (William D. Green CEO, Accenture). Emerging Market companies fit into the following categories according to Accenture:

- *Fully fledged globalizers* tend to be older, more established companies that have attained a scale and geographic span on a par with big western multinationals, i.e. Tata group, CEMEX.
- *Regional players* aim to break out of their domestic market in search of greater scale, but for reasons of cultural affinity and geographic proximity fix their sights initially on neighbouring markets. One example is Vina capital from Vietnam, who are now moving into south east Asia.
- *Global sourcers* are interested principally in selling to their domestic market but, because of resource constraints at home, they source internationally.
- *Global sellers* are the mirror image of global sourcers, in that they primarily manufacture or source at home, but are seeking new consumer markets abroad in order to increase sales.
- *Multi-regional niche players* tend to be smaller companies operating across multiple regions in niche sectors, usually on the basis of innovative technology or processes.

According to Accenture, emerging markets are crucial players in sustainability for many reasons.

- **Talent:** People have become one of the most highly sought after and valuable resources on earth, fought over by multiple competitors. The supply of labour is shifting dramatically. Of the 438 million people to be added to the global workforce by 2050, 97 % will come from developing countries. As developing countries become more powerful, companies that operate there are also luring nationals back to their home countries, and away from the more developed countries.

- *Resources:* With increased levels of business comes an increased need and thus competition for resources such as energy, commodities and raw materials. Since 2000, these economies have been responsible for 85% of the increase in world energy demand. 'In this context the challenge for leaders is fast becoming one of how to manage the complex balance between three overriding imperatives: of economic growth, energy security (of supply for resource-poor countries and of demand for resource-rich areas), and sustainability.'

- *New consumers:* With up to a billion new consumers in these emerging markets, there are plenty of opportunities to grow market share. This is particularly true as emerging market populations which originally were largely built on supplying low cost goods and services to western economies are fast becoming important consumer markets in their own right. Growth is fuelling rising employment and creating a new middle class. Emerging economies will account for more than half of global consumption by 2025.

- *Because they are growing:* From the emerging economies, there are now 70 companies in the Fortune global 500 list of the world's biggest companies, up from 20 a decade ago. Within the last year alone, the number has grown by nine. These companies are expanding and acquiring new businesses at a frenetic pace, conducting more than 1100 mergers and acquisitions in 2006. Many everyday brands in western markets owned by companies in the developing world, i.e. Tetley in the UK owned by Tata.

- *Innovative business models:* Because they have learnt a different set of lessons to businesses in the developed world, emerging market companies are doing well at mastering the challenges of a new multi polar world. Being more street wise business operators, they are managing a broad range of risks more comfortably. Many have mastered the art of improvisation, and are adept at turning apparently unpromising situations to their advantage through overcoming talent shortages, innovative educational and training programmes, incubating consumer demand through BOP business models or adapting products and technologies to local market conditions.[25]

Developing Value: The Business Case for Sustainability in Emerging Markets aims to help business managers understand the opportunities, risks and bottom line implications of sustainability strategies (www.sustainability. com/developing-value). Accenture has two publications with more information called Multipolar Business World (www.accenture.com).

The challenge will be to see how these emerging countries and companies in these countries choose to embrace sustainability in their operations at home and abroad. As *The Economist* put it: 'could the rise of the new champions reflect the advance of bad forms of capitalism at the expense of good forms? . . . How can western firms compete in countries where bribes are seen as an ordinary cost of business?' There are many other uncertainties about emerging markets, in particular local governments and their attitude to the rule of law. 'Will theft of intellectual property be punished? Will lax regulatory enforcement allow your company's supply chain to be contaminated?'[26]

Challenges

- *Uncertainty:* Uncertainty is present in how we value all environmental and social problems as well as the policies that are being put in place to address these problems. Any analysis that fails to recognize this runs the risk of not only being incomplete but also misleading.
- *Free Riders:* Free riders are those who don't take on their fair share of responsibilities, but who benefit from those that others take on.

Free riders in the field of sustainability take the form, for example, of firms that sign up to international initiatives and use the logo but who fail to pay their dues or follow the requirements listed for membership.

- **Everyone needs to do their part:** In order for sustainability to move forward, businesses need to do their part but so do consumers, buyers, government and other actors.

- **Determining the tradeoffs:** Although we would like to believe that all sustainability initiatives are win-win, the fact is that many are not in the short-term. This leads us to have to make tradeoffs in our daily decisions and daily lives. How much are we willing to pay? What are we willing to do? How far are we willing to go?

- **Getting incentives right:** Reportedly only a small fraction of houses being rebuilt in New Orleans meet new stricter building codes. Better-built houses are more likely to survive a storm, but the builders and homeowners know the government will pay them to rebuild if it happens again. This is referred to as a moral hazard 'where people behave differently if they are insured against risk. In this case you have a moral hazard when people choose to build in disaster proven areas because they don't have to take on the full cost of their decisions.'[27]

- **Determining what optimum means:** If you were to ask environmentalists, they would say that optimum level of pollution is zero, but economists don't necessarily see it that way. Pollution is a by-product of many things that we value and, therefore, some amount of pollution is warranted. For example even renewable energy produces some quantity of pollution. The question therefore is how much is optimum?

Trends and new ideas

– Alternative trading system	– From free to fee
– A new economic model	–Valuing future generations
– Estimating the cost of inaction	

Alternative trading system The Seikatsu Club Consumers' Co-operative Union won the Honorary Right Livelihood Award in 1989 because it was a form of 'alternative economic activity against industrial society's prioritization on efficiency.' This network made up of Japanese housewives has approximately 600 consumer co-operatives with 22 000 000 members in Japan. The co-operative takes advance orders from its members for daily goods such as eggs and milk and thus is able to ensure proper sourcing and good prices. It also works together to ensure the right quality by refusing to purchase products that are detrimental to the environment or human health. The club has gone beyond providing daily goods such as eggs and milk to providing other services such as recycling, health, education and childcare. By 2005 the total annual retail sales reached US $610 million making it a force to be reckoned with.

Other models exist where goods and services are traded without money also referred to as Local Exchange Trading Systems. Members earn credit by providing a good or service that they can later use to pay someone else from the network to provide them with a good or service. Transactions are recorded in a central location that all members have access to. Banco Palmas in Brazil works with the official country currency and a social currency issued by the bank called the Palmas currency. The bank is owned and managed by the community and offers loans for productive activity to stimulate local enterprise and consumer credit, including a local Palmacard credit card, for products and services produced inside the community. Their intention is to create a local financial system based on a network of producers and consumers.

> Ashoka Changemakers and the Banking on Social Change competition (www. Changemakers.net).

A new economic model The conventional neoclassical economic model is based on perpetual growth and is seen as the way to achieving wellbeing. The news media have been full of articles describing how it took just a few days for governments to abandon decades of economic doctrine to try to rescue the financial system. Why shouldn't it take as long to introduce a plan to introduce a new, more relevant economic model?

In October 2008 UNEP and leading economists launched the Green Economy Initiative which 'will encourage and enable economic, planning, finance, labour, environment, and other policymakers to support increased investments in environmental assets and green production while ensuring a fair and just transition towards a green economy'. The ambitious plan calls on world leaders, to promote a massive redirection of investment away from the speculation that has caused the bursting 'financial and housing bubbles' and into job-creating programmes to restore the natural systems that underpin the world economy. Its mission is to communicate a global plan for a green industrial revolution to be supported by strong and convincing evidence of income generated, decent jobs created and poverty reduced through investing in a new generation of assets including: Ecosystems (or environmental infrastructure), clean and efficient technology, renewable energy, biodiversity-based products and services (such as organic foods), chemical and waste management and mitigation technologies, and green cities with ecologically friendly buildings, construction and transport systems. All this could create millions of green jobs.

The Green New Deal (www.unep.org/greeneconomy). Also take a look at some of the winners of the Nobel Prize in Economics who have been exploring sustainability (www. nobelprize.org/nobel_prizes/economics/laureates). Several organizations are also looking at new economic models including The Foundation for the Economics of Sustainability (www.feasta.org), Centre for the Advancement of the Steady State Economy (www.steadystate.org) and the New Economics Foundation (www.neweconomics.org).

Estimating the costs of inaction One of the areas slowing down global action in sustainability is the perceived high cost of taking action. In response, there has been an increased effort to calculate the costs of not taking action in areas such as water and sanitation, clean air and climate change. A report submitted to a UN biodiversity conference in 2008 said mankind was causing €50 billion ($68 billion) of damage to the planet's land areas every year, through factors including pollution and deforestation[28]. The 2006 Stern Report put a £ 2.3 trillion price tag on the consequences of ignoring climate change. It said 'The costs of action to the global economy would be roughly 1 percent of GDP, while the costs of inaction could be from 5–20 percent of GDP'. The OECD also published a report that looked at the costs of inaction on a range of key environmental challenges such as air and water pollution, natural resource management, environment-related industrial accidents and natural disasters. For example, the costs of natural disasters (e.g. floods, windstorm, earthquakes, etc.) to the poorest countries are estimated at being as much as 13% of annual GDP. Although the cost of taking the required action today seems significant, many agree that the costs if we take action today are trivial compared to how much this will cost us in the future.

> The Stern Review on the Economics of Climate Change (www.hm-treasury.gov.uk/sternreview_index.htm) and OECD Costs of Inaction on Key Environmental Challenges 2008 (www.oecd.org/env/costofinaction).

From free to fee We've seen plastic shopping bags move from being a free resource to one that consumers are required to pay for in some countries. In the past, many resources were free (fish, water and air to name a few). Future generations will increasingly be living in an environment where these same resources will be priced. We may even begin to see environmental goods such as clean tap water or air being marketed. It is easy to imagine new housing developments that use the clean air in their neighbourhood as an important selling point. The opposite is also starting to happen; sustainable products that were once more expensive to produce will become increasingly less expensive as the materials they use are more readily available and savings from not using chemicals, petroleum and other expensive inputs starts to show.

Valuing future generations If valuing current generations and their environmental needs wasn't difficult enough, policy makers also have to contend with how to value future generations. The question then arises—how much should be reserved for the needs of the future when making decisions that affect us today? In calculating the costs of greenhouse gas reductions one needs to see how these compare to the benefits of the reduced risk of climate change many decades, even centuries into the future. Should a dollar spent today to prevent climate change weigh equally against a dollar in benefits 100 years from now?

This is where discount rates come in. Sure, discounts rates don't sound very exciting, but they are increasingly important and used in cost-benefit analysis and long-range environmental planning. The decision of which rate to choose can have serious implications; higher discount rates make investments less attractive, while lower discount rates make them appear more attractive. For example if we estimated the benefits of climate change mitigation at approximately $1 trillion 100 years from now, and we used a discount rate of 5% that $1 trillion would only be worth $7.6 billion today. Instead if we choose a rate of 0.1% then that $1 trillion 100 years from now would be worth over $900 billion today, more than 100 times the amount. The Stern review chose 0.1% per year to calculate the present value of the benefits of climate change mitigation for future generations. Many environmentalists argue that the discount rate should be zero because it is immoral to value our well being over those in the future. There is no correct discount rate.[29]

What Environmentalists Need to Know about Economics (2008) by Jason Scorse available to download free at (policy.miis.edu/faculty/scorse.html) is a great introduction to everything relating to economics and the environment and it has a chapter on this topic. Nobel Laureate Robert Salow's essay on 'Sustainability: An economists perspective explores the idea of future generations' (cda.morris.umn.edu/~kildegac/Courses/Enviro/3008/Solow.pdf).

What you can do . . .

❑ Think of what the current incentives and disincentives are that guide people's behaviours as a basis for putting in place solutions

❑ *Be careful about making decisions purely based on price:* A company may be able to quote a lower price for a service because they have no mechanisms in place to minimize their environmental impact.

Want more?

The World Bank Environmental Economics and Indicators has many resources including the *Little Green Data Book* available free online (www.worldbank.org). Other sources include The International Society for Ecological Economics (www.ecoeco. org), Vox is research-based policy analysis and commentary from leading economists (www.voxeu.org). *The Economist* (www. economist.com) and Environmental Economics Economists on Environmental and natural resources (www.env-econ. net). McKinsey has created a study of the world's leading cities grouped based on innovation (whatmatters.mckinseydigital. com/flash/innovation_clusters).

Read: *Common Wealth: Economics for a Crowded Planet* by Jeffrey D. Sachs (2009), which argues that the crises facing humanity are daunting—but solutions to them are readily at hand. *Capitalism as if the World Matters* by Jonathon Porritt (2005) looks at the question of whether capitalism, as the only real economic game in town can be retooled to deliver a sustainable future. *Limits to Growth* and *Limits to Growth: The 20 Year Update* by Donella H. Meadows, Jorgen Randers and Dennis Meadows (1972 and 2004) looks at the consequences of a rapidly growing world population and finite resource supplies. *Ecological Economics* by Herman E. Daly (2003 and 2008) is an introductory-level textbook for an emerging paradigm that addresses this fundamental flaw in conventional economics. *Small is Beautiful* by E. F. Schumacher (1973) critiques Western economics to a wider audience and was ranked among the 100 most influential books published since World War II. *The Natural Advantage of Nations: Business Opportunity, Innovation and Governance in the 21ˢᵗ Century* by Karlson Hargroves and Michael H. Smith (2005) looks at how it is possible and profitable to achieve sustainable development in our lifetimes.

Environmental valuation

'Is it true that the service of pollination, provided mainly by bees for free, is estimated to be at least worth US$ 4 billion a year to the agricultural sector in the US alone? Or that coral reefs provide ecosystem services vital to off-shore fisheries and shoreline protection worth as much as US$ 600 000 per square kilometre? Or that the world's protected areas (accounting for only 12 % of total land surface) sustain a rapidly growing eco-tourism sector, support local livelihoods, and overall produce benefits for society in excess of US$ 4,000 billion a year? The answer is yes, but there is the paradox: 20 % of the world's coral reefs and 35 % of all mangroves have been destroyed, and two-thirds of all ecosystem services degraded, some perhaps beyond repair.'

WBCSD[30]

Despite growing awareness about the importance of ecosystems and biodiversity, as well as a commitment by the international community to achieve, by 2010, a significant reduction of the current rate of biodiversity loss, ecosystems continue to be mismanaged, misunderstood and destroyed. As stated by the World Bank, 'There are many reasons for the gap between aspiration and reality. One of the most important is that economic policies and markets generally fail to value biodiversity or the

(continued)

conservation of ecosystems. With few exceptions, there is little financial reward for conserving biodiversity, nor much penalty for destroying it'.[31]

The Millennium Development Goals

1. Eradicate extreme poverty and hunger
2. Achieve universal primary education
3. Promote gender equality and empower women
4. Reduce child mortality
5. Improve material health
6. Combat HIV/AIDS, malaria and other diseases
7. Ensure environmental sustainability
8. Development a global partnership for development.

Businesses often place zero value on natural assets and natural systems. For example, a fishing fleet counts the cost of vessels, fuel, people and transportation, but it treats fish as free. This can lead to a 'tragedy of the commons' problem: as fish become scarcer, they become more valuable, which encourages more fishing. Valuation is difficult, because typically neither the economic value nor the degradation of these services is included. At the same time, the alternate goods and services needed to replace them – such as water treatment plants in the case of water – do contribute to GDP, which can be rather misleading.

Valuing natural resources may seem straightforward; one only has to consider market transaction prices. However, market prices do not cover the true value of these resources, or the broader ecosystems of which they are part. For example, an ecosystem service plays a significant role in many transactions, as breeding grounds for fish and barriers for storms, or the role of biodiversity on water and air purification. Ecosystems provide a range of services including:

- Provisioning: in providing goods such as food, water and fibre.
- Regulating: in regulating biophysical processes and controlling natural processes.
- Cultural: by providing recreational, aesthetic or spiritual value.
- Supporting: in supporting processes such as soil formation, photosynthesis and nutrient cycling.

Markets are likely to undervalue ecosystem services if these are not in some way quantified and recorded. Only then can these values be used when deciding on alternative uses of ecosystems or the activities that will impact them.The Millennium Ecosystem Assessment (MEA) is one of the first attempts at valuing ecosystems and evaluating on a global scale the full range of services people derive from nature and therefore the consequences of ecosystem change for human wellbeing.

The World Bank and IUCN use the following criteria to calculate total economic value:

*   *Direct use value*: ecosystem goods and services that are used directly by humans, for consumptive uses such as harvesting food, timber or fuel, and non consumptive such as recreational and cultural activities.
*   *Indirect use value:* ecosystem services that provide benefit outside the ecosystem itself, for example natural water filtration, storm protection function of mangrove forests, etc.
*   *Option value:* derived from preserving the option to use ecosystem goods and services in the future that are not used in the present.
*   *Non use value:* for the enjoyment people may experience simply by knowing that a resource exists even if it they never expect to use that resource directly.

The MEA uses cost-benefit analysis as the main method for valuation. Typically, this determines the costs of a project as well as the benefits then translates them into monetary terms. Projects with benefits that outweigh the costs generally move forward. However, this type of analysis may be misleading, as the true or total value is not included. Although costs are often known, environmental benefits often lack market value. Benefits are often collected over time, while costs are up front. As a result, it is often difficult to understand what is being measured or to determine values for what is being measured.[32]

The MEA can make use of several methods to determine the value of a benefit.The decision of which one to use usually comes down to time and resources available.

*   **Market Price Method:** estimates economic values for ecosystem products or services that are bought and sold in commercial markets. For example, a cultural site could be valued based on the entrance fees collected.
*   **Hedonic Pricing Method:** uses information from a surrogate market to estimate the implicit value of an environmental good or service. For example, housing prices can be used to estimate how much extra people are willing to pay for residential property in areas free from traffic.

(*continued*)

- *Travel Cost Method:* estimates economic values associated with ecosystems or sites that are used for recreation. Assumes that the value of a site is reflected in how much people are willing to pay to travel to visit the site.
- *Productivity Approach:* estimates economic values for ecosystem products or services that contribute to the production of commercial goods. For example, the benefits of different levels of water quality improvement would be compared to the costs of reductions in polluting runoff.
- *Damage Cost Avoided, Replacement Cost and Substitute Cost Methods:* estimate economic values based on costs of avoided damages resulting from lost ecosystem services, costs of replacing ecosystem services, or costs of providing substitute services. For example, the costs avoided by providing flood protection.
- *Preventive Expenditure Method:* based on actual expenditure incurred to prevent, eradicate or reduce adverse environmental effects.
- *Contingent Valuation Method:* Estimates economic values for virtually any ecosystem or environmental service. The most widely used method for estimating non-use, or 'passive use' values. It asks people to directly state their willingness to pay for specific environmental services, based on a hypothetical scenario. For example, people would state how much they would pay to protect a particular area.
- *Contingent Choice Method:* Estimates economic values for virtually any ecosystem or environmental service based on asking people to make tradeoffs among sets of ecosystem or environmental services or characteristics. It does not directly ask for willingness to pay—this is inferred from tradeoffs that include cost as an attribute. For example, a person would state their preference between various locations for a landfill.
- *Benefit Transfer Method:* Estimates economic values by transferring existing benefit estimates from studies already completed for another location or issue. For example, an estimate of the benefit obtained by tourists viewing wildlife in one park might be used to estimate the benefit obtained from viewing wildlife in a different park.[33]

Want more?

A list of European Valuation studies is available at: www.europa.eu.int/comm/environment/enveco. Millennium Ecosystems Assessment reports can be found at www.millenniumassessment.org. Ecosystem Valuation describes how economists value the beneficial ways that ecosystems affect people designed for non-economists (www.ecosystemvaluation.org). Several organizations such as the World Bank, the IUCN, the WRI, UNEP and the Global Environment Facility are working on valuating ecosystem services. Natural Capital Project (www.naturalcapital.org).

Business and the world's poor

'Beside their philanthropic efforts and their policy influence, companies can contribute significantly to meeting the development goals through their core business operations, either by involving the poor in their supply chain activities, or by supplying appropriate products and services to improve people's livelihoods in developing countries.'

WBCSD

In the year 2000, the world's leaders came together and signed the Millennium Development Goals: 15 goals related to poverty, education, health and gender issues for the world to work together to reach by the year 2015. Business's contribution to the achievement of these goals has been through partnerships, aid donations and other philanthropical activities, but increasingly its impact has been through a focus on exploring business opportunities directed at and working with the world's poor by creating opportunities for them to improve their own lives. As stated by the WBCSD 'business is good for development and development is good for business'.

Market-based approaches to poverty reduction focus on enabling opportunity rather than providing aid. Traditionally there has been an assumption that the very poor were unable to help themselves and therefore needed charity and aid. However, as the World Resource Institute writes, the fact is that even within the poorest communities there are still commerce and market processes. 'A market-based approach thus focuses on people as consumers and producers and on solutions that can make markets more efficient, competitive, and inclusive – so that the BOP (Bottom of the Pyramid) can benefit from them. It looks for solutions in the form of new products and new business models that can provide goods and services at affordable prices.'

(continued)

Who are They?

The base of the pyramid (BOP) is an expression that refers to the 4 billion low-income consumers that constitute the foundation of the economic pyramid. BOPs are generally 'not integrated into the global market economy and do not benefit from it.'They are often rural, very poorly served, dominated by informal economy and as a result relatively inefficient and uncompetitive. According to the WRI they share the following characteristics:

- **Significant unmet needs**: many have no bank accounts, access to modern financial services, phones, water and sanitation services, electricity and basic health care.
- **Dependence on informal or subsistence livelihoods:** most lack access to markets to sell their labour, handicrafts or crops and therefore have no choice but to sell to local employers or middlemen, who often exploit them.
- **Impacted by a BOP penalty:** many in this segment actually pay more, either in terms of cash or effort to obtain basic goods than most in developed countries and is often of lower quality.

	Market size	% po	% buying power
Africa	429b	95 %	71 %
Asia	$3.47trill	83 %	42 %
Eastern E	$458b	64 %	36 %
LA and C	509b	70 %	28 %

(**Source:** The World Resource Institute's The Next 4 Billion, Market size and business strategy at the base of the pyramid http://www.wri.org/publication/the-next-4-billion, p. 9.)

Why?

Business is increasingly interested in the world's poor for several reasons:

- **Companies realize they can make a difference:** Companies have the potential to make a positive impact in communities and influence the business environment, support international norms relating to corruption and human rights, share know how and engage in multi-stakeholder dialogues.
- **Part of a long-term strategy:** Companies are starting to see the need to break out of mature markets and include this large potential market as part of their company's growth strategy.

- **Vast amount of opportunities:** Over two billion people live on less than $2 per day and by 2050, more than 90% of the world's population will be living in developing countries. Individuals with incomes below $3000 in local purchasing power represent a $5 trillion global consumer market, those between $3000 and $20 000 a $12.5 trillion dollar consumer market.
- **Conditions are improving:** Often the necessary conditions for doing business such as transparency, effective legal systems, low levels of corruption and efficient government bureaucracy remain poor in many countries (for example in Canada it takes 2 days to incorporate a business compared to 203 days in Haiti). Although there are still challenges in working in certain markets, countries are investing time and effort to strengthen their governance, legal structures and investment structures.
- **Better partners available:** There are an increasing number of partners such as not-for-profits, foundations and multilateral organizations that are not only willing but able to work with the private sector in these countries. This also provides the opportunity to share risks.
- **Public expectations of companies are changing:** Communities and consumers are expecting companies to become more involved in issues such as poverty alleviation and be accountable to the impact they have on developing countries.
- **Transfer lessons learnt to other markets:** Working in these new markets can bring about innovative ideas and products that can be used in other developing and emerging markets in which a company operates.
- **Building better capacity locally and internationally:** Building better communities creates better employees, partners, etc. but also enhances the skills and knowledge of employees and a company.

How?

Companies are getting involved in development and poverty alleviation in several ways:

- **By collectively engaging** in public policy dialogues and through national or international coalitions, such as the Global Business Coalition Against HIV/AIDS and the UN Global Compact.

(continued)

- **Buying products or services from the poor** as suppliers, employers and distributors. Companies such as Unilever and Starbucks are working with small scale producers to source raw materials.
- **By providing products and services** companies are providing access to pro-poor financial services (Citigroup, Deutsche Bank, Credit Suisse), information technology (Microsoft, Dell, IBM) and access to water and energy (EDF, Suez, General Electric). Health care companies are engaged in R&D initiatives, preferential pricing and product donations.
- **Through community investment** companies continue to donate money into communities to help strengthen them and empower entrepreneurs.
- **By creating innovative business models** that reach and are accessible to the world's poor.

Companies are currently developing and testing out new ideas and business models to work with the poor across the full value chain of the company, from R&D, raw material sourcing, production, distribution and marketing to consumption. According to C. K. Prahalad and Stuart L. Hart's *The Fortune at the Bottom of the Pyramid* (2002), 'Doing business with the world's 4 billion poorest people . . . will require radical innovations in technology and business models. It will require MNCs to re-evaluate price-performance relationships for products and services. It will demand a new level of capital efficiency and new ways of measuring financial success. Companies will be forced to transform their understanding of scale, from a "bigger is better" ideal to an ideal of highly distributed small-scale operations married to world-scale capabilities.'[34]

DuPont Thailand had a programme that donated lunches to pupils in rural locations. It decided to treat the programme as a marketing opportunity in order to find ways to expand the programme beyond the two schools with which they were working. In 2002 they identified several schools to run a farming programme using DuPont corn seeds, material and farming supervision. The crops were sold to local dealers earning the school over $ 10,700, which was invested back into their lunch programmes. DuPont invested $ 5600 in the project and exceeded sales forecasts in the region for similar seeds as local farmers had seen the success of that particular variety of corn in their area.

Many businesses, such as P&G, have already learnt numerous lessons about the challenges of entering these markets. Based on conversations with UNICEF, the company decided to provide products with micronutrients like iodine and iron that children in certain countries were missing and that were key to their growth. P&G came up with a product called NutriStar, a low-cost, powdered milk drink with micronutrients. It was launched in the Philippines using strategies similar to those used to launch other products in developed markets, including a campaign to educate people of the benefits. However, a local competitor copied the product, without all the nutritional content and sold it at a lower price. They built on the demand produced by P&G for a product with micronutrients, but did not provide the same product.

Some things to keep in mind:

- **Focus on core competencies:** Focus on what the company does well and build from there. Often it requires a shift in mindset. Look for business and non-business partners locally who could handle those competencies that you lack across the supply chain, including helping to understand what the real needs of the market are.
- **Focus on high standards:** It is key that businesses live up to high standards in these new markets. There is sometimes a low level of trust in business in these areas so companies need to make a real, honest effort.
- **Start early as it takes time:** Allocate resources and R&D into testing new business models and ideas on the ground. Also review what your company has done before as there could be expertise hidden away internally.
- **Provide unique products and services:** This either means create new ones that are appropriate to BOP needs, or adapt an existing product. This also includes enabling access to these goods and services through innovative packaging strategies (i.e. single use), novel distribution strategies (service rather than a product), and financing options (prepayment, collective billing systems or incentives for paying).
- **Localized value creation through franchising:** Through agent strategies that involve building local ecosystems of vendors or suppliers, local entrepreneurs and SMEs. Local phone entrepreneurs and resellers, mini-hydro power systems, community based treatment systems.
- **Don't just rely on market research:** Businesses interested in reaching these markets need to immerse themselves in the lives of their target customers in order to understand challenges relating to access, awareness, affordability etc.
- **Two-way learning:** There is a lot that companies can learn from these communities. Keep an open mind.

(continued)

Want more?

- For more on the Millennium Development Goals see www.un.org/ millenniumgoals and www.unmillenniumproject.org. The UN Millennium Project lists a selection of what they call 'Quick Wins' which are activities that could bring 'vital gains in wellbeing to millions of people and start countries on the path to the Goals' (www. unmillenniumproject.org/resources/quickwins.htm).
- The World Resource Institute's The Next 4 Billion, market size and business strategy at the base of the pyramid (2007) and many other resources available at www.nextbillion.net/.
- For more on business and development see the WBCSD programmes and publications on development and sustainable livelihoods at www.wbcsd.org including A Business Guide to Development Actors (2004) and Doing Business with the Poor: a field guide (2004).
- The World Bank has several resources including Poverty Reduction Strategy Papers that help to identify which agency to work with and understand the development priorities. Development Marketplace at www.developmentmarketplace.org. The World Bank has a website www.doingbusiness.org which provides information on doing business in countries across the world.
- **Read:** *The Fortune at the Bottom of the Pyramid: Eradicating Poverty Through Profits* by C.K. Prahalad (2004), where he talks about the immense untapped buying power of the world's billions of poor people which represent an enormous opportunity for companies who learn how to serve them. *The Next 4 Billion: Market Size and Business Strategy at the Base of the Pyramid* (2007) looks at the 4 billion low-income consumers at the base of the economic pyramid.

'Business cannot succeed in a society that fails.'
Bjorn Stigson, WBCSD, President

8   Entrepreneurship

'The social entrepreneur wouldn't be happy just to give someone a fish or teach them to fish - they'd want to reinvent the fishing industry'

BILL DRAYTON, ASHOKA

While large companies usually receive the majority of attention, it is the small and medium sized enterprises (SMEs) that make up 90% of all businesses in the world, and are responsible for between 50-60% of total employment. They are the fastest growing part of the economy and account for the major share of exports and the bulk of new jobs in most countries. SMEs are responsible for providing the products and the services that larger companies rely on. They are also largely responsible for innovation. The Babson Center for Entrepreneurship in the USA estimates that in the last hundred years, 95% of the significant innovations in products and services came from firms with fewer than 20 employees.[35]

However, SMEs are often slow to get involved in sustainability. There is an increased recognition that SMEs are actually a large part of the problem when it comes to unsustainable business practices. In many countries, environmental health and safety inspections of SMEs are either not required or are not being performed as rigorously as with large enterprises. Although one small business may not think that it can have any impact, collectively they can and do have a major impact.

While sustainability needs many SMEs to clean up their act, it also relies on SMEs to push the agenda forward. There is a major need for new, innovative business ideas and services and often SMEs are better positioned than larger companies to provide these. In addition to SMEs, there are a growing number of entrepreneurs both outside and within organizations, who have the ability to identify underserved markets and come up with innovative ideas to provide new sustainable products and services, either for profit or not for profit.

Why is it important?

- *Innovation:* There are opportunities and demand for a growing number of new more sustainable products, services and technologies. SMEs and entrepreneurs are in an ideal position to explore and develop these opportunities.
- *Building a stronger business:* Many of the points introduced in the business case introduction are just as relevant to SMEs as they are to large companies, perhaps even more so. Sustainability policies and practices can help a small company identify and manage risks, cut costs, explore new revenue generating opportunities, find, retain and have more productive staff and increase efficiency.
- *Business partners are asking for it:* For those SMEs that supply, or want to supply larger companies, these larger companies are increasingly looking to work with companies that share their social and environmental values. Failing to take these issues seriously can result in a loss of business opportunities.
- *No longer invisible:* Gone are the days when SMEs could slip under the radar. Laws and regulations that once mostly affected larger companies are starting to apply to smaller ones as well.
- *Flexibility:* SMEs are able to respond to the changing business environment with greater speed and flexibility, meaning they will be able to integrate sustainability directly into their business plans more efficiently.

- **Reach and opportunities:** SMEs and entrepreneurs may be able to identify and reach markets and groups that are currently not being effectively reached, resulting in new opportunities. This is especially true with the growing number of active social entrepreneurs working around the world.
- **Influence:** SMEs can have an important impact on larger companies. There are many examples now where SMEs with a strong sustainability culture have been bought by larger companies who are interested in capturing and diffusing their approach to sustainability.

The key concepts

SMEs have a potentially large impact because of their sheer numbers. As there are so many different types of SMEs, there are several different ways these groups are having an impact and can benefit from sustainability. While the key concepts presented below are all important for SMEs, it is worth noting that the other chapters in this book are equally applicable.

• What are the different business model options for sustainability in new companies	→ *Social/environmental ventures*
• Entrepreneurs focused on large scale change	→ *Social entrepreneurs*
• Working from inside a company as an entrepreneur	→ *Intrapraneurs*
• Exploring new business opportunities that are sustainable	→ *Generating Ideas*
• Finding money for new sustainability ventures	→ *Funding*
• Towards success	→ *Box: Advice for Social and Environmental Entrepreneurs*

Social/environmental ventures

An entrepreneur is someone who starts a new organization, usually in response to a new opportunity identified. Entrepreneurs need to decide very early on what kind of business they will be pursuing as legally there are different requirements in different countries. The choice will determine what your goals are and what you are trying to accomplish. According to the Global Social Venture Competition, a social venture is one that plans to be financially sustainable or profitable and be self-sufficient on its earned revenue. It also has a quantifiable social and/or environmental bottom line incorporated into its mission and practices. Some different options are listed below.

- *Sell a sustainable product:* This business can be one where the opportunity is specifically 'green' such as a new clean technology, green consulting or selling other products or services that are seen as being sustainable. For example, Green and Black Chocolates is a company that makes organic, fair trade, high quality chocolate. As a profitable venture, Green and Black was bought by Cadbury and the products are now available internationally. This has in part allowed it to have a wider audience and push the market for fair trade chocolate.
- *Operate in a sustainable way:* You can also have a traditional business that does not sell a 'green' product per say, yet as part of its mission is working in the field of sustainability. For example a company that has in place a very detailed sustainability strategy that outlines where they will source from, what materials are used and how their employees are treated. The company also uses sustainability principles and tools to focus on cutting costs and increasing revenues.
- *Create a blend:* Increasingly you see not for profits and for profits blending together. Some not for profits provide consulting services or sell different products. Other companies sell products and services at a profit, but direct a percentage of that profit to different charitable activities, which either they pursue through a foundation, or which they donate to other organizations working in areas that are important to the business.

The reason often given by smaller companies for not looking at these issues is that they just don't have the resources to explore sustainability, or the same support networks that larger companies have. However, this is changing. Regardless of what you choose to do there are numerous local, national and international support networks for companies of all shapes and sizes. For example, small companies in North America can join BALLE, the Business Alliance for Local Living Economies, a network of sustainable businesses committed to building local economies. BALLE is comprised of nearly 60 local networks of independent businesses in a variety of locales across the US and Canada, and represents more than 20 000 entrepreneurs (www.livingeconomies.org).

The Efficient Entrepreneur is an online tool that provides practical advice for how SMEs can take steps to reduce costs, increase productivity and satisfy clients while at the same time reducing business risks and protecting the environment. (www.efficient-entrepreneur.net). Kauffman Foundation is one of the largest foundations devoted to entrepreneurship in the world? (www.kauffman.org).

Social/environmental entrepreneurs

Although definitions of what exactly constitutes a social entrepreneur vary, the term social entrepreneur is used to refer to people who create businesses, both big and small, where social and environmental issues are at the core of their business offerings. According to the Skoll Foundation, social entrepreneurs, 'seize opportunities that challenge and change forever established but fundamentally inequitable systems.' The Schwab Foundation refers to a social entrepreneur as a leader or pragmatic visionary who:

- Achieves large scale, systemic and sustainable social change through a new invention, a different approach, a more rigorous application of known technologies or strategies, or a combination of these.

- Focuses first and foremost on the social and/or ecological value creation and then tries to optimize the financial value creation.
- Innovates by finding a new product, a new service, or a new approach to a social problem.

According to the Skoll Foundation, the difference between standard and social entrepreneurship does not come down to motivation – with entrepreneurs spurred on by money and social entrepreneurs driven by altruism. 'The truth is that entrepreneurs are rarely motivated by the prospect of financial gain, because the odds of making lots of money are clearly stacked against them. Instead, both the entrepreneur and the social entrepreneur are strongly motivated by the opportunity they identify, pursuing that vision relentlessly, and deriving considerable psychic reward from the process of realizing their ideas'. Instead they say the real difference lies in the value proposition itself. Social entrepreneurs aim for value in the form of large-scale, transformational benefit that accrues either to a significant segment of society or to society at large.[36]

There are many examples of social enterprises working around the world. The microcredit movement introduced further in the Finance chapter is one of the best-known examples. Another is Riders for Health created by the Grand Prix motorcycle racing community. This enterprise looks to tackle a simple yet critical element of the African health care system: transportation. By providing motor bikes and maintenance support services, Riders for Health have extended the reach of health care providers to 11 million Africans (www.riders.org).

In the book *The Power of Unreasonable People*, John Elkington and Pamela Hartigan present ten characteristics of successful social entrepreneurs, who:

- Try to shrug off the constraints of ideology or discipline
- Identify and apply practical solutions to social problems, combining innovation, resourcefulness and opportunity
- Innovate by finding a new product, a new service, or a new approach to a social problem

- Focus—first and foremost—on social value creation and, in that spirit, are willing to share their innovations and insights for others to replicate
- Jump in before ensuring they are fully resourced
- Have an unwavering belief in everyone's innate capacity, often regardless of education, to contribute meaningfully to economic and social development
- Show a dogged determination that pushes them to take risks that others wouldn't dare
- Balance their position for change with a zeal to measure and monitor their impact
- Have a great deal to teach change makers in other sectors
- Display a healthy impatience (e.g. they don't do well in bureaucracies, which can raise succession issues as their organizations grow—and almost inevitably become more bureaucratic).

> There are several foundations actively working to advance social entrepreneurship including the Skoll Foundation (www.socialedge.org), The Schwab Foundation (www.schwabfound.org). Ashoka (www.ashoka.org) and Acumen Fund (www.acumenfund.org). University Network for Social Entrepreneurship works with professors, researchers, practitioners and students to develop social entrepreneurship as a vocation and carry its principles into other disciplines and sectors (www.universitynetwork.org). Institute for Social Entrepreneurs (www.socialent.org).

Intrapraneurs

Entrepreneurs are not just individuals working outside an organization to develop new ideas. Individuals can also become entrepreneurs from within a company or organization, an idea increasingly being referred to as intrapraneurship. Consulting firm SustainAbility provides this definition of intrapraneurs:

'1 Someone who works inside major corporations or organizations to develop and promote practical solutions to social or environmental challenges where progress is currently stalled by market failures.

2 Someone who applies the principles of social entrepreneurship inside a major organization.

3 One characterized by an "insider-outsider" mindset and approach.'[37]

Larger companies, although slow to change, can bring about significant weight when they do change. Employees working for these companies are in a unique position to push for change as they have a good understanding of the inner workings of the company. Working from within can also give them access to resources such as people and finances to make a difference. Working within the company enables them to incubate their social idea at lower risk than if they were to go at it on their own. If the idea becomes successful, they have helped drive the future success of the company.

Promoting and supporting intrapraneurship from within, regardless of the size of the company or the size of the project, can bring about potentially substantial advantages. Intrapraneurship allows companies to test out new ideas and business models and potentially develop new products and services. This concept is not necessarily anything new. Many companies have discovered the advantages to having teams, also known as 'skunk works', working apart from the main, bureaucratic engine of the company. This freedom allows them to be creative in ways they could not from within the company's mainstream structures. Grameen Bank and Danone Foods paired up to create a unique community based joint venture in Bangladesh which is based on social and environmental concerns. In 2006 they launched a yoghurt product called Shoktidoi designed to provide for the nutritional needs of Bangladeshi children at an affordable price (6 euro cents) that can be bought by even the poorest families. The plant hires local workers and relies on developing microfarms which supply raw materials used to produce the yoghurt. A distribution system called 'Grameen Ladies' make sales door-to-door. The business provides income to more than 1600 people within a radius of 30 km around the plant. The plant has a rainwater recovery system and the yoghurt pots are made of a material that is entirely biodegradable.

Companies have explored several different ways of doing this including:

- *Islands:* This involves initiatives being incubated away from the mainstream business so that they can enjoy a degree of freedom. As author Guy Kawasaki puts it 'Just about everything you learn and do inside a large company is wrong for intrapraneurship ... Generally, you should do everything the opposite from the tried and true existing way of large companies'.[38] One of the best ways to do this is to work from a separate building filled with people who love what the team is doing.

- *Bridges:* Some projects will have clear but relatively loose links to the host company, often enjoying more freedom than traditional business units. Shell's wind division in the North Sea was physically located outside corporate headquarters but with access to Shell's capital and other resources. Their companies and brand give them access to resources they wouldn't enjoy as a traditional entrepreneur.

- *Symbiosis:* Intrapraneurs that incubate their initiatives right inside the host organization. Unilever's Shakti Programme looks at increasing market share in rural villages in India by providing women with training in selling, commercial knowledge and book-keeping. These women can then choose to set up their own business or become Shakit distributors. This department sits in the centre of Hindustan Unilever's sales department and is completely integrated into the business. Shakit plans to double the number of women entrepreneurs from 45 000 today to 100 000. These types of approaches allow intrapraneurs to have more of an impact on the workings of the rest of the organization.

> The Social Intrapreneur (www.sustainability.com/downloads_public/TheSocialIntrapreneur.pdf).

Generating ideas

Dale Vince started in 'green energy' in 1996. Major electricity companies laughed at him, because at the time, no one was talking about green energy, but they aren't laughing anymore. Today his business Ecotricity provides 100 % green energy and is worth millions of dollars. In 2008 they had 33 000 customers (up from 25 000 in 2007) including 2300 small businesses (up from 900 the year before) including long-standing customers like the Body Shop and Ben and Jerry's. Today one in six of the wind projects in England have been planned and built by Ecotricity (www.ecotricity.com). Small businesses usually think about how to reach new markets before anyone else does, and typically move faster. So how do they find their inspiration? Entrepreneurs need to ensure that they are targeting real markets. Some tips on identifying these:

- *Putting a sustainable spin on something that currently exists:* This involves turning an already existing business into a 'green' one. Whole Foods Market is a food store that sells only natural and organic products. It started as one small store in 1980 in Texas and now has over 270 stores in North America and the UK.
- *Something that you think could be done better:* Sometimes the idea already exists, but with some tweaks it can be reinvented to make it much better. Clif Bar, an industry leader in all organic energy bars, began with the founder being frustrated by the taste of the available energy bars. He thought he could make a better bar. Two years later, Clif Bar became a reality and today they focus on continually improving their products, their company and the planet (www.clifbar.com).
- *Identify a need that can be better fulfilled:* Many entrepreneurs simply see a need for something and come up with innovative ideas on how to better fill that need. The founder of Adventerra Games saw a need for fun activities to get kids and their families excited about saving the earth. The result is a small company (www.adventerragames.com) that invents, produces and distributes board games in four different languages that help kids and their families learn about the planet and how they can make a difference by changing their behaviours and habits. Players win the games by saving water or energy or by recycling correctly. The games are often donated by businesses or foundations to local schools or school districts.

- *Understand environmental laws, regulations and standards as drivers:* Current regulations on pollution, safety, product content and performance, labelling, reusing and recycling, and protection of endangered habitats and species can all present substantial business opportunities for those who know how to identify and asses them. The lengthy time it takes for these to come into effect often presents a window of opportunity during which entrepreneurs can judge whether a profitable business will result.

- *Exploit new demand for sustainable technology:* Reducing the volume and toxicity of waste and developing products made from secondary materials, also known as clean tech, have become big business. Serious Materials develops high performance green building materials. They focus on creating better products that do not require new consumer behaviour to adopt the greener building solution (www.seriousmaterials.com).

- *Create the environment for others to be more sustainable:* Rather than just becoming a green dry cleaner, the Bancroft family went one step further. Family-owned GreenEarth Cleaning, founded in 1999, is the world's largest solution provider for environmental friendly dry cleaning. Customers now have the choice to use environmentally safe dry cleaning processes. It is now used by quality dry cleaners operating more than 1000 stores worldwide and works with companies such as P&G, GE and Sanyo (www. greenearthcleaning.com).

There are many websites and books to help take your ideas to reality. One is Entrepreneurship, a website which assists nations in developing the environment to allow entrepreneurs to organize and operate a business successfully (www.entrepreneurship.org). Ecopreneurist is a collection of regular blogs of green entrepreneurial ideas from around the world (ecopreneurist.com). Global Ideas bank is a website full of interesting ideas for social invention (www. globalideasbank.org)

Funding

As an entrepreneur, where you look for funding will depend to a certain extent on the chosen company structure (non-profit or for profit for example). There are an increasing number of different financing options for all sorts of different companies in this area. As with any new business, social enterprise funding sources are similar to those of traditional business ventures and can include:

- *Family and friends, or personal savings:* Often entrepreneurs start out by using their own resources and savings, or by taking loans from family and friends who believe in their vision.
- *Foundations:* A foundation is a not for profit group that gives out grants to other organizations and individuals. Each foundation chooses to fund based on different criteria. Many of the large foundations are from the US including the Rockefeller Foundation (www.rockfound.org), Bill and Melinda Gates Foundation (www.gatesfoundation.org), David and Lucile Packard Foundation (www.packfound.org), MacArthur Foundation (www.macfound.org), Ted Turner/UN Foundation (www.unfoundation.org), Ashoka (www.ashoka.org/) and The Ford Foundation (www.fordfound.org), to name but a few. Foundations can be private individuals but increasingly are set up by companies such as the Shell Foundation (www.shellfoundation.org).
- *Investment funds:* For example the Global Environment Fund invests in businesses around the world that provide cost-effective solutions to environmental and energy challenges. They have approximately $1 billion aggregate capital under management (www.globalenvironmentfund.com).
- *Partnerships and in kind donations:* Funding does not just have to come in the form of cash, it can also come in the form of other kinds of resources including people or organizations donating time, office space, trading of services or products, or even advice. Combining forces with another entrepreneurial team can make your business case stronger and provide additional opportunities for financing from banks and investors.

- *Venture capital (VC):* Several large VC firms have specials divisions focused on social, green and cleantech ventures. In the not for profit sector, there are also social venture funds developing which operate similarly to traditional venture funds but expect a different level of returns. The Acumen Fund is a non-profit global venture fund that uses entrepreneurial approaches to solve the problems of global poverty (www.acumenfund.org). Green VC provides additional news and resources on green venture capital, funding and start-ups (www.greenvc.org).

- *Angel Investors:* Angel Investors are high net-worth individuals with extensive business experience that invest in companies. They generally provide advice and a funding amount that bridges self-funding and large venture capital investments. These investors add value to the organizations they invest in because they bring expertise along with capital investment.

- *Business plan competitions:* There are a growing number of sustainability awards and business case competitions which have various prizes, including cash rewards associated with them. Some of these can be quite significant. For example, the Global Social Venture Competition is a global MBA student business plan competition for social ventures. Winners get mentorship, exposure and cash prizes (www.gsvc.org).

- *Government and local grants:* Government grants can be a good source of funds for starting social enterprises. Grant writing, application processes and making deadlines can be challenging, so be sure to understand all requirements as early as possible. There are several websites that can be resources to finding available grants: www.businesslink.gov. uk has a well defined grant section for UK businesses, www.grantslink. gov.au in Australia and www.grants.gov can be a source for US based start-ups. Many other countries have similar sites of their own.

- *Going public:* An IPO is a way for a privately owned SME to take in additional capital for growth. When Google went public, it included in the provisions of the original IPO that 1% of its equity, 1% of its profit and 1% of its manpower would go to solving major world problems.

US International Grant-making Project: www.usig.org/ (information on grant-making, particularly grant-making that cross borders, resources for potential grantees, etc.). Investors Circle is a network of over 200 angel investors, professional venture capitalists, foundations, family offices and others who are using private capital to promote the transition to a sustainable economy (www. investorscircle.net).

- **Sell:** Some larger companies interested in green business are choosing to buy green companies rather than reinvent the wheel. When Danone took over Stonyfield Farm, the CEO of Stonyfield Farm said he accepted the deal because he wanted to change Danone from inside in order to have a greater leverage on the food market. While Danone took an 80 % share in Stonyfield Farm, they left him in complete control.

Challenges?

- **Resources:** Insufficient technology, expertise, training and capital can be a barrier for SMEs interested in adopting environmental and social responsibility. The need to deal with more pressing matters such as upgrading the quality of technology, management and marketing often prevents them from taking a more sustainable approach.
- **Balancing priorities:** Finding time to incorporate sustainability practices into a start-up or SME can be challenging, as entrepreneurs and SMEs typically have a lot of things to be thinking about and seemingly never enough time to do them all.
- **Tailored Initiatives:** There are a growing number of initiatives open to larger businesses focused on different sustainability issues. However, there is still a lack of initiatives tailored for small companies although some organizations are starting to work on this (i.e. GRI reporting guidelines for SMEs).
- **Give more recognition:** Most of the leaders we hear about in sustainability are those that have the time and budget to communicate

their successes. The kind of sustainability practices which are common amongst SMEs, such as their role in the local community, also need to be celebrated.

Trends and new ideas

– Microbusinesses	– Working with Big Business
– Social Stock Exchange	– Marketing on a shoestring

Microbusinesses Microfranchises are 'small businesses that can easily be replicated by following proven marketing and operational concepts.' These can sell for anything between $ 25 and $ 6000. The same idea is being explored to provide development solutions. For example, The HealthStore Foundation, based in the US gives healthcare workers in Kenya microloans to open their own for profit Child and Family Wellness Shops that distribute medical products and services to remote communities in Kenya. Applying the basic principles of successful franchising, the foundation then trains the franchisees in uniform procedures, carefully selects locations and conducts regular inspections to ensure quality and consistency. The franchise can also exploit economies of scale to obtain safe and effective drugs at low costs.[39] Microleasing is another opportunity available. In the case of Honey Care in Kenya as well, beehives are sold, or leased, to individuals who are also provided with basic training in bee-keeping, basic record-keeping and management skills. The group also offers the farmers a stable and year round market for their honey by agreeing to buy their honey at a guaranteed and mutually acceptable price for a period of two years or more allowing farmers to plan ahead.

Social stock exchange In order to develop strong social enterprise, large amounts of capital and support need to be made available. Therefore, many organizations are starting to explore alternatives to the traditional stock exchange by putting in place exchanges that focus on developing social value rather than financial value. Global Exchange for Social Investment launched in 2002 works to create such a global social capital market. It works to link charitable donors, entrepreneurs and investors in funding social businesses in low-income regions around the world (www.gexsi.org). Social Stock Exchange in Brazil launched in 2003 brings together non-profit organizations with the Sao Paulo Stock Exchange investors who are interested in supporting those efforts (www.bovespa.com.br). The South African Social Investment Exchange launched in 2006 makes carefully selected social development projects available as investment opportunities with a social return. Investors can buy shares in SASIX projects and can track online how their investments are performing and view the impact they are having (www.sasix.co.za). Keep an eye out for other social stock exchanges being developed in England, Germany, New Zealand, Portugal, the US and Thailand.

Big business working with SMEs For businesses, working with entrepreneurs can be one of the most effective ways to explore and ultimately serve underserved markets. Enabling small, local firms to supply goods and services to larger enterprises creates more efficient supply chains by optimizing cost, quality, flexibility and other considerations. This can also allow a larger company to gain local knowledge and contacts required to operate effectively and profitably. It also often forces small companies to improve their standards and practices to meet the stricter requirements of the larger company. Often larger companies include working with and supporting local SMEs as part of their sustainability initiatives. In 2007, HP globally invested $47.1 million (or 0.51% of pre-tax profits) in educational, economic development, environmental and local community investment projects. There are several ways for large companies to work with SMEs:

- *Creating links* with local SMEs in the different areas of the value chain; for example procurements, agriculture, manufacturing, subcontracting, etc. Large grocery store chains like Tesco and Whole Foods Market focus on regional sourcing of a multitude of items sold in their stores as a way to reduce overall costs and the impact of their enterprise on the environment.

- ***Work to strengthen the SME environment*** and its role in local economic development by supporting their activities, providing financing, training centres, etc. COOP Italia, a very large retailing enterprise, is helping its 350 SME suppliers to meet CSR standards by providing training and support; and TriSelect is a French urban waste recycling business that offers distance learning for low-skilled employees to improve their knowledge of health and safety in the work place.[40]
- ***Creating new distribution networks.*** Amanco, for example, worked with a farming cooperative in Mexico to develop a new distribution system that enables Amanco to sell its irrigation systems to small farms in poor rural areas.
- ***Deliver better quality products.*** SC Johnson is the largest buyer in Kenya of Pyrethrum produced by some 200 000 subsistence farmers. SC Johnson worked with KickStart to provide these farmers with better access to manually operating irrigation pumps – this has not only helped the Kenyan farmers, but it has ensured the long-term availability, quality and lower cost of natural pyrethrum for SC Johnson products.

Marketing on a shoestring In 1997 according to Interbrand, the Body Shop which had less than 0.5 % of the global cosmetic market, was the 28th most valuable brand in the world. How? These companies, who have today grown into international leaders, looked to market their products in whatever way they could, on-line, on-pack, in-store, through their positions on different issues (in this case animal testing) and through strong relationships with NGOs. Some common threads to the marketing approach of these companies are:

- ***Intuition led:*** based on the founder's intuition and vision rather than on market surveys, finding innovative low costs techniques to use because of tight budgets.

- *Guerrilla marketing:* on-line, on-pack and in-store campaigns where companies take strong stands on issues which among other things spotlight the controversial practices of their competitors and highlighting the comparative benefits of their products. The Body Shop took on animal testing, Ben and Jerry's took on bovine growth hormones.
- *Strong relationships with NGOs:* through charitable donations, cause-related marketing, joint campaigns or activities in which they are involved.
- *Limited use of mass advertising:* either due to cost constraints or the necessity to communicate a sophisticated positioning, they remain consistent with their activist approach. Most companies have been reluctant to use 'traditional' forms of mass media advertising.
- *Their communications focus on high quality:* these companies go beyond social and environmental selling points, (i.e. Patagonia's outdoor clothes have a lifetime guarantee).
- *Accountability and Transparency:* Ben and Jerry's was the first company to voluntarily report on social performance in 1989.[41]

What you can do . . .

- ❑ Embed the different sustainability practices introduced in this book into your existing business.
- ❑ Report: Many entrepreneurs and small businesses are also choosing to report. Of course the scope and scale is not at the level of large companies. GRI has a special section for SMEs for sustainability reporting. i.e. making certifications more attractive and useful to SMEs, or getting SMEs to report sustainability as a cluster such as the wine and fruit growers of Chile do.
- ❑ Start your own: Identify needs that are not currently being met appropriately and think of ways to provide for these. Attend academic programmes and networking groups to learn more about entrepreneurship and to help you develop your ideas.

Want more?

- World Bank Business Environment Snapshots provides information about how easy (or difficult) it is to do business in more than 200 countries (rru.worldbank.org/).

- The Global Entrepreneurship Monitor (GEM) research programme is an annual assessment of the national level of entrepreneurial activity. GEM 2007 conducted research in 42 countries (www.gemconsortium.org).

- Social Innovation Conversations brings social change ideas through audio lectures, speaker series and conference recordings downloadable for free (sic.conversationsnetwork.org).

- SMEs and the European Union includes a documentation centre for SMEs including an awareness-raising questionnaire and examples of best practice (ec.europa.eu/enterprise/csr/sme. htm). Small Business Journey outlines the way for small businesses to realize more value by behaving responsibly (www. smallbusinessjourney.com). SME Toolkit is research by the IFC and IBM which offers resources to help small businesses in emerging markets grow and succeed (www.smetoolkit.org). Business and Development Network SME resources can be found at www.bidnetwork.org. New Ventures, a programme of the World Resource Institute, promotes sustainable growth in emerging markets (www.new-ventures.org).

Read: *How to Change the World: Social entrepreneurs and the power of new ideas* by David Bornstein (2004), which provides examples of people around the world who have found innovative solutions to a wide variety of social and economic problems. *The Power of Unreasonable People: How Social Entrepreneurs Create Markets That Change the World* by John Elkington, Pamela Hartigan and Klaus Schwab (2008) shows how social entrepreneurs are solving some of the world's most pressing economic, social and environmental problems.

Some advice for entrepreneurs

- *Failure is an option:* The fact is that the majority of entrepreneurial projects fail. If failure isn't an option, then there is no room for experimentation or risk or growth. Most successful entrepreneurs talk more about their failures and the lessons they learnt that enabled them to have some successes.
- *Keep an open mind:* Think as if there were no borders, no constraints. What could you do? Often companies spend their time trying to preserve the status quo rather than trying to open new markets.
- *Money does matter:* Whether or not you are starting a for profit, a not for profit or a charity you still need to approach any new venture as a business. Even not for profits need money to operate.
- *Focus on solving a problem, not selling a solution:* Often people are quicker to recognize the problem than the value of a particular solution. Position your product or service as a solution to a particular problem that is easily recognizable by your target audience.
- *There is no right or wrong way to do it:* There is no one way to be an entrepreneur. There are no rules as to what you do and when you do it. For many people it is just something they have in them. The combination of personal drive and focus combined with a winning idea makes it happen.
- *Focus on people:* It doesn't matter how great you think your idea is, if people don't buy it, want it or need it, it won't go anywhere. Without good people working with you, life will be difficult so treat your people well.
- *Network:* Almost every person that you speak to could possibly support your success through offering contacts, ideas, references, time or even just an ear to allow you to practice speaking of your organization so that you are more effective in future conversations with investors or so forth.
- *Continuous focus on your key priority:* Whether it is getting members signed, selling the product . . . make sure this is a driver every day as all of the little stuff and side ideas can really distract from this key success factor.
- *Do not be afraid to reposition based on new information gained:* If it is discovered that the original idea is not the ideal solution, avoid becoming discouraged, focus on the specific area

of problem or issue and adjust it to become the ideal solution . . . continuously remoulding the idea so that it achieves the driving goal.

- ***Don't do it alone:*** Great ideas are usually not developed alone, but with a partner. If it isn't a co-owner or formal partner, there at least has to be one person to brain storm with that knows the plan as intimately as you do and cares about it almost as much. So much the better if they have good intuition in the areas you don't.
- ***Support:*** Many people with knowledge, connections, influence or simply time to burn on Internet research want to help entrepreneurs. Find them; you don't have to do it all yourself.

Checklist for getting started . . .

- ❑ Identify a problem, what would you like to change? What do you think could be done better? What is missing?
- ❑ Think about many possible solutions. Have some of them already been started? Did they work? If they didn't why didn't they?
- ❑ Pick a solution and devise a strategy. How are you going to sell that solution in practice?
- ❑ Think about all the strengths and weaknesses of the ideas.
- ❑ Build the business case. How are you going to be self-sufficient? Are you looking to make a profit? Will the profit be reinvested into the company?
- ❑ Explore the potential social and environmental impacts your solutions could have. Look at quantifying these.
- ❑ Assemble your team. Find a partner—two minds are always better than one.
- ❑ Network and create partnerships. Which groups can help you bring your solution forward?
- ❑ Gather resources to get started such as office space and initial cash.
- ❑ Get working! If you succeed congratulations, if you don't, learn from mistakes and start again.

9 Ethics and Corporate Governance

'Let's start with what is legal, but always go on to what we would feel comfortable about being printed on the front page of our local paper, and never proceed forward simply on the basis of the fact that other people are doing it.'

WARREN BUFFETT

If marketing, accounting, finance and the other core topics introduced in this book are the various pieces of the sustainability puzzle, each playing its part in creating more sustainable companies, ethics forms the glue that holds these pieces together. Business ethics goes beyond choosing to 'do the right thing' in day-to-day operations and business decisions; it is a core principle of good management and sustainability. Without good management, strong corporate governance and open and transparent relationships with customers, business partners and stakeholders, sustainability issues, policies and goals can go nowhere. Ethics enters into every aspect of sustainable business, such as quality standards, honest payment terms for both customers and suppliers, staff relationships and tax returns to mention only a few. Regardless of your position in a company, ethics is a foundational part of your job.

Despite its importance, ethics is often forgotten, pushed aside or taken for granted. Most companies have some set of ethics and management codes in place, by which the company stands, but many employees just assume that their company is properly managing ethical issues. Thus general managers play an important role in ensuring that ethical standards are upheld, and in promoting sustainability principles throughout their work place.

Why is it important?

- *Investors are looking for good governance:* Investors are interested in companies that have good, strong management practices and principles and see sustainability as a proxy for good management.
- *Quality of relationships:* A company or manager that conducts business ethically and legally develops higher quality relationships with customers, suppliers, employees and others, which can directly improve the business.
- *Reputation:* Companies with policies and practices based on less than the highest ethical standards, or that are enforced with a relaxed attitude to compliance, risk damaging their reputation. This is especially true today as news, both positive and negative, travels fast.
- *Financial costs:* There is clear evidence that in many countries corruption adds more than 10% to the cost of doing business, and as much as 25% to the cost of public procurement. Other unethical behaviour can have significant costs such as fines for non compliance, lost customers and damages to brands due to loss of reputation, to name just a few.
- *Legal risks:* Many forms of unethical behaviour, such as corruption, are illegal both in the country in which they occur and in the country the company is originally from. This is particularly relevant in companies based in OECD countries and was universally recognized in 2003 with the adoption of the UN Convention against Corruption.

The key concepts

General management comprises the actions that managers and companies need to take in order to ensure legal and ethical underpinnings of their organization and operations. Many people consider ethics and general management to be vague topics however there is plenty of practical and specific guidance available for businesses to operate ethically. This includes:

• Upholding universal human rights	→ ***Business and human rights***
• Promoting worker rights and standards	→ ***Labour and working conditions***
• Making difficult decisions	→ ***Ethics and the individual manager***
• Creating strong control systems in organizations	→ ***Corporate governance***
• Stopping the misuse of power	→ ***Corruption***
• Stopping the misuse of power for private gain	→ ***Bribery***
• Moving the sustainability agenda forward	→ ***Box: The role of the CEO***

Business and human rights

In 2008, the Declaration of Human Rights turned 60 years old. The Declaration, which has been translated into more than 360 languages, is the foundation of international human rights law. It is codified in international law through two treaties: the International Covenant on Civil and Political Rights and the International Covenant on Economic, Social and Cultural Rights, each of which has been ratified by over three-quarters of all countries. These, in addition to the International Labour Organization conventions and laws, provide a universal benchmark for minimum standards of behaviour. According to the Office of the High Commissioner for Human Rights (OHCHR), 'Human rights are fundamental principles and standards that enable individuals everywhere to have freedom to live in dignity. All human rights are universal, interrelated, interdependent and indivisible.'

In order to assist business in understanding the growing number of declarations related to human rights, the UN Norms for Business with regards to human rights were compiled. These norms include:

- *Right to equal opportunity and non-discriminatory treatment.* Business should ensure equality of opportunity and treatment for the purpose of eliminating discrimination based on race, colour, sex, language, religion, political opinion, national or social origin, social status, indigenous status, disability or age.
- *Right to security of persons.* Business should not engage in, or benefit from, war crimes; crimes against humanity; genocide; torture; forced disappearance; forced or compulsory labour; hostage-taking; extrajudicial, summary or arbitrary executions; other violations of humanitarian law; or other international crimes against the human person. Business should observe international human rights norms as well as the laws and professional standards of the country or countries in which they operate.
- *Rights of workers.* Business should:
  - not use forced or compulsory labour
  - respect the rights of children to be protected from economic exploitation
  - provide a safe and healthy working environment
  - provide workers with remuneration that ensures an adequate standard of living for them and their families
  - ensure freedom of association and effective recognition of the right to collective bargaining.
- *Respect for national sovereignty and human rights.* Business should:
  - recognize and respect applicable *norms* of international law, national laws and regulations, as well as administrative practices, the rule of law, the public interest, development objectives, social,

economic and cultural policies (including transparency, account-ability and prohibition of corruption) and the authority of the countries in which the enterprises operate.

- not offer, promise, give, accept, condone, knowingly benefit from, or demand a *bribe* or other improper advantage.

- refrain from any activity which supports, solicits or encourages States or any other entities to abuse human rights.

- respect economic, social and cultural rights as well as civil and political rights, and contribute to their realization; in particular the rights to development, adequate food and drinking water, the highest attainable standard of physical and mental health, adequate housing, privacy, education, freedom of thought, conscience and religion and freedom of opinion and expression, and shall refrain from actions which obstruct or impede the realization of those rights.

- *Obligations with regard to consumer protection.* Business should take all necessary steps to ensure the safety and quality of the goods and services they provide, including observance of the precautionary principle. They should not produce, distribute, market, or advertise harmful or potentially harmful products for use by consumers.

According to the UN Global Compact, 'Business should support and respect the protection of internationally proclaimed human rights and make sure that they are not complicit in human rights abuses.' An organization can do this in two ways:

Sphere of influence concerns the boundaries of a company's human rights responsibilities, whose human rights the company should be concerned with, and which human rights a company should pay particular attention to. Each company has a particular sphere of influence based on their geographic presence, industry, size and particular business relationships, which can include the workplace (rights of employees), supply chain (partners do not engage in rights abuses), marketplace (products do not harm customers), community (no negative impacts on the communities in which they operate) and government (using influence to develop public policy that promotes and rewards good behaviour).

Complicity is about business ensuring that it does not assist or encourage human rights abuse committed by governments, rebel groups, other companies or individuals. It is made up of two elements:

- An action or omission (failure to act) by a company, or individual representing a company, that 'helps' (facilitates, legitimizes, assists, encourages, etc.) another, in some way, to perpetrate a human rights abuse;
- The company was or should have been on notice that its action or omission could provide such help.[42]

For the full text of the Declaration of Human Rights and a short online course on Human Rights and Business go to www.unhchr.ch/udhr. Some other organizations that have information on this topic include Voluntary Principles for Security and Human Rights (www.business-ethics.com) and (www.voluntaryprinciples.org), Business for Human Rights (www.business-humanrights.org). The Global Compact (www.unglobalcompact.org/Issues/human_rights). Fifteen leading corporate law firms from around the world will participate in a UN-led effort to identify whether and how national corporate legal principles and practices currently foster corporate cultures that are respectful of human rights (www.csrwire.com/News/14385). The UNEP Finance Initiative has developed a toolkit on human rights which provides a very good overview and additional resources (www.unepfi.org/humanrightstoolkit). Aim for Human Rights' Guide to Corporate Human Rights Impact Assessment Tools (www.aimforhumanrights.org).

Labour and working conditions

Today globalization has made rights and standards more relevant than ever and companies need to uphold local and international labour standards. The International Labour Organization is a specialized agency of the UN responsible for protecting and promoting worker safety and standards. Such standards provide the following benefits:

- To ensure that economic development remains focused on improving the lives of human beings rather than treating labour as a commodity, which can be bought or sold for the highest profit or lowest price.
- To provide an even playing field by helping governments and employers to 'avoid the temptation of lowering labour standards in the belief that it could give them a greater comparative advantage in international trade'.
- To improve economic performance because although many companies believe that there are significant costs associated with meeting such standards there is growing research 'that indicates that compliance often accompanies improvements in productivity and economic performance'.

The ILO has established an extensive series of labour standards that include eight 'fundamental conventions' that cover freedom of association and protection of the rights to organize, the right to collective bargaining, forced labour, minimum age, child labour, equal remuneration, abolition of forced labour and discrimination. International labour standards also include such areas as occupational safety and health, wages, employment security, vocational guidance and training, maternity protection.

Apart from international standards, groups have come together to ensure fair prices. According to the Fair Trade Labelling Network, 'Fairtrade is about better prices, decent working conditions, local sustainability, and fair terms of trade for farmers and workers in the developing world. By requiring companies to pay sustainable prices (which must never fall lower than the market price), Fairtrade addresses the injustices of conventional trade, which traditionally discriminates against the poorest, weakest producers. It enables them to improve their position and have more control over their lives.' Today Fair trade organizations around the world come together under the Fairtrade Labelling Organizations International (FLO). According to the FLO by the end of 2007, there were 632 Fairtrade certified producer organizations in 58 producing countries, representing 1.5 million farmers and workers.

The International Labour Organization provides detailed information on all labour standards. Read their 'Rules of the game, a brief introduction to international labour standards' (www.ilo.org). Also see labour laws in your country. The FairTrade Labelling Network (www.fairtrade.net/) and The World Trade Organization (www.wto.org/).

With their families and dependents, FLO estimates that 7.5 million people directly benefit from Fairtrade. The sales of Fairtrade certified products have been growing at an average of 40 % per year in the last five years. In 2007, Fairtrade certified sales amounted to approximately 2.3 billion worldwide.[43] The key objectives of the standards are to:

- ensure a guaranteed Fairtrade minimum price which is agreed with producers
- provide an additional Fairtrade premium which can be invested in projects that enhance social, economic and environmental development
- enable pre-financing for producers who require it
- emphasize the idea of partnership between trade partners
- facilitate mutually beneficial long-term trading relationships
- set clear minimum and progressive criteria to ensure that the conditions for the production and trade of a product are socially and economically fair and environmentally responsible.

Ethics and the individual manager

So why do managers make unethical choices? Our ethical judgement is influenced by our moral principles, which come both from our background (i.e. religion, upbringing, social and cultural norms) and also from norms learned from working in a particular industry or firm. Research shows that there are four main reasons why managers make bad choices:

- *A belief that the activity is not 'really' illegal or immoral.* To prevent this, be clear about the kinds of activities that are acceptable, those that will be tolerated and what behaviour will be condoned.

- *A belief that the activity is in the individuals' or the corporations' best interests.* Often this belief results from pressure to achieve short-term results. To prevent this, do not focus too much on short-term gains while neglecting the long-term consequences of management decisions.
- *A belief that the activity is 'safe' because it will never be found out or publicized.* To discourage this belief, engage in communications that increase the perceived probability of being caught, persecuted and punished, and announce misconduct.
- *A belief that because the activity helps the company, the company will condone it and even protect the person who engages in it.* To prevent this, stress the responsibility of senior managers to clearly communicate the norm that company loyalty should not go against the laws and values of the society.[44]

Sometimes unethical decisions are made as a result of 'groupthink'. It has often been observed that a group of people working together will sometimes make unethical decisions that few, if any, of them would make individually. This appears to be due to the reluctance of individuals to press for the serious consideration of sensitive ethical issues.

Managers encounter complex business problems on a day-to-day basis that have strong social and ethical components. These problems have no simple solution and neither are the optimal decisions nor their consequences always obvious. The Ethics Resource Centre recommends applying the following ethics filters to decision-making:

- *Policies:* Is it consistent with my organization's policies, procedures and guidelines?
- *Legal:* Is it acceptable under the applicable laws and regulations?
- *Universal:* Does it conform to the universal principles and values my organizations has adopted?
- *Self:* Does it satisfy my personal definition of right, good and fair?

They have also come up with a six-step ethical decision-making model for use by managers and their teams.

Define the problem: Describing why the decision is called for and identifying the most desired outcome(s).

Identify available alternative solutions to the problem: Consider more than five in most cases. At a very minimum three options should be identified to allow people to escape from having to choose between two opposing options.

Evaluate the identified alternatives: Look at the likely positives and negatives for each and differentiate between what information you know for a fact and what you believe might be the case.

Make the decision: Ensure that all members of the team have clear information about the problem and alternatives.

Implement the decision: Once decided, tangible steps should be put in place to move forward with the solution. A decision only counts if it is implemented.

Evaluate the decision: Did it fix the problem? Is it better now, or worse, or the same? What new problems did the solution create? What lessons were learned that could be applied to help next time a similar problem arises.[45]

Ethics Resource Centre (www.ethics.org), Business Roundtable Institute for Corporate Ethics (www.corporate-ethics.org). Caux Round Table Principles for Business: ethical and responsible behaviour (www.cauxrountable.org).

Corporate governance

The OECD defines corporate governance as the system by which business corporations are directed and controlled. The corporate governance structure specifies the distribution of rights and responsibilities among different participants in the corporation, such as shareholders, board members, managers, employees and other stakeholders, and spells out the rules and procedures for making decisions on corporate affairs. Corporate governance also refers to the rules governing the process through which the company objectives are set, and the means of attaining those objectives and monitoring performance.

The OECD published its Principles of Corporate Governance in 2004, which represent certain common characteristics that are fundamental to a good corporate governance framework. These principles are:

- *Ensuring the basis for an effective corporate governance framework:* Promote transparent and efficient markets, be consistent with the rule of law and clearly articulate the division of responsibilities among different supervisory, regulatory and enforcement authorities.
- *The rights of shareholders and key ownership functions:* Protect and facilitate the exercise of shareholders' rights.
- *The equitable treatment of shareholders:* Ensure the equitable treatment of all shareholders, including minority and foreign shareholders. All shareholders should have the opportunity to obtain effective redress for violation of their rights.
- *The role of stakeholders in corporate governance:* Recognize the rights of stakeholders established by law or through mutual agreements and encourage active co-operation between corporations and stakeholders in creating wealth, jobs and the sustainability of financially sound enterprises.
- *Disclosure and transparency:* Ensure that timely and accurate disclosure is made on all material matters regarding the corporation, including the financial situation, performance, ownership, and governance of the company.
- *The responsibilities of the board:* Ensure the strategic guidance of the company, the effective monitoring of management by the board and the board's accountability to the company and the shareholders.

When analysing a company's corporate governance structures, companies such as Deutsche Bank look at four factors:[46]

- *Board independence:* This is the board's ability to act independently from management in the best interest of shareholders, including the board's structure, composition and overall capabilities.
- *Shareholder treatment:* This addresses questions relating to the treatment of minority shareholders as well as issues around capital structure and its impact on shareholder rights.

- *Information disclosure*: This focuses on the quality, extent and timeliness of the information provided by companies to analysts and investors as well as internal verification mechanisms.
- *Corporate compensation*: This addresses the compensation of directors and executives as well as systems to monitor and measure this compensation.

Global Corporate Governance Forum (www.gcgf.org), World Bank Corporate Governance Toolkit (rru.worldbank.org/Toolkits/ CorporateGovernance/), Conference Board Centre for Corporate Citizenship and Sustainability (www.conference-board.org/ knowledge/citizenshipcenter), European Corporate Governance (www.ec.europa.eu/internal_market/company/ecgforum/index_ en.htm), International Corporate Governance Network (www.icgn. org) OECD Corporate Governance (www.oecd.org/corporate).

Corruption

Corruption is defined as 'the misuse of entrusted power for private gain'. According to the World Bank, corruption is the single greatest obstacle to economic and social development. The bank estimates that it costs more than 5% of the world's GDP or approximately $ 3 trillion. For business, corruption is estimated to add 10 % or more to the costs of doing business in many parts of the world and up to 25% to the cost of procurement contracts in developing countries.[47] Further research found that moving a business from a country with low levels of corruption to a country with medium or high levels of corruption is the equivalent to a 20% tax on foreign business.[48] The Global Compact and Transparency International suggest three practical steps to fight corruption:

1. *Internal:* Introduce anti-corruption policies and programmes within the organizations and business operations.
   - Top management must send consistent messages, directing all managers to apply stringent codes and high standards, while at the same time making it clear that these codes are not open to interpretation.

- A company should adopt its own business principles and ethics code, and publish it to employees.
- Training and continuous efforts must be made to ensure that principles and codes are integrated into other management systems.
- Adopt internal reporting procedures to ensure that appropriate systems are in place to ensure that if something does happen, the company is the first to know.

2. *External:* Report on anti-corruption work and activities in the annual communications and share experiences and best practices.

3. *Collective:* Collective action among businesses can help business managers in making the right decisions. For example, Publish What You Pay, a coalition of over 200 NGOs, calls for the mandatory disclosure of the payments made by oil, gas and mining companies to all governments for the extraction of natural resources (www.publishwhatyoupay.org).

The growing number of international initiatives aimed at helping companies to stop and deal with corruption, indicates how important anti-corruption practices have become in the global business community. The UN Convention against corruption was adopted by the General Assembly of the UN in 2003 (www.unodc.org/unodc/en/corruption) and the 9th of December is International Anti Corruption Day. The Global Corruption Barometer is a survey that assesses general public attitudes towards and experience of corruption in dozens of countries around the world. The Corruption Perceptions Index ranks more than 150 countries by their perceived levels of corruption as determined by expert assessments and opinion surveys (www.transparency.org).

International Chamber of Commerce anti corruption website (www.iccwbo.org/policy/anticorruption), World Economic Forum Partnering Against Corruption Initiative (www.weforum.org/paci), World Bank Anti Corruption Knowledge Centre (www.worldbank.org/publicsector/anticorrupt/index.cfm), UN Global Compact resource section on corruption (www.unglobalcompact.org/Issues/transparency_anticorruption).

Bribery

Bribery is a major part of corruption. According to the Transparency International, bribery is 'an offer or receipt of any gift, loan, fee, reward or other advantage to or from any person as an inducement to do something which is dishonest, illegal or a breach of trust, in the conduct of the enterprise's business.' According to Transparency International's Business Principles for Countering Bribery, the different forms of bribery include:

- *Bribes:* An enterprise should prohibit the offer or actual transfer of a bribe in any form, including kickbacks, on any portion of a contract payment, or the use of other routes or channels to provide improper benefits to customers, agents, contractors, suppliers or employees of any such party or government officials. The enterprise should also prohibit employees from accepting bribes.
- *Political contributions:* an enterprise, its employees or agents should not make direct or indirect contributions to political parties, organizations or individuals engaged in politics, as a way of obtaining advantage in business transactions. The enterprise should disclose these contributions.
- *Charitable contributions and sponsorship:* ensure that these sorts of contributions are not being used for bribery. An enterprise should publicly disclose all its charitable contributions.
- *Facilitation payments:* These are small payments made to secure or expedite the performance of a routine or necessary action to which the payer of the facilitation payment has legal or other entitlement. Recognizing that facilitation payments are a form of bribery, the enterprise should work to identify and eliminate them.
- *Gifts, hospitality and expenses:* The enterprise should prohibit the offer or receipt of gifts, hospitality or expenses whenever such arrangements could affect the outcome of business transactions and are not reasonable and bona fide expenditures.

Several recent initiatives such as the OECD Anti-bribery Convention and the anti-bribery provisions of the revised OECD guidelines for

Multinationals attempt to curb its effect and in fact for the 37 countries that have signed the convention, bribery is illegal. The ICC Rules of Conduct to Combat Extortion and Bribery provides the following guidance on how to approach anti-bribery policies:

- Enterprises should make their *anti-corruption policy* known to all agents and other intermediaries and make it clear that they expect all activities carried out on their behalf to be compliant with their policy.
- In order to prevent bribery and extortion, enterprises should implement *comprehensive policies or codes* reflecting these Rules of Conduct as well as their particular circumstances and specific business environment. These policies or codes should include (a) training, (b) confidential channels to raise concerns, (c) disciplinary procedures and (d) applicability to all controlled subsidiaries, foreign and domestic.
- All *financial transactions* must be properly and fairly recorded in appropriate books of accounts available for inspection by board of directors,(i.e.no off the books or secret accounts);transactions should be inspected within established independent systems of auditing and comply with all provisions of national tax laws and regulations.
- The *board of directors* (or other body) with the ultimate responsibility for the enterprise should take reasonable steps to ensure compliance with these Rules of Conduct.

Information on the OECD Anti-bribery convention including ratification and enforcement can be found at www.oecd.org. The Business Principles for Countering Bribery provide a framework for companies to develop comprehensive anti-bribery programmes, both large and SMEs. They also have a six-step process for implementing anti-bribery policies and programmes (www.transparency.org/global_priorities/private_sector/business_principles). More on ICC and Bribery can be found at www.iccwbo.org and www.unglobalcompact.org under Transparency and Anti-Corruption.

Challenges?

- *What is legal versus what is ethical:* Just because a practice is not illegal, this does not mean it is ethical. Ethics is much wider than law.
- *Implementation:* Ethics programmes, codes of conduct and other mechanisms put in place to stop unethical behaviours provide little help if managers at all levels do not know or implement it consistently. It is not enough to have an ethics statement, it needs to be understood, used and enforced.
- *Consistency:* Even companies with strong ethical policies and processes will encounter problems with ethics. Create a safe environment where employees can raise concerns about possible misconduct and wrong doings. Despite the proliferation of help lines and ethics offices, employees still suffer from a 'fear of retaliation'.[49]
- *Pressures to be unethical:* A study based on in-depth interviews with 30 recent graduates from the Harvard MBA working in banks, consulting and advertising firms found that many young managers received explicit instructions from their middle-manager bosses or felt strong organizational pressures to do things that they believed were unethical or even illegal.[50]
- *Misleading the public:* As sustainability becomes a hot topic in more countries, more groups appear that are trying to tap into this market. While some are working to raise awareness, others are not quite what they seem—they are, in a sense 'greenwashed' organizations. Full Frontal Scrutiny, a joint project by the Consumer Reports WebWatch and the Centre for Media and Democracy, looks at raising awareness of what it calls front groups, organizations that state a particular agenda while hiding or obscuring their identity, membership and or sponsorship. This can include organizations that avoid mentioning their main sources of funding or have misleading names (for example, the National Wetlands Coalition actually opposes policies to protect US wetlands) (www.frontgroups.org/).
- *Incentives:* The fact is that there is still a place in society for both responsible and irresponsible companies. Good companies, even good employees, aren't penalized for doing the 'right thing' but they are not necessarily rewarded either.

Trends and new ideas

– Transparency and Honesty	– The company of the future
– Management 2.0	– Whistleblowing

Transparency and Honesty Honesty is the best policy, in life and in business. In fact, increased honesty is helping businesses move forward in sustainability, and protect them when they encounter problems. In its Footprint Chronicles, Patagonia allows consumers access to the complete picture of the impact a product has on the environment, the good, the bad and the ugly. They openly recognize that they sometimes have a negative impact, and they are working to minimize these (www.patagonia.com/usa/footprint). Mountain Equipment Co-op (MEC) in Canada disclosed in 2008 a list of factory names and locations from where they source MEC-brand products, the first Canadian retailer to do so. In their annual report they also discuss their progress made in being a more sustainable company and openly discuss their challenges (www.mec.ca).

Management 2.0 According to Management Lab (MLab), 'Both practitioners and scholars are caught in the paradigm trap of management 1.0, reliant on the old staples of standardisation, specialisaton, hierarchical planning and control, and extrinsic rewards, propped up by the doctrine of shareholder value. In their time highly productive, these innovations are now increasingly obstructive barriers to progress.' MLab wondered what would happen if you asked progressive business thinkers to reinvent management for the 21st century, to throw away years' worth of assumptions and to radically re-imagine the ways in which companies could work? Some of the thoughts collected include:

- *People:* Manage as if everyone mattered, stakeholders, employees. Work to maximize system success. Enable communities of passion. Increase trust and reduce fear.

- *Purpose:* Seek orientation in a higher and broader purpose. Purpose generates energy, passion and commitment.
- *Rewards:* Stretch executive timeframes and perspectives. Change incentives to reward executives and investors who nurture the small projects that have the potential to become big ones over time. Develop holistic performance measures.
- *Question:* Substantially reduce the gravitational pull of the past. Explicitly challenge industry (and corporate) orthodoxies.
- *Structure:* Expand the freedom for autonomous action. De-organize – dissolving (formal) hierarchy, eliminating silos and collapsing the distance between centre and periphery. Abolish the myth of the imperial CEO. Lead from behind.
- *Decisions:* De-politicize decision-making. Surface conflict, allow minority views to be heard. Exploit the wisdom of the crowd in critical decisions.
- *Information:* Create a democracy of information. Create an internal market for ideas, talent and resources.
- *Creativity:* Overcome the prejudice that people aren't creative; create space and time to give them time to reflect, dream and innovate. De-stigmatize failure and build cultures that reward much more small-scale innovation (www.managementlab.org/files/LabNotes9.pdf).

The company of the future What would a corporation look like that was designed to seamlessly integrate both social and financial purposes? That is the question that a US multi-stakeholder initiative called Corporation 20/20 (www.corporation2020.org) is looking to answer. They have developed a set of principles to guide the design of the new company which include:

1. The purpose of the corporation is to harness private interests to serve the public interest.
2. Corporations shall accrue fair returns for shareholders, but not at the expense of the legitimate interests of other stakeholders.

3. Corporations shall operate sustainably, meeting the needs of the present generation without compromising the ability of future generations to meet their needs.
4. Corporations shall distribute their wealth equitably among those who contribute to its creation.
5. Corporations shall be governed in a manner that is participatory, transparent, ethical and accountable.
6. Corporations shall not infringe on the right of natural persons to govern themselves, nor infringe on other universal human rights.

Whistleblowing Whistleblowers, those who release information about suspected corruption and unethical behaviour within an organization, are often seen as bad individuals, and whistle blowing actions are often seen as being disloyal and creating a distrustful atmosphere. The fact is this could not be any further from the truth. Having in place a system where individuals within the company and who deal with the company such as suppliers and buyers are encouraged to report unethical or corrupt behaviour can be an important tool that allows the company to detect and fix eventual problems. In addition, these systems can play a key role in preventing significant financial consequences in the company, or in extreme cases, have the consequence of bringing down the whole company, if such fraud were to become public. According to a 2007 study by KPMG, 25 % of the incidents of fraud uncovered among 360 incidents analysed, came to light thanks to a whistleblowing system put in place by companies. However, only 33 % of companies surveyed in Europe had hot lines for employees to report incidents of possible fraud. In 2008, the International Chamber of Commerce launched a set of guidelines aimed at helping companies establish and implement internal whistleblowing programmes (www.iccwbo.org).

- Create a whistleblowing programme as part of internal integrity practices.
- Handle reports early on, in full confidentiality.

The World Bank's Anti-corruption programme includes a list of blacklisted companies and individuals, as well as a phone line to report corruption in bank related projects. (www.worldbank.org)

- Appoint a high-level executive to manage the whistleblowing unit.
- Communicate in as many languages as there are countries of operation.
- Abide by external legal restrictions.
- Allow reporting to be anonymous or disclosed, compulsory or voluntary.
- Acknowledge, record and screen all reports.
- Enable employees to report incidents without fear of retaliation, discrimination or disciplinary action.

What you can do . . .

❑ Examine the culture of the organization: What are the norms of behaviour? What is valued?

❑ Write a code of ethics: Adopting someone else's code of ethics will not work. A company, with the full support of the CEO and the board as well as the employees, must put together an ethics code that represents the values and needs of the employees.

❑ Issue the code and make it known: Publish and send the code to all employees, suppliers and business partners; post it on the web to make sure everyone knows it and how to use it.

❑ Provide training and examples: Practical examples of the code in action should be introduced into all company internal (and external) training programmes as well as induction courses. Managers should sign off on the code regularly and a review mechanism should be established.

❑ Build a robust ethics infrastructure that is self-sustaining: Have an independent committee that is responsible for ensuring that systems are in place to assure employee compliance with the Codes of Ethics. This can include, protection for people who 'blow the whistle', establishing 'hotlines' or 'helplines' where employees can seek guidance.

❑ Provide space for your employees to bring up issues that are of concern to them: When faced with a situation where you are not sure what is the correct thing to do, ask yourself 'What would I feel if this were done to me or to someone I love?' 'What decision would I make if my mother and father were looking over my shoulder?'

Want more?

- Several rankings exist of the most ethical companies including '100 Best Corporate Citizens' (www.thecro.com) and *Business Ethics Magazine* 100 Best Corporate Citizens (www.business-ethics.com/BE100_all).

- The Conference Board is a global organization based in the US working to help businesses strengthen their performance and better serve society (www.conference-board.org).

- Baseswiki is an online tool developed by Harvard Kennedy School and the UN Secretary General's Special Representative for business and human rights which focuses on the non-judicial mechanisms available around the world to help companies and their external stakeholders resolve disputes (www.baseswiki.org).

- Business in Society Gateway is a comprehensive online resource centre on business in society issues and corporate responsibility (www.businessinsociety.eu).

Read: *The Market for Virtue: The Potential and Limits of Corporate Social Responsibility* by David Vogel (2006) provides an analysis of the CSR movement in the US and Europe.

The role of the CEO

'Senior management commitment is key to a company's successful approach to corporate responsibility; while it is essential that senior management assign clear responsibilities, resources and authority to company managers for addressing corporate responsibility issues on an ongoing basis, leadership in these matters rests with the chief executive, the chairman and board directors.'

International Chamber of Commerce

The World Economic Forum conducted a survey of CEOs around the world which indicated that business leaders have three responsibilities:

1. *Our companies' commitment to being global corporate citizens is about the way we run our own business.* The greatest contribution we can make to development is to do business in a manner that obeys the law, produces safe and cost effective products and services, creates jobs and wealth, supports training and technology cooperation and reflects international standards and values in areas such as the environment, ethics, labour and human rights.
2. *Our relationships with key stakeholders are fundamental to our success inside and outside our companies.* Being global corporate citizens requires us to identify and work with key stakeholders in our main spheres of influence: in the workplace, in the marketplace, along our supply chains, at the community level and in public policy dialogue.
3. *Ultimate leadership for corporate citizenship rests with us as chief executives, chairmen and board directors.* Although it is essential that we assign clear responsibilities, resources and leadership roles to our managers for addressing these issues on a day-to-day basis, ultimate responsibility rests with us (www.weforum.org/pdf/GCCI/GCC_CEOstatement.pdf).

According to the Globally Responsible Leadership Initiative (GRLI), 'business leaders at many organizational levels, whilst aware of some of the challenges, are often ill equipped to deal with these global issues. Some dismiss them as irrelevant to their personal responsibilities and accountabilities. Others steer clear of questioning the economic systems upon which their working environment is based.' The GRLI believes that there are at least four urgent challenges for leaders:

- They should think and act in a global context.
- They should broaden their corporate purpose to reflect accountability to society around the globe.
- They should put ethics at the centre of their thoughts, words and deeds.
- They – and all business schools and centres for leadership learning – should transform their business education to give corporate global responsibility the centrality it deserves.

It has been said time and time again that without the support of senior management initiatives cannot have their full impact. The role of the CEO is not only to steer the ship in the right direction, but also to be able to see over the horizon and be able to plan ahead. As such, the chief executive plays a key role as a champion on sustainability strategies:

- CEOs can make sure the issues are part of information conversations that take place on a daily basis and make sure it is part of their language.
- CEOs can make sure they walk the talk by sending clear and consistent messages about the importance of sustainability in the organization, and matching this with their own actions.

They are the ultimate supporter and enabler of the issues within their organization, and thus have a vital role to play in a company's adoption of sustainability.

Want more?

The Globally Responsible Leadership Initiative is a global community working to promote support and execute the development of a next generation of globally responsible leaders (www.grli.org). The International Business Leaders Forum works with business, governments and civil society to enhance the contribution that companies can make to

(continued)

sustainable development (www.iblf.org). Finally, CEOs and senior managers are increasingly writing articles and blogs which include their organizations commitment to sustainability. Consulting firms also have CEO surveys on a yearly basis including PwC and McKinsey.

Read: Several CEOs of leading sustainability companies are releasing books about their work, for example, *Mid-Course Correction: Towards a Sustainable Enterprise: The Interface Model* by Interface CEO Ray Anderson (1998).

10 Finance

'If you want to make capitalism sustainable, you might as well start with capital'

NICK ROBINS

Martin Hancock, the former chair of the UNEPFI from Westpac tells the story of a man who turned to him during a conference on sustainable banking and whispered, 'It must be serious if the banks are coming around the table.' Indeed, sustainability must be making real progress if the finance sector, known for being conservative, is starting to become interested. One might even argue that finance is the most important sector in sustainability, as it reaches every corner within companies and throughout the economy.

According to the IFC, 'The biggest impact of banks, investors and insurers on sustainable development is not their own environmental footprint but their pivotal role in allocating financial capital between different economic activities, both at home and abroad.'[51] The financial sector plays a key role by sending a signal to companies that can enable them to invest in longer-term opportunities. Financial institutions, such as banks, are also responsible for managing social and environmental risks in decision-making and lending, as well as helping identifying opportunities for innovative product development in new areas related to sustainability. In addition to what they choose to finance, the financial sector can have a crucial impact by not investing in products, initiatives or projects that are unsustainable or damaging to society and the environment.

Why is it important?

- **To better understand companies:** Screening for environmental social and governance (ESG) factors can lead to a more thorough understanding of both the risks and opportunities and how these will impact the bottom line both today and in the future.
- **Anticipating problems:** Many investors are reacting to bad corporate governance news rather than anticipating potential problems. A greater consideration of these issues allows investors and financial professionals to see the problems before they occur and plan accordingly.
- **Increase profitability:** For companies that are able to move beyond merely looking at risks and to start identifying and acting on opportunities, there are many avenues to explore, for example in sustainable energy, cleaner production, biodiversity conservation and the fast growing environmental technology industries.
- **Intangibles:** ESG issues can have a strong impact on intangible assets such as reputation and brand, which can represent over two-thirds of the total market value of a listed company. As the Chartered Financial Analyst Institute puts it, 'Investors should consider what a company does to maintain and protect one of its most important assets: its reputation'.[52]
- **Part of your fiduciary responsibilities:** According to UNEPFI, 'appropriate consideration of these issues is part of delivering superior risk-adjusted returns and is therefore firmly within the bounds of investors' fiduciary duties'.
- **As a proxy for good management:** Groups such as Goldman Sachs's Sustain use management of environmental, social and governance issues as a proxy for overall strong company management. 'Because the world is more difficult to operate in, we think there are certain factors companies will need to manage if they are to succeed'[53] Investors have a preference for companies with strong governance and are prepared to pay a premium for this.

- *Increased demand:* There is an increased demand for sustainable finance, especially from high net worth individuals.

The key concepts

Sustainability affects both the financial sector and financial activities undertaken by a company.

• Incorporating sustainability issues into investments	→ *Sustainable Investment*
• The responsibilities of those people who manage money	→ *Fiduciary Responsibilities*
• Providing global indexes to benchmark sustainability performance	→ *Tracking progress*
• Doing proper due diligence	→ *Mergers and Acquisitions*
• Exploring sustainability issues within projects	→ *Project Finance*
• Providing financial services to the poor	→ *Box: Microfinance*

Sustainable Investment

Sustainable investment (SI), also referred to as socially responsible investment or responsible investment, is a term used to describe an investment process which takes environmental, social, ethical and governance considerations into account. This process is in addition *to*, or is incorporated *into*, the usual investment selection and management processes and can be adopted across asset classes (private equity, real estate, etc.). SI has developed new approaches over the past few decades. There is still demand for, and suppliers of, each of the different forms of SI:

- *Negative screening*: SI started with banks choosing not to invest in sectors or companies that were seen as 'bad' because of their policies, actions, products (e.g. tobacco and weapons) or services (e.g. gambling). For example the Co-operative bank in the UK has a long list of areas, determined in part by customers, where they will not invest.

- *Positive screening:* Portfolios are chosen based on a set of non-traditional criteria, which can include environmental, social, governance and ethical issues. These screens are seen as having an impact on both financial and non-financial measures. Common positive screens include energy efficiency, environmental management and employment standards.

- *Best in class:* A subsection of positive screening, this involves selecting the best performers based on environmental, social and governance parameters. Investors are presented with the 'best in class' for each sector based on a set of ESG criteria. There are a growing number of indexes that provide information on these companies.

- *Engagement:* Fund managers actively engage with companies in which they invest to seek improvement on environmental, social and governance issues if their research indicates a shortfall in these areas.

- *Shareholder activism:* Owners will exercise their right to vote and their right to raise resolutions in order to achieve better management outcomes from the companies they invest in. Even ESG resolutions that attract less than majority support can still capture the attention of a corporate board and lead to change. GE's Ecoimagination was created in part, because of an environmental resolution raised by a group of nuns, and went on to gain 24% support.[54]

- *Integrated into decision process:* Sustainability issues are incorporated into investments in the same way as other financial information, although the trend is more recent so few managers can currently claim full integration. One example of a group working in this area is GenerationIM. They don't have one team doing the sustainability analysis and another doing the financial. Instead each analyst is trained to develop both capabilities.

- *Community investing:* Investor capital is used to finance or guarantee loans to individuals and organizations that have historically been denied access to capital by traditional financial institutions, such as disadvantaged urban and rural communities (www. communityinvest.org).

There are a wide range of different types of sustainable investment, some of which—at the 'ethical' or deep green end—are very much about saving the earth or meeting other social or environmental objectives, which deliberately take precedence over financial objectives. Investors in this type of product, driven by ethical values more than financial value, make up a small minority. Many responsible investments, on the other hand, are focused much more on the potential for more attractive returns over the longer term. Financial returns are still the driver but there is a much clearer recognition that it is simply not possible to maintain high financial returns over a long period of time if they are achieved at the expense of people or the environment.

As a growing number of investors begin to understand the relevance of ESG to the bottom line, they are looking for guidance on how to proceed. For this reason, there is a lot of excitement around the United Nations Principles for Responsible Investment (UNPRI), which was launched in 2006 to help investors integrate consideration for ESG issues into investment decision-making and provide a platform for investors to share knowledge and best practices. The UNPRI is a set of six principles and possible actions and guidance on how to implement these principles which includes:

> We will incorporate ESG issues into investment analysis and decision-making processes.
>
> We will be active owners and incorporate ESG issues into our ownership policies and practices.
>
> We will seek appropriate disclosure on ESG issues by the entities in which we invest.
>
> We will promote acceptance and implementation of the Principles within the investment industry.
>
> We will work together to enhance our effectiveness in implementing the Principles.

We will each report on our activities and progress towards implementing the Principles.

(WWW.UNPRI.ORG)

The Principles for Responsible Investment also has an Academic Network, a web-based tool for knowledge exchange within the responsible investment community which provides freely accessible avenues for research, education and network-building on critical responsible investment issues (www. academic.unpri.org).

Natural Capital Institute Responsible Investing is a public database for the US and Canada found at www.responsibleinvesting. org. Other websites of interest include www.sristudies.org, www. socialinvest.org, www.eurosif.org. UKSIF offers a free online training course for financial advisors on green and ethical investment at www.uksif.org/consumers-advisers/advisers/online_course. Mercer provides several resources on responsible investment including a dictionary on the language of responsible investment (www.mercer.com/ri). Generation Investment Management, co-founded by Al Gore in 2004 has an investment approach based on the idea that sustainability factors—economic, environmental, social and governance criteria—will drive a company's returns over the long-term. By integrating those issues with traditional analysis they aim to deliver superior investment returns (www. generationim.com).

Fiduciary responsibilities

Today, the majority of investments are in the form of pension funds, mutual funds or institutional investment funds. The value of assets managed by the investment industry worldwide is estimated at over

$42 trillion. Funds are overseen on behalf of individuals by a relatively small number of trustees who act as fiduciaries to oversee large pools of retirement savings. Legally, their job is to act in the best interest of the savers whose money is in the funds.

However, are they? Discussion has recently been centred on what exactly the best interests of those individuals are. A report by UNEP and Freshfields Law Firm says,

> 'This is where the interesting questions concerning fiduciary responsibility come to the fore: are the best interests of savers only to be defined as their financial interest? If so, in respect to which horizon? Are not the social and environmental interests of savers also to be taken into account? Indeed, many people wonder what good an extra percent or three of patrimony are worth if the society in which they are to enjoy retirement and in which their descendents will live deteriorates. Quality of life and quality of the environment are worth something, even if not, or particularly because, they are not reducible to financial percentages.'

Many funds fail to look at these issues for two reasons. Many fiduciaries question whether they are legally allowed to take action on such issues, despite the growing body of evidence that ESG issues can have a material impact on the financial performance of their portfolio. However as the report says, 'On that basis, integrating ESG considerations into an investment analysis so as to more reliably predict financial performance is clearly permissible and is arguably required in all jurisdictions.' Much of this boils down to the simple rule of the Precautionary Principle: whereby if one may, through exercising a degree of caution, avoid exposing oneself (or one's investments) to risk, one should certainly take appropriate steps to do so.

The second reason that many funds fail to integrate ESG into their investment decisions relates to the culture of investing. The report The Prudent Investors says that investors have a 'herd mentality', that they assume safety in numbers by following largely similar strategies when it comes to investing. In part they do this because of the pressure felt to justify their existence based on a quarterly if not daily basis by focusing on short-term profit opportunities. According to William Donaldson, former Chairman of the Securities and Exchange Commission, 'Over time, analysts have become obsessed with the question of whether a company meets its quarterly EPS numbers and not with whether a company is built to last. And because of the considerable clout of the sell-side analyst, this shift from long-term thinking to short–term results has echoed through to company management and to professional investors.'[55]

Fortunately things are changing. The current financial crisis is leading to major changes in public attitudes and regulations, deep self-examination with the financial community. The focus is on filling the gaps in the regulatory apparatus and legislative frameworks that allowed banks to get into such deep trouble with such unsustainable investments. In some countries, such as France, ESG issues must be considered for investment, and have been put into the investment management mandate issued to fund managers by the French retirement reserve fund. In addition, although the majority of individuals who hold their savings in these funds do not know what their money is being invested in or have any say in the matter, this is changing with rising awareness levels (see trends). For example Calvert Social Index, which measures the social performance of the largest 1000 US based companies have a service called Know What You Own, which allows you to see what is in your US mutual funds and if the companies held meet Calvert's social standards (www.calvert.com).

There are several reports that present information on this topic: The Prudent Trustee by Jed Emerson and Tim Little (www.genfound.org) a legal framework for the integration of environmental, social and governance issues into institutional investment, October 2005 UNEPFI and (www.unepfi.org/fileadmin/documents/freshfields_legal_resp_20051123.pdf). A climate for change—A trustee's guide to understanding and addressing climate risk (www.carbontrust.co.uk).

Tracking performance

Indices are starting to track the environmental, social and governance performance of leading sustainability driven companies around the world. They provide asset managers with reliable and objective benchmarks to manage sustainability portfolios. These indices are used as the research basis of responsible investment decisions, and facilitate tracking of the performance of responsible investments.

The information is collected through surveys sent directly to businesses and is complemented by additional information collected through various media and stakeholder reports, and other publicly available information. In some cases analysts personally contact individual companies to clarify points that arise from the analysis of the information collected. Indices often include evolving selection criteria and all information is available to the public.

For businesses, participation in these programmes can have several benefits:

- Communication of their sustainability efforts to a wide audience thus enhancing their reputation and brand as a good corporate citizen.
- Third-party authentication for their ESG efforts, if the ESG firms rate them well or include them in indexes.
- Access to additional investment through inclusion on sustainability indexes.
- Understanding of their own strengths and weaknesses, identification of potential opportunities for improvement and self-benchmarking against competition through the response process and research firm feedback.

There are several indexes tracking the financial performance of leading sustainability driven companies internationally.

Launched in 1999, the Dow Jones Sustainability Indexes chooses companies based on a set of criteria and weightings covering economic, environmental and social areas (www.sustainability-index.com). Every year the 2500 largest companies in the world based on free-float market capitalization are invited to take part in the assessment which looks at:

- *Economic dimensions:* Codes of conduct, compliance, corruption and bribery, corporate governance, risk and crisis management.
- *Social dimensions:* corporate citizenship, labour practice indicators, human capital development, social reporting, talent attraction and retention.
- *Environmental dimensions:* eco-efficiency, environmental reporting.

FTSE4Good Index series was launched in 2001. To be included in the indices, companies need to demonstrate that they are working towards environmental management, climate change mitigation and adaptation, countering bribery, upholding human and labour rights and supply chain labour standards. A small number of sectors such as tobacco and weapon companies have been excluded. They also undertake engagement programmes to work with companies to help them understand changes in the criteria and provide guidance and support to companies working to meet the index's evolving standards. Companies who do not are taken off the list (www.ftse4good.com).

Indices are also active at the national level. Brazil Nuevo Mercado, part of Sao Paulo Stock Exchange in Brazil has stricter reporting rules and expanded Shareowner rights, in order to attract investment from outside the country. The promise of greater transparency and higher corporate governance standards by the companies listed has led to great increases in foreign capital invested in Brazilian listed companies.[56] Jantizi social index consists of 60 Canadian companies that pass a set of broadly based environmental, social and governance rating criteria (www.jantzisocialindex.com/).

As the number of indexes and research projects grow, so does the number of surveys companies are being asked to fill out. Challenges for companies range from company resource constraints including staff, time, costs and management system limitations. The main issue is ease of participation. Recommendations are that financial institutions and information requestors should take steps together to improve the information–request process in order to increase the likelihood of participation, including spreading out the timing of requests, ensuring adequate time to response, expanding online information collection, shortening the information requests and standardizing quantitative metrics as much as possible.

Want more?

- Each year www.sustainablebusiness.com announces the world stop 20 sustainable stocks. Other indexes include The London Stock Exchange's Corporate Responsibility Exchange Sustainability indexes (www.londonstockexchange.com) and the KLD Indexes (www.kld.com). For more information on the different indices mentioned above read their fact sheets available on each of their websites. SAM and PwC launched the Sustainability Yearbook which breaks down the leading companies into Gold, Silver and Bronze classes as well as picking out the companies in each sector that have made the greatest progress (www.sam-group.com).

- Other groups to look at include Henderson (www.henderson.com/sri) and Ethibel, an independent consultancy agency based in Belgium for SRI that advises banks and brokers offering ethical savings accounts and investment funds (www.ethibel.org). Innovest analyse companies' performance on environmental, social and strategic governance issues with a particular focus on their impact on competitiveness, profitability and share price performance (www.innovestgroup.com). Also see the Ethical Investment Research Service (www.eiris.org). UNEPFI publication Understanding Corporate Sustainability Disclosure Requests (www.unepfi.org).

Mergers and acquisitions

The following scenario is unfortunately far too common. Company X did not do proper environmental due diligence on the properties of a company they bought. They only realized after the deal that the company they just bought had been dumping toxic waste for 10 years in its yard. Because of legislation changes after the event, the company is no longer able to sell the acquired company without cleaning up the mess first.

For a deal that may have cost a few million to begin with, the clean up costs have now exceeded $400 million.

Sustainability issues should be of particular concern for those involved in mergers and acquisitions. The reason is, quite simply, that there is a lot of money at stake. Sustainability issues can affect both the viability and the ultimate value of deals. Leading practices can lead to a premium while lagging companies who have no plans in place to respond to increasing regulatory and marketplace demands for change can result in a discounted price.

Sustainability concerns can and should be incorporated into all steps of the M&A process, from the criteria used to identify, screen and prioritize potential targets, to the valuation of the company. Most important is that a company's sustainability policy, as seen in the business case, is part of an effective strategy to identify and manage risks. Here are a few tips:

- *Understand the strengths and weaknesses:* A buyer should learn exactly how advanced the target company's assessment of sustainability is. Sellers should understand their position in sustainability and accurately convey that to a buyer.
- *Incorporate sustainability metrics:* Begin to incorporate sustainability metrics, goals and targets into the deal valuation process, for example, energy and water consumption, carbon footprint, etc.
- *Consider the potential impact of changes:* This concerns everything from consumer preferences, changes in regulations, to variations in prices both in the present and future.
- *Consider the people aspects:* Determine whether the target company's management can effectively address sustainability

---

Want more?

How Green is the Deal? The Growing Role of Sustainability in M&A, Deloitte. 2008 (www.deloitte.com). An information graphic on the structure of the organic industry shows the acquisition of different organic brands (www.msu.edu/%7Ehowardp/organicindustry.html).

requirements, and whether the people responsible for sustainability initiatives are capable and are receiving the necessary organizational support.[57]

Project Finance

Environmentalists who have for decades been raising awareness on the negative social and environmental impacts of certain large infrastructure projects are now beginning to make the connection between the projects they campaign against and the financiers who back those projects. At the same time, financiers have begun to understand that social and environmental risks pose a threat to long-term shareholder value and must be taken seriously.

Project finance, according to the Equator Principles, 'is a method of funding in which the lender looks primarily to the revenues generated by a single project both as the source of repayment and as security for the exposure'.

In 2002, led by the World Bank Group's International Finance Corporation, banks working in the project finance sector developed the Equator Principles, a common and coherent set of environmental and social policies and guidelines that could be applied globally across all industry sectors. The Principles are voluntary guidelines to ensure that projects, whether they are large infrastructure projects such as dams or smaller projects, are financed in a manner that is socially responsible and reflects sound environmental management practices. The Principles have become the market standard for assessing environmental and social issues in financing large projects, and have been adopted by 59 financial institutions from 21 countries (85% of the global project finance sector). Banks apply the principles to all new projects financed globally with a total project capital cost of $10 million or more (revised down in 2006). Projects are classified into three levels according to potential social and environmental impacts. Category A (high risk) is for projects with potential significant adverse impacts such as a new mine, category B (medium) is for limited impacts that are site-specific and easily mitigated such as tourism and category C (low) is for projects with minimal or no adverse impacts such as telecommunication. The principles include:

1. *Review and categorization:* When a project is proposed for financing, the bank will, as part of its internal social and environmental review and due diligence, categorize each project based on the magnitude of its potential impacts and risks.
2. *Social and environmental assessment:* For each project, a social and environmental assessment should take place which includes proposing mitigation and management measures where appropriate.
3. *Applicable social and environmental standards:* For projects located in non-OECD countries and those located in OECD countries not designated as high-income, IFC performance standards must be followed.
4. *Action plan and management system:* Based on these assessments, banks make agreements with their clients on how to mitigate, monitor and manage social and environmental risks.
5. *Consultation and disclosure:* Experts from the government, the borrower or third parties will consult with the communities affected by the projects in a structured and culturally appropriate manner.
6. *Grievance mechanism:* To ensure that consultation, disclosure and community engagement continues throughout construction and operation of the project, the borrower will receive and facilitate resolution of concerns about the projects' social and environmental performance raised by individuals or groups.
7. *Independent review:* An independent social or environmental expert will review compliance with the equator principles.
8. *Compliance:* Banks will comply with all relevant international and industry standards and all local laws and regulations.
9. *Independent monitoring and reporting:* They will ensure ongoing monitoring and reporting over the life of the loan including invitation of an independent expert to assess compliance and monitor progress.
10. *Reporting:* Banks commit to reporting publicly at least annually about their Equator Principles implementation processes and experience.

The Equator principles website has more resources on project finance as well as the activities of the institutions that have signed onto the principles (www.equator-principles.com). The IFC applies certain minimum standards to all the projects it finances to minimize their effect on the environment and on affected communities (www.ifc.org/ifcext/enviro.nsf/Content/ PerformanceStandards).

Challenges?

- *From short term to long-term:* The financial sector is built around institutional incentives that reward short-term more than long-term results. Pressure to meet quarterly targets and market expectations makes it challenging to focus on long-term results.
- *Shareholders and customers:* There is still a disconnection between shareholders' professed values and what they expect from their investments. The same is true of customers who are pressuring banks to move forward on these issues without supporting the banks' efforts by actually using these products. There are many reasons why this is the case including staff and customers not being aware of the different sustainability products on offer and a continuing cynical belief that all responsible investment products will underperform financially.
- *Competencies:* Most analysts have limited knowledge of sustainability, and new analysts are not receiving enough training to use non-financial criteria in financial valuation. Work done by the WBCSD and UNEFI has shown that 'young analysts still appear unconvinced over the materiality of most environmental, social and governance issues to business; and are unable to consider them because of inadequate information, training or tools; unwilling to depart from business as usual because of conflicts with remuneration, career advancement and culture'.
- *Silo thinking:* Many products and discussions are focused only on one topic, for example climate change. But is that really your biggest

and only risk? The range of sustainability issues is very broad, and all aspects should be considered.

- *Cost payback analysis:* The number of years required for some sustainability projects to pay for themselves may appear high with a traditional payback analysis. However, many times these are revealed to be more than cost effective over the long-term.
- *Access to better information:* The current availability of data varies widely between companies, sectors and regions, and is based on different voluntary and mandatory reporting regulations.

Trends and new ideas

– New Landscape for Corporate Ownership	– Long-term value
	– A new kind of bank
– A new definition of profit	– Innovative financing strategies

New landscape for corporate ownership Shareholders in large companies are no longer limited to the wealthy, privileged few. Today, working people around the world have their pensions and other life savings invested in shares of the world's largest companies. For example, the biggest shareholding body in Canada is the teachers and civil servants of Ontario, while in Denmark it is the workers' pension fund. The College Retirement Equities Fund, the pension plan for US editors, itself controls about 1% of all US stock market capitalization and CALPERS the California Public Employees Retirement System is almost as big. Through pension, insurance and savings institutions millions are inheriting power. So, as WEF puts it, 'Each pensioner owns a tiny interest in a vast number of companies. From the telecoms of Panama to the chemical companies of Germany, from the electronic companies of Silicon Valley to the oil wells of Nigeria, millions of citizens are the beneficial owners'. This is important for two reasons. First it means that the responsibility of investors will increasingly be to meet the intrinsic interests of owners in the long-term, owners who represent people internationally. Second this group of people could start speaking up as they become more aware and engaged.

At the other end of the spectrum, approximately 10 million individuals worldwide hold at least $1 million in financial assets, a number which is increasing rapidly. These investors are increasingly interested in green tech and alternative energy investments in their portfolios (12% of HNWI and 14% of ultra-HNWI). 'North America was the only region in which social responsibility was the primary driver of HNWIs' green investing. Among all HNWIs worldwide, approximately half pointed to financial returns as the primary reason for their allocations to green investing.' A study by Eurosif in Europe found that sustainable investments by HNWI are predicted to exceed S1 trillion by 2012.[58]

Insurance and sustainability The insurance sector is the world's largest economic sector, which reaches virtually every customer and business around the world. Without insurance, businesses and individuals would be afraid to take the risks that are necessary for the continuous development of capitalist society. In 2005 the worldwide volume exceeded $3.4 trillion roughly split 60/40 between life and non-life categories of insurance. Therefore, it is in the insurer's interest to reduce risks and improve sustainability. According to UNEPFI, 'The insurance industry is a strong lever for implementing sustainability due to its size, the extent of its reach into the community and the significant role it plays in the economy.'

The sector is increasingly concerned with climate change, health, man-made risks, and environmental liability, to name a few. Two types of insurance products have appeared in response: (1) products which differentiate insurance premiums on the basis of environmentally related characteristics; and (2) products specifically tailored for clean tech and emission reduction activities. Argentina's government is the first in the world to require companies involved in potentially hazardous activities to purchase insurance covering environmental damage to the country.[59]

> UNEPFI has done some work on Sustainability and the insurance sector including the development of Principles for Sustainable Insurance (www.unepfi.org). Climate Wise is an initiative to develop the insurance industry's strategy on climate change that currently includes over 40 members (www.climatewise.org.uk).

Focus on long-term value The economic and financial events of 2008 sent out a clear message about the consequences and costs of short-termism, in particular in the US. The Aspen Institute's long-term value creation guidelines for corporations and investors focus on re-asserting long-term orientation in business decision-making and investing, and moving away from the excessive short-term pressures in today's capital markets that result from intense focus on quarterly earnings and incentive structures. This encourages corporations and investors to pursue short-term gain with inadequate regard to long-term effects. The principles include defining metrics for long-term value creation, focusing corporate–investor communication around long-term metrics, and aligning company and investor compensation policies with long-term metrics (www.aspenbsp.org).

A new kind of bank It is probably safe to assume that most individuals are not happy with their banks for some reason or another, from hidden fees to lousy service. Combine extraordinarily high customer dissatisfaction with the current global financial turmoil and it's easy to conclude that Banking is an area just begging for innovation and change. Now some banks are stepping up to answer the call for change—from new product offerings to redefining the whole concept of banking to be more transparent, and inclusive. In the UK, the Co-operative Bank has gained over 205 000 customers and continues to grow, largely due to the explicit ethical policy first launched in 1992, which is based on continued customer consultation. In Europe, Triodos is committed to transparency and the realization of social, environmental and cultural objectives in day-to-day banking. As a result, it only finances enterprises and organizations that add social, environmental and cultural value.

For those who choose to stick with their bank, many mainstream banks have now started exploring how to be more sustainable by sending statements, invoices and other notices by email to save paper (for an example see HSBC at www.hsbc.com/1/2/sustainability). In addition, the number of sustainability-related financial services and products offered to retail and business customers has exploded. 'Green mortgages' are available with considerably lower interest rates for clients who purchase new energy efficient homes and/or invest in retrofits. A range of green loans are available in all categories including home equity loans and car loans. An increasing array of credit cards donate approximately half a percentage point of every purchase, balance transfer or cash advance to different charities and organizations.

Where individuals and small businesses are getting fed up with the big banks, they are turning to a growing number of successful community based banks. These banks are often more focused on small business loans and personal service to the community. Umpaqua Bank in the US sets up its branch locations like neighbourhood hubs with a focus on community and a range of green products and free events and seminars. US-based ShoreBank Pacific reported its tenth consecutive quarter of record earnings, its assets increased by 11% for the quarter and 34% for the year. San Francisco based New Resource Bank formed in 2005 with the aim to build a bank that was 'by the people for the people' of their community.

The Collevecchio Declaration, signed by over 100 NGOs, calls on big banks and investors to take their responsibility for the environment and socially harmful impacts of their activities (www. foe.org/camps/intl/declaration.html). 'Green Financial Products and Services', published by the UNEPFI in August 2007 has a long list of different products now being offered by banks (www.unepfi. org/fileadmin/documents/greenprods_01.pdf). FT and IFC give out sustainable banking awards: 2008 winners for sustainable bank of the year were Banco Real, Brazil and Rabobank, Netherlands (www. ftconferences.co.uk/sustainablebanking).

What you can do . . .

☐ Propose these options to your customers: Follow the work being done in sustainable finance at the national and international level. Read up on the different options that could be of interest to your customers and clients and propose the appropriate options to them.

☐ Think through financial decisions: Use full cost and life-cycle thinking when making financial decisions that incorporate both quantitative and qualitative measures over the short- and long-term. Picking the cheapest contractor for example could lead to an inferior job which could lead to hidden and significant long-term costs.

☐ Know what you own: Research the companies that make up the pension fund your clients are participating in or mutual funds that you are considering for recommendation. A fund with a subset of companies with poor environmental records could be bad.

☐ Look at investing your money in sustainable investments: Look into, for example, community investing. Money goes to loans given to not for profits, co-ops and social housing. Deposit and interest tend to be guaranteed so you can't lose money (www.communityinvestment.ca).

☐ If you own shares: When you own stock in a company, you own a small part of that company and therefore enjoy certain rights. Go to the company's annual shareholder meetings, speak to other shareholders or to the CEO directly and ask for action through shareholder resolutions. If more than 50% of shareholders agree with your proposal, then the company must comply with the resolution. The number of companies that have changed practices because their shareholders demanded it is actually quite startling. See www.amnesty.ca/sharepower and The Corporate Action Network's Share Power Campaign at www.amnestyusa.org.

Want more?

- The Chartered Financial Analyst Institute (CFA) has done some work in ESG including a manual for investors on these issues (www.cfainstitute.org). The GRI has a special supplement for the financial services sector that provides guidelines for reporting (www.globalreporting.org). CFO released 'The role of finance in environmental sustainability efforts' (www.cfo.com).

- Several international initiatives are working to build understanding of the impacts of environmental and social considerations on financial performance. The UNEP Finance Initiative is a global partnership between UNEP and the financial sector with over 170 institutions on board including banks, insurers and fund managers. Signatories (representing more than $15 trillion) include most of the major banks around the world. Many of the resources are also available to the public on their website from their different work streams on asset management, property, insurance, climate change, biodiversity and ecosystems, water, human rights and performance indicators (www.unepfi.org).

- Coalition for Environmentally Responsible Economies (CERES) is a coalition of investor groups, environmental organizations and investment funds that engage directly with companies on environmental and social issues. Based in the US, it currently has more than 70 members and 60 companies who follow the CERES principles. These principles cover the following areas: protection of the biosphere, sustainable use of natural resources, reduction and disposal of wastes, energy conservation, risk reduction, safe products and services, environmental restoration, informing the public, management commitment, audits and report (www.ceres.org).

- The Enhanced Analytics Initiative is an international collaboration between asset owners and asset managers aimed at encouraging better investment research, in particular research that takes account of the impact of extra-financial issues on long-term investments. The initiative currently represents total assets under management of €1.8 trillion (www.enhancedanalytics. com).

- Network for Sustainable Financial Markets is a group of academics and finance sector professionals and other experts exploring how to make the financial markets deliver long-term sustainable value (www.sustainablefinancialmarkets.net).
- The Climate Principles is a voluntary framework to guide the finance sector in tackling the challenge of climate change. Members include HSBC, Munich Re and Credit Agricole (www.theclimategroup. org/about/corporate_leadership/climate_principles).
- The Interfaith Centre on Corporate Responsibility is an association of 275 faith-based institutional investors. Each year ICCR members sponsor over 200 shareholder resolutions on major social and environmental issues (www.iccr.org). Investor Environmental Health Network is a partnership with investment managers who through dialogue and shareholder resolutions encourage companies to adopt policies to reduce and eliminate toxic chemicals in their products (www.iehn.org).

Read: *Sustainable Banking and Finance: People—The Financial Sector and the Future of the Planet* by Marcel Jeuken and J. Smits (2001) is an introduction to the world of banking and finance.

Sustainable Investing: The Art of Long Term Performance by Cary Krosinsky and Nick Robbins (2008) provides an overview of the world of sustainability investment, written by international leaders in SRI, ethical and sustainable investment from Wall Street and London.

Microfinance

'We are aiming at a world where a wide variety of strong institutions jostle and compete with one another for poor people's business, innovating and improving services to earn their loyalty'

CEO of CGAP[60]

For the most part, the financial sector works well in countries where individuals have a place to put their money, borrow and have access to a variety of other financial services. The story is very different in developing countries, where many people have no or little access to funds, and when they do have money, they have nowhere to put it.

Historically, banks dismissed the opportunity to provide services to the poor because it was not seen as a viable alternative, and the barriers to working in certain countries, and reaching the customers, were seen as insurmountable. In the 1970s the shift to microfinance began – as different groups in Columbia, Brazil and India started testing the disbursement of microloans to individuals (often women, pensioners, artisans and small farmers), which could be used to start or build up their businesses.

The initiatives were a success. One woman in Bolivia who sold flowers from a street corner in La Paz, together with three other women, was able with a small loan from ACCION International to buy flowers in bulk at a much cheaper rate. Because of her strong repayment record, she was approved for larger loans until she was able to borrow on her own. Today she has been able to send all three of her children to school and even has money left to make improvements on her house.

Some 97 to 99% of loans from well performing microfinance institutions are repaid. Experts point to several reasons for this repayment success. First, these loans represent one of few, often the only, opportunities poor people have to access money. Second, prompt repayment of loans allows individuals to have access to more funds and other financial services, which builds a continuing cycle of creating a better, more sustainable life for themselves. Also, in some cases group lending is used where a number of individuals provide collateral or guarantee a loan through a group repayment pledge. The incentive to repay is enhanced based on peer pressure to pay (the stick) and peer support to help a member in difficulty (the carrot): the group has a structural incentive to get involved because if one person in the group defaults, then other group members are required by the contract to pay back the loan.

Microfinance is seen as a win-win solution. The availability of financial services to the world's poorest gives them opportunities and options to go beyond meeting basic needs, to increase their household income, to save and take on credit. Many microfinance institutions report having better returns on equity than large banks do. ACCIÓN International serves 4.94 million clients with a portfolio of $12 billion and a 97% rate of repayment. Another institution in the slums of Bangladesh accepts deposits of minimum 2 c, has 10 000 clients and is self-sustaining.

(continued)

Today the boundaries between microfinance and the formal financial sector are starting to break down and the term 'microfinance' now encompasses an ever-growing range of organizations and services, experimentation and new entrants, new delivery channels and new clients. In effect, microfinance is now going mainstream – with national and international banks such as ICICI, Citigroup, Deutsche Bank and HSBC testing the waters, excited about the potential for profit in this new area. Development finance institutions such as the International Finance Corporation are also getting involved.

Despite the successes, there is still much work that needs to be done.

- *From a charity to a business:* Work needs to be done to change something that started as a charity into a proper business. This includes bringing down the cost of operation, which at the moment is very high, increasing efficiency and focusing on human capital.
- *Information sharing:* There is the need to increase transparency regarding performance, which is currently low and share information systems such as client credit histories.
- *Interest-rate ceilings:* Some countries impose interest-rate ceilings that discourage firms from entering the market, because these ceilings make small loans cost more than large loans.
- *Expensive:* Because of the small size of the loans and fixed transaction costs the interest on the loan can be high. However, informal lenders can charge 100–150% per annum, so while microfinance is expensive, it still offers funds at rates way below the informal loan market.
- *Beyond business loans:* Microfinance is slowly expanding to provide a larger variety of services for the poor including credit, savings, remittances, insurance and different kinds of loans for both consumers and for businesses.
- *Source of money:* The money in microfinance has historically come from charities, governments and international organizations with growing interest from large banks and private investors. Going forward, microfinance applicants will increasingly be funded by domestic savings and local banks with the aim to help build domestic financial markets. Increasing interest from mainstream social investors, a very fragmented sector, will continue to cause shifts and consolidations.

It isn't just the financial institutions getting into microfinance. In Kenya the M-Pesa telecommunications system allows people to send money over mobile phones. Cash is handed over to registered retailers who credit customers' virtual accounts. Customers can then send between 100 and 35 000 shillings via text message to another person who then can pick up the money at another registered retailer using a secret code and ID. M-Pesa is making it easier for people to have access to their money.

Individuals are also getting involved in microfinance. Kiva, for example, is a person-to-person microlending website where individuals can browse through real individuals in need of funding including entrepreneur profiles. Once a person chooses who they want to loan to and make the loan, they receive email journal updates and track repayments (usually over 6–12 months) (www.kiva.org).

Want more?

- UN Capital Development Fund has an online course on microfinance which provides a good introduction (www.uncdf.org/mfdl).The year 2005 was the International Year of Microcredit and the website has quite a few resources on the topic (www.yearofmicrocredit.org). CGAP is an independent policy and research centre dedicated to advancing financial access in the world's poor.They also provide global estimates on the numbers of borrowers and other facts (www.cgap.org). The Microfinance Gateway is a large online resource on microfinance including research, publications, articles, news and job opportunities (www.microfinancegateway.org), The Microfinance Information Exchange provides in-depth information on the outreach, efficiency, profitability and portfolio quality of microfinance institutions (www.themix.org).
- Some networks and providers of Microfinance include ACCION (www.accion.org) and FINCA (www.villagebanking.org), Oikocredit (www.oikocredit.org), Grameen Bank (www.grameen-info.org), Freedom From Hunger (www.freefromhunger.org) and Rabobank (www.rabobank-ict.nl/ssr). Forbes magazine also did a ranking of the 50 top microfinance institutions in 2007.The top 5 were ASA in Bangladesh, Bandhan in India, Banco de Nordeste in Brazil, Fundacion Mundial de la Mujer Bucaramanaga in Colombia and FONDEP Micro-Credit in Morocco (www.forbes.com).

(*continued*)

- Rating agencies such as Moody's (www.moodys.com), Fitch (www. fitchratings.com) and Standard & Poor's (www.standardandpoors. com) have begun either to rate microfinance transactions like bond issuances or to rate the institutions themselves, and provide research on the subject. Microrate is a rating agency dedicated to the evaluation of microfinance institutions (microrate.com).

Read: *Creating a World Without Poverty: How Social Business Can Transform Our Lives* by Muhammad Yunus (2008) who won a Nobel peace prize in 2006 for his work in microfinance with Grameen Bank.

11 Marketing

> *'Green marketing is mostly about making (break-through) green stuff seem normal - not about making normal stuff seem green.'*
>
> JOHN GRANT

Marketers are both the supervillains and superheros of sustainability. As supervillains they spend their time encouraging people to buy more, promoting unsustainable consumption. As the WWF puts it 'Marketers are blamed for a multitude of sins: encouraging ever greater consumption of alcohol, fatty foods, empty calories, water and biological resources; using too much packaging; limiting the useful life of products so that people are forced to replace them earlier than necessary; producing greenhouse gases. The list seems never-ending'[61]. On the other hand, as superheroes, 'the real power lies in the hands of the marketer—we, the creative folks who have the power to design and promote cleaner products and technologies and help consumers evolve to more sustainable lifestyles' according to Jacquelyn Ottman, a marketing and sustainability expert.[62]

The way that people buy and consume products has an impact on the planet and society. So as superheroes, marketers can use their power to inspire and orient positive changes in consumer behaviour in several ways. First, they work to identify, anticipate and satisfy customer requirements profitably by identifying opportunities for more sustainable products. Second, they market their products in a responsible way that does not promote over consumption or misinformation through green-washing. Third, they communicate information about the product and how best to use and dispose of it.

Why is it important?

- *Opportunities:* Although surveys differ (estimates range widely from 5 to 75%), a potentially large percentage of consumers are ready and looking to purchase products on sustainability grounds but currently don't because these products are either not accessible or unavailable. It is a growing market that is not yet being effectively reached.
- *Bad news can spread quickly:* Whether the news has substance or not, the rise of social networks and influencers means that you are not the only one developing your marketing message. Not having a consistent, well thought-out message will be picked up and can have a lasting negative effect on your brand.
- *Good news can also spread quickly:* If you take sustainability seriously, and it shows through in your products and marketing campaigns, others will do the marketing for you by spreading the news as best practice. In some markets, such as organics and fair trade products, governments and NGOs run awareness campaigns that indirectly promote products with these labels.
- *Boost brand value and build trust:* Companies are increasing their brand valuation by investing in sustainable business practices. By being transparent in their communications with stakeholders, companies can build trust and loyalty with their customers. Such goodwill proves invaluable in hard times. Customers are looking for companies and brands that they feel are genuinely committed to society and the environment.
- *Internally and externally:* Marketers have a crucial job in providing consistent messages about sustainability and the company not only to external customers, but also, perhaps more importantly, to employees and internal teams.

- **Impact is in the use:** Considering that the majority of the impact of a product (80%) is actually in the way that it is used and disposed of, marketers can play a key role in educating the consumer on how to best use and dispose of the product in order to reduce the full life-cycle effects of the company's products.[63]

The key concepts

Marketers are present throughout the life-cycle of a product and have many opportunities to embed sustainability in their work in the following ways:

- Identify who your customer is   → **People**
- Identify what your customer wants   → **Products**
- Determine how much to charge for   → **Price** those products/services
- Determine how best to sell those   → **Place** products/services
- Determine the best way to present   → **Packaging** and protect those products
- Communicate your sustainability   → **Eco-labels** commitments and characteristics
- Increase awareness about the issues   → **Social marketing** that are important to your company
- Help raise money for causes that are   → **Cause-related** important to your stakeholders   **marketing**
- How to promote your sustainability   → **Box: Advertising Dos** commitments   **and Don'ts**

People

Increasingly, customer concern for the environment and society is translating into a demand for more sustainable product options and choices. The extent of this increased demand, however, is a contentious issue.

Numerous studies propose numbers of consumers being prepared to buy 'green' that range widely from between 5% to 75%. Private research firms and the producing companies themselves are working to segment the green consumers to better understand who their customer is and what they want. This has resulted in an ever growing variety of groupings, for example:

- Those who will buy sustainable products no matter what.
- Those who will buy green but expect high standards and quality.
- Those who are not sure what to think but do want to buy green if it is easy and straightforward.
- Those who are completely confused as to what to buy and therefore end up not buying green.
- Those who stay away from green products and are uninterested in this area altogether.

The majority of consumers are in the middle group. They are ready to purchase green but influenced by a variety of different sustainability factors to different degrees.

It has proved difficult to isolate the so-called 'green consumer' for several reasons:

- Some studies tend to overstate green behaviour by focusing on what people say they do, but not on what they actually do.
- Other studies understate the potential by focusing on only one element of green products (i.e. whether a consumer would buy products that are organic but not looking at products designed to increase efficiency).
- The potential market can be overlooked by looking only at the demand for existing products but not the potential demand for products that do not yet exist in this area.
- Decisions are based on a range of factors often combined together. Consumers will choose a hybrid car for both environmental and cost saving reasons, or may choose organic food because it tastes better and is healthier, not just because it is better for the environment.

- As mainstream products become more sustainable, consumers will be buying green whether or not they consciously realize it.
- Consumers are not always familiar with or may not truly understand the meaning of the terms used in the surveys such as green, sustainability, etc. They do not necessarily know what exactly a green product is or how to recognize a green company.
- By attempting to relate a consumer's environmental concerns to what they purchase, we may be looking at the wrong place. Many of the significant contributions the consumer can make towards environmental quality actually come from product use, maintenance and disposal.

Therefore, when considering why people would purchase sustainable products, it is more important to understand the compromises and tradeoffs consumers are being asked to make. Getting to this stage will then allow companies to focus on providing the products that people actually want and need, thereby making it simple for consumers to do their part. Some of the hurdles to be overcome are:

- *Performance:* Many consumers still see 'green' products as being inferior. Consumers are looking for green products that work as effectively, or better than non-green options. Often, they will not buy green products on the basis of environmental benefits alone, and instead are looking for added selling points.
- *Price:* Consumers don't want to pay much extra or sacrifice quality for greener products. They will only pay a premium if they feel that premium is justified, based on the guarantee of certain environmental or social factors, or added value to the consumer.
- *Personal benefit:* Consumers are looking for products that aren't just making an impact far away, but that directly impact them as well. They will be more likely to respond to product attributes that will personally benefit them such as 'safe', non-toxic, cost effective rather than just biodegradable or fair trade.

- **Convenience:** Consumers will tolerate only minimal inconvenience in using green products and don't want to have to go out of their way to buy them. Products need to be easy to use and available at mainstream distributors.
- **Information:** Many consumers may be interested in buying more sustainable products but currently lack the right information at the right time to make those decisions. They don't necessarily expect companies to have perfect green credentials, but will look for a commitment to improve and evidence backed by facts, for example through recognized eco-labels.

So, when it comes to consumers, anything goes. If a product is of high quality, readily available and a reasonable price it has the potential to capture market share. In an interview with Harvard Business Review, Steve Bishop from Ideo said 'don't bother with the green consumer'. He said that companies spend time trying to connect with those people who really understand the issue, the green niche so to speak, but in the process risk alienating their base who have different values and who are interested in solving their own personal needs before saving the planet. The solution? Rather than focusing on the features of a product, focus on consumer needs in order to cater to all consumers.

Those involved in marketing sustainable products should be interested in the following categories of consumers:

- There is the ever-growing '*conflicted consumer*'[64]. This group, which is estimated at being anywhere between 25% to over 50% of consumers in some markets, believe that the companies they currently buy from are unethical and are building resentment towards the brands. Examples include certain fast food restaurants for the perceived damage of their food to children. This is a group of apparently loyal customers that are ready to leave as soon as a more ethical alternative product or service becomes available.
- Another important consumer group for green products is *women*. Women are spending about 85 cents of every dollar spent and make more than half of family and business-to-business spending

decisions.[65] As they continue to progress in the work environment women are taking sustainability labels seriously and are asking companies to react to these issues.

- Product *'evangelists'* are your free sales force, they are the ones that do not just believe in your product, but they believe in it so much that they will tell others about it. Finding the right tools to engage with this group will increase sales, loyalty and generate consumer insight.
- With increased levels of awareness about sustainability issues, *young people* are not just getting involved, but are increasingly influencing their parents' decisions in this area.

Sustainability consumers often get put into a group described as LOHAS (Lifestyles of Health and Sustainability). For more information on this group in the US visit (www.lohas.com). Much of the research in this area is done by companies themselves or research companies who charge for access to the results. This includes companies like the Roper Organization, who has been conducting a Green Gauge survey in the US since 1990 (www.gfkamerica.com). GlobeScan Green Behaviour Segments (www.globescan.com/csrm_overview.htm). You can also find information about demand for different products from specialist organizations. For example to find out more about the demand for fair trade products see www.fairtradefederation.org or for social investment see www.socialinvest.org.

Products

A sustainable product is one that provides environmental, social and economic benefits over its full life-cycle. Today most work is being done on separate parts of the life-cycle, but in the future we will increasingly see products that really do aim to be sustainable as a whole. Some could argue that there is no such thing as a truly sustainable product. All products need energy, water and materials to be designed, produced and used. But much work is being done to reduce the impacts of products across the life-cycle.

Companies have two fundamental choices when it comes to creating sustainable products. First, they can take an existing product and make it greener. This involves many of the concepts introduced in eco-design including using more sustainable materials, production processes, disposal, etc. Second, they can identify customers' needs and wants and develop entirely new products that are able to better address these in a more sustainable way.

Consumers are looking for a variety of different kinds of sustainable product options (or combination of) including:

- *Products that present a solution:* This could be a product that is a better alternative to what is currently available. The focus is on identifying a need and providing a product that satisfies that need.
- *Products that are safer:* Several sustainability products, for example those that use less chemicals and have more natural ingredients such as organic, aim at providing healthier, safer options for consumers (i.e. green cleaning products such as 7th generation and Ecover).
- *Products that save money:* Many green products on the market right now, especially new technologies (both very simple or complex) allow consumers to not only reduce their energy or water use for example, but also save them money (i.e. solar panels which enable a consumer to both generate their own power and sell excess power into the grid).
- *Products that make them feel good:* Certain products may or may not have any intrinsic sustainability characteristics but the companies producing them or the products themselves support causes that the consumer perceives to be important. Supporting those products makes the consumer feel as if they have done their part in making the world a better place (i.e. Fairtrade)
- *Products that make them look good:* Some consumers are looking for products that look like they are green in order to communicate to others their green credentials (i.e. hybrid cars or green luxury goods).
- *Products that make it easy to switch:* Consumers are looking for products that make their life simpler, not more complicated and they are looking for products that make it easy to switch. Consumers

are also looking for products, brands or retailers that are doing the work for them, such as products that all uphold certain standards so that they do not have to think about every single purchasing decision.

- **Products that are high quality:** Consumers are looking for products that are high quality (i.e. Patagonia creating sustainable outdoor clothing provides a lifetime guarantee on all of its products).
- **Products that aren't doing harm:** Consumers are increasingly interested in supporting products that are not doing harm to society and the environment, in particular as the levels of awareness increase about the impacts of many of these product and processes.

Marketers have a role to not only question the underlying assumptions behind product development, but also, in some cases, to question the product altogether. Some producers may assume that consumers need to physically own a product in order to be satisfied with their purchase. But generally, it is the use of the product itself rather than the purchase that generates that satisfaction. With this in mind, marketers should rethink not only the way that products are designed, but how the entire product experience is designed. Can the product be rented, borrowed, reused, repaired. Will it need to be disposed of? Traditional discussions around the purchase itself need to make way for more discussions about what happens after the purchase.

See the Operations chapter for more information on the design of sustainable products. IDEO in collaboration with BSR has created some different design toolkits based on designing for social impact and human-centred design (client.ideo.com/socialimpact or hcdtoolkit).

Price

A post on the blog of TerraCycle's founder explains some of the dilemmas that companies faced with price. The company launched a line of eco-friendly cleaners that are just as good as synthetics and, in some cases, better. They are packaged in used soda bottles and retail at $2.99, cheaper than other eco-brands, but 70 cents more expensive than Windex or other household cleaners. 'So here's the question' asks Tom Szaky, 'Our sell through at our retailers is very strong, so we could keep our price at $2.99, and be the best price in the eco-field but still be a premium to the national brand. Or we could cut our margin and either match or even beat the prices of the conventional brands. It would hurt margin, but it should increase market share. It would be a bold but tempting move since we may be able to gain market share beyond the "eco-cleaner" category. What do you think we should do?' The question generated much debate on the website, including this post 'While your price may be higher, I would think the "value" you provide may be higher as well. My wife and I try to buy only eco-friendly products and actually "feel" better when we do (and that's worth at least 70 cents). Maybe focus on dominating the eco cleaners, then as more and more people "go green" you can clean up! (pun intended)'[66]

Pricing products is a tricky business, whether they are green or not. Getting the price right is crucial; price it too high and you may miss the mainstream market and, price it too low and consumers may see it as a lesser quality product. In addition, as Ken Peattie puts it, 'How much more would you be willing to pay for greener products' contains a powerful message which promotes the image of the environment as an additional cost burden on business and consumers. 'It would perhaps be more appropriate to ask consumers "Do you want to continue buying products that are inexpensive because they damage the environment".[67] While the pricing of the product from the company's side often rests on their actual costs, what a consumer is willing to pay for a more sustainable product is more related to the perceived value it brings to both the customer and to the environment and society as a whole. Determining how much a consumer is willing to pay for a sustainability product comes down to these points:

- *The Perceived value (financial):* This has to do with the total value that the customer is getting from the product or service itself, and how much value they are getting from this product as opposed to another one. This includes:

- *Operating costs:* CFC light bulbs for example may be a little bit more expensive than traditional light bulbs to buy, but they will cost the consumer less over time because they last longer and use less energy, which results in reduced energy bills.
- *Indirect costs:* Is the product worth enough to the consumer that they are willing to go out of their way to buy it? Is it higher quality, or does it result in increased consumer satisfaction? Is the product easy to find, easy to use?
- **The Perceived values (ethical):** This does not have to do with the product itself, but rather with the claims that the product makes. How much does the consumer value the environmental and social guarantees the product is making? This also depends on how much knowledge the consumer has about different issues, and therefore whether they are able to understand the positive changes that the company has made to society or to the environment. It also has to do with how far they believe the impacts being claimed to be true. This includes:
  - *Direct impact:* Supporting a product that was made using sustainable materials, sustainable processes, fair trade, recyclable materials, etc. For example, a consumer choosing to buy paper that is recycled and FSC certified knows that they are protecting forests and supporting the responsible management of the world's forests.
  - *Indirect impact:* For example some companies will link parts of their profit to social and environmental causes relevant to or of interest to their business. This is either through the price you pay, or as a percentage of profits. Customers then feel that they are doing something good by buying the product, especially if they care for the cause, and that if they are being asked to pay a premium it is going to the right place (see cause-related marketing).

In many countries, more and more products in all price categories are different shades of green, some from small companies that specialize in sustainable products, and others from big companies who have products that uphold these principles. In Australia Natural Instinct beauty and household products sell at the same price as other similar, non-green options and are of equal or higher quality. More than ever, consumers have many choices, at many price points, and sustainability is a larger factor in making price decisions.

Place: retailers and sustainability

The place in the marketing mix generally refers to where and when consumers will acquire a particular product or service. This includes several elements such as where the product is made (see greening offices for more on this) and how the products are transported (see the operations chapter for more). Here we will focus on where the product is being sold; the retailer. In this context, retailer includes any organization that sells and delivers a product to the consumer, and it can include supermarkets, specialty stores, fast food restaurants and department stores.

Retailers have often been perceived as not only playing a passive role in sustainability, but in some cases being part of the problem. According to UNEP the world's 200 largest retailers account for 30% of worldwide demand. Therefore, actions by retailers have a significant effect in this area, and in many cases, retailers are actually leading the changes. One example is Wal-Mart, whose website states, 'With roughly 61,000 suppliers, 176 million customers each week and more than 2 million associates, we have the ability to reach and influence people on a level unattainable by any other company'. Their strategy, known as Sustainability 360, includes goals and targets in their supply chain, in the products they sell, their employees and the communities they operate in and source from. Wal-Mart aims to be supplied by 100 % renewable energy, to create zero waste, and to sell products that sustain our resources and the environment.

Retailers have a number of areas to review in building and improving sustainability:

- **Store management:** They must make sure their own operations are sustainable, and that they are controlling and managing their own environmental and social impacts through implementing systems in energy and water conservation, waste management, and recycling. For example, Kohl department stores in the US now has 40% of the power it uses provided by solar panels on the roof of its department stores, and plans to increase this to 80% in California. Because of the high upfront costs of the panels, SunEdison, a solar energy services company, paid for the panels and is selling the electricity that comes off them to Kohl.

- *Where products come from:* The sourcing of consumer products includes working with suppliers to favour development of products that are more sustainable. For example, Starbucks started integrating conservation principles in its best-buying practice, and by working with Conservation International implemented C.A.F. E. standards which set ambitious goals to ensure high quality coffee would be grown and processed in a manner that is both socially and environmentally responsible.

- *Eliminating unsustainable products:* Some retailers are eliminating products they consider to be unsustainable from the store and, where possible, offering more sustainable alternatives. After a six month consultation with its over 100 000 members, The Co-op, a food retailer in the UK revised its product portfolio in support of more sustainable options, including banning the sale of eggs from caged hens in favour of free range and organic eggs.

- *Educating the customer:* Retailers are providing more sustainable options for their customers to choose from. They are also educating their staff about these options and pricing and promoting them appropriately. Spanish supermarket Eroski offers as part of their campaign for more responsible consumption, a school for consumers where they can learn, among other things, how FSC certified forests are managed (www.consumer.es/escuelas).

- *Where the product is placed:* Within the retail location, make more sustainable products easier to find and easier to buy. Green products in some countries are confined to the health food aisle or store. This can limit the number and kinds of customers these products could potentially attract. Office Depot publishes a special catalogue with its green offerings (over 2200 items), and in store these offerings are placed alongside less green alternatives. This increased sales of green products by nearly 10% in 2007 (www.officedepot.com/buygreen).

- *How the product is sold:* Retailers are also exploring new ways to get the products to consumers in the first place. Allegrini, an Italian producer of biodegradable detergents has developed Casa Quick. Casa Quick takes its detergents in mobile vans from house to house and allows families to refill their bottles paying only for the quantity taken. Consumers receive a kit of plastic flasks which are easy to carry from house to van.[68]

- *Presentation of products in-store:* Several international companies such as Unilever, IKEA, McDonalds and PepsiCo are working together through the global initiative Refrigerants Naturally! to combat climate change by replacing harmful gases with natural refrigerants in point-of-sale cooling machines (www.refrigerantsnaturally.com).

- *Retailing differently:* The REI (an outdoor company) store in Boulder, Colorado is not just a LEED certified green building but also a community centre. The floor plan is designed around a central resource area with meeting rooms, information kiosks and a children's play area (www.rei.com/greenbuilding/boulder).

- *Reverse logistics:* Retailers can also provide a spot for consumers to bring back products for reuse and recycling. Many electronic stores already have facilities to collect used batteries and supermarkets will collect used plastic bags. Terracycle, a company that makes products from waste, has a collection system for non-recyclable waste such as tape roles, paint brushes, chip bags and candy wrappers in the front of major retail stores such as Home Depot across the US.

The Retail and Industry Leaders Association's Sustainability Initiative helps leading retail companies meet environmental standards relevant to the retail industry and pursue responsible environmentally sustainable activities and business practices (rila.org). Sustainability Issues in The Retail Sector survey (www.ipsos-mori.com/_assets/reports/sustainability-issues-in-the-retail-sector.pdf). Initiatives are happening with both small and big retailers. For big see Home Depot, Walmart, Tesco, Marks and Spencer.

Packaging

Packaging is the first part of the consumers' tangible experience with your product. If a product or a company promotes itself as green and then uses excessive or unsustainable packaging, it is not sending a consistent message to the customer. Packaging should not only be seen as something that protects the product, it should also be seen as an opportunity to connect with the customer and transmit information about the product, what it is made of, how to best use it and how to dispose of it when a consumer is finished using it. There are two components to sustainable packaging:

1. **The packaging:** Companies can look at making the packaging itself more sustainable. This includes looking at:

   - *Materials used:* According to the Sustainable Packaging Coalition, sustainable packaging is packaging that:
     - is beneficial, safe & healthy for individuals and communities throughout its life-cycle;
     - meets market criteria for performance and cost;
     - is sourced, manufactured, transported, and recycled using renewable energy;
     - maximizes the use of renewable or recycled source materials;
     - is manufactured using clean production technologies and best practices;
     - is made from materials healthy in all probable end-of-life scenarios;
     - is physically designed to optimize materials and energy; and
     - is effectively recovered and utilized in biological and/or industrial closed loop cycles.
   - *Reducing the amount of packaging:* The European Packaging Directive, for example, sets strict requirements to prevent the use of excessive packaging. Wal-Mart as part of its goal to reduce packaging used by suppliers by 5% by 2013 has a packaging scorecard

that allows manufactures to rank their current use of packaging based on raw materials used, package size, recycled content, material recovery value, etc.

- *Proper packaging:* Getting rid of all packaging is not the answer either. According to the Institute of European Environmental Policy, under-packaging can be as much of an issue as over-packaging in terms of wasted energy and resources from ruined goods. Packaging needs to be considered in the context of the design and manufacture of the product.

- *Packaging across the life-cycle of the product:* Producers must think about how much is being used and what kinds of materials are being used as part of the packaging whether it is primary (the packaging customers see), secondary (the packaging used to ship to retailers) or tertiary (the packaging used to ship the products from the manufacturers.

- *Simple:* Amazon's Frustration-Free Packaging initiative is designed to free customers from difficult packaging. Instead of being pack-aged in hard to open and hard to recycle plastic and cardboard packaging, Amazon works with leading manufacturers such as Microsoft and Mattel to package products in a simple, recyclable cardboard box.

- *The design of the packaging:* O2 redesigned their packaging to encourage customers who didn't need a charger to opt out of receiving a new one when they upgraded their phone. This had a multiple knock-on effect allowing phones to be posted through letter boxes (reducing courier deliveries), giving customers the option of having a tree planted in their name and offering a simple way to recycle their current phone.

- *Eliminating packaging:* In 1985 Swiss retailer Migros began sell-ing toothpaste tubs without the unnecessary boxes they usually come in. Although sales initially dropped, after in-store signs edu-cated customers, Migros went on to remove excess packaging from everything from yoghurt to drinks.[69]

2. **The messages on the package:** Companies should also take the opportunity to communicate with the consumer through the packaging in the following ways:

- *Sustainability information:* Several companies take the space on the packaging as an opportunity to communicate their commitments and actions in this area. Companies can provide information on the sustainability goals of the company and information on the causes that are important to the company as well as how the consumer can get more involved.
- *Materials used (or not used):* Timberland's EcoMetrics label is a sort of nutritional label for shoes that lets customers know exactly what went into making the shoes. It lists the product's energy use, global warming contribution and materials efficiency.
- *How to use:* Labels are also the ideal location to give users simple and easy to understand information about how best to use the product in order to minimize the negative impacts, and also maximize the positive impacts.
- *How to dispose:* Labels are also being used to provide information for consumers on what to do with the product, or packaging once they are finished with it. This can involve:

  - *Providing details on how the product itself can be returned, repaired or reused:* Kiehls, a 150-year-old skin and hair product company has a loyalty card which is stamped every time a customer returns an empty Kiehls container. Once you get a certain number of stamps you can get free products. Other companies provide financial incentives, for example a deposit that is refunded if you return the used packaging or a discount on your next purchase.

  - *Providing details on how to dispose and recycle:* Marks and Spencer in the UK provides clear information on its packaging telling the consumer what parts of the packaging is recyclable and which are not.

The Sustainable Packaging Coalition works with member companies to promote more sustainable packaging options (www.sustainablepackaging.org). The Packaging Design Library showcases packaging innovation and solutions that implement sustainable attributes (spcdesignlibrary.org). See www.thecoca-colacompany.com/citizenship/packaging.html as an example of what one company is doing with their packaging. See operations for more information. 'Starting a Packaging Project: Tips for Non-Packaging Designers' (www.indes.net/e-publishing/idnref2.html). The Reusable Packaging Association has created an online calculator to help businesses determine the cost savings of converting to reusable packaging from single-use corrugated packaging (usereusables.com).

Eco-labels

As the market for socially and environmentally preferable products continues to grow, so does the need for customers to sift through the increasing number of environmental and social claims used in the marketing of these products and services and to understand what they mean. Eco-labels, found on a wide variety of products, tell consumers about certain environmental or social standards the product complies with. Labels exist for a wide range of product and service qualities, including, but not limited to, energy and other resource efficiency, sector specific labels, organic and other food related labels, social labels such as fair trade, recycling, product content and design.

The variety and types of eco-labels continue to grow, and many eco-labels are introduced throughout this book in the relevant areas. According to the ISO standard on eco-labels (14020) there are three major categories of eco-labels.

Type 1: Third party claims are awards given by a third party requiring a product to meet certain independently set criteria. These show leadership characteristics rather than just presenting information and are often accompanied by public awareness campaigns to educate consumers about what the label means. (For more on this see ISO 14024) Examples would include:

- Regional and national eco-labelling schemes such as the EU Flower (www.eceuropa.eu/environment/ecolabel), Germany's Blue Angel considered the first and oldest environmental label (www.blauer-engel.de), Nordic Swan (www.svanen.nu), Japan's Eco Mark (www.ecomark.jp), Taiwan's Green Mark (greenmark.epa.gov.tw), India's Indocert (www.indocert.org) and New Zealand's Environmental Choice (www.enviro-choice.org.nz).
- Sector or issue-specific labels which have a narrower focus than national programmes such as the Rainforest Alliance certification which promotes and guarantees improvements in agriculture and forestry (www.rainforest-alliance.org), the fair trade label which guarantees producers were paid fair prices (www.fairtrade.net) or industry specific such as the chemical industry (www.responsiblecare.com).

Type 2: Green claims are the manufacturers' or retailers' own declarations. Since these are not given by a third party, it is more difficult for consumers to compare them with other brands or to fully understand what the claim means. (For more on this see ISO 14021) Examples include:

- Statements such as '100% recycled', 'natural' and 'environmentally friendly'. Where not regulated by law, or no evidence is shown, these statements are often not reliable and are found on products that are not always what they claim to be.
- Company private labels. Private label initiatives have a wide range of truthfulness and usefulness. An example of a well-regarded private label is the Philips' Green Logo, which is used on electronic products that meet certain environmental criteria across the whole life-cycle. Products with the logo have been certified by external auditors that they are 10% more efficient than other products on the market within a given product category (www.greenproducts.philips.com).

Type 3: Environmental declarations quantify information about a product based on life-cycle impacts and should allow products to be compared easily because they consist of quantified information about aspects such as energy output. Unlike other labels they do not judge product, leaving that task to consumers. Rather they provide something similar to a nutrition label found on food products but instead this label outlines environmental impacts throughout the life-cycle. Compared to type 1 and type 2, much less work has been done in this area but some examples include labelling products with their carbon footprints (www.carbontrust.com) and energy efficiency labels on household goods. InterfaceFLOR, a manufacturer of modular carpets in the US received a third party verified EPD.[70] (For more on this see ISO 14025, also see the Global Type 3 Environmental Product Declarations Network—www.gednet.org)

Good eco-labelling initiatives involve the participation of government, industry and commercial associations, retailers and companies, consumers, as well as other interested parties such as academics, media and the international community. A product must comply with all the required criteria to be awarded a label and must be retested regularly. According to the Global Eco-Labelling Programme, an effective labelling programme should:

- Be *voluntary:* It should be the decision of the business to participate in the programme.
- Distinguish *leadership:* Claims should not imply a product is exceptional if all other products share the same general characteristics.
- Be based on *sound scientific and engineering principles* with a strong focus on life-cycle considerations to assure customers that all aspects of the products development have been taken into account.
- Be *credible:* Often eco-labels are managed by well-respected and recognized third party organizations and used by well-respected companies, which increases the product's credibility.
- Be *measurable* and *comparable:* Claims should be made only if they can be verified. Methods used can include international standards, recognized standards or methods developed by industry, provided that they have been subjected to peer review.

- Be based on *open and accountable processes* that can be monitored and questioned. They should operate in a business-like and cost effective manner.[71]

Several challenges exist in this area. The range of existing and new eco-labels is making it confusing for customers to understand what it all means, especially when private company labels are added to the mix. Some labels have strict requirements to adhere to while others require very little effort to get certified. No one label covers all sustainability issues and it is unlikely that labelling will be standardized in the foreseeable future. However, we are still in the early days of eco-labelling.

Industry also has many labels that are introduced in the relevant sections of this book. The Global Eco-labelling Network is a non-profit association of third-party, environmental performance labelling organizations founded in 1994 to improve, promote and develop the 'eco-labelling' of products and services (www.globalecolabelling.net). The European Eco-label catalogue aims to help European consumers to distinguish greener, more environmentally friendly products of high quality (www.eco-label.com). The Consumers Union Guide to Environmental Labels is a US site that looks at providing information to consumers about eco-labels (www.greenerchoices.org/eco-labels).

Social marketing

Social marketing refers to programmes and campaigns that aim to raise public awareness in order to introduce more sustainable behaviours relating to the environment (i.e. such as energy or water conservation and waste reduction) or society (i.e. health, voting). Social marketing does not look to sell a product or service, but rather encourage or modify a behaviour by applying traditional marketing principles and techniques to influence a particular audience's behaviours for individuals' and society's benefit.

The goals of social marketing can include:

- accepting a new behaviour (e.g. composting food waste),
- rejecting a potentially undesirable behaviour (e.g. starting smoking),
- modifying a current behaviour (e.g. increasing physical activity from 3 to 5 days of the week),
- abandoning an old undesirable one (e.g. talking on a cell phone while driving).

For all can be either one time action (install a low flow showerhead) or promoting repeated behaviour (take a 5 min shower).[72] Examples include the Rock the Vote campaign in the US which aimed to engage the political power of young people through the use of music, popular culture and new technology to incite young people to register and vote in every election.

Governments and not-for profits regularly run these sorts of campaigns but increasingly industry is doing so as well, as a way to gain support for their sustainability efforts. As NGO Utopies puts it, 'these campaigns often seek to encourage consumers to behave responsibly and are usually the work of companies which, having incorporated social responsibility into the products or services they supply, require a matching commitment from their customers for their actions to be really effective'.[73]

Among the best-known private-sector social marketing campaigns are the Body Shop's campaigns against animal testing in the mid-1990s and those against female stereotypes and in favour of free trade since 1997. The 'look behind the label' campaign at Marks and Spencer in the UK was an educational campaign aimed to teach its customer base to appreciate the changes that were about to take place relating to fair trade, sustainability, non-gm and animal welfare. It then followed with Plan A, outlining all the steps that the retail company was going to take to be more sustainable. In France Leclerc conducted a campaign about the impact of plastic bags in 2003 that was followed by the adoption of an amendment banning non-biodegradable plastic bags.

Social marketing applies traditional marketing techniques to sell a particular behaviour rather than a product or service. These include:

1. ***Understand the problem.*** Do market research. Take a look at successful campaigns that have taken place around the world as a starting point. Identify and remove barriers to change. Understand why people don't want to change and help them get over those hurdles.

2. ***Select a target market.*** This is the group of people that the campaign will be focused on. In the case of Rock the Vote it was youth. Focus on target markets that are ready and willing to act rather than one that is resistant to change.

3. ***Product.*** The product is often a message with clear instructions on how to act. Many people are ready and willing, they just don't know how. Make sure the message is simple and doable. The message will sometimes be accompanied by a physical product that helps with that change. For example encouraging people to use less water could be accompanied by a list of easily accessible places to buy low flow showerheads.

4. ***Price.*** The price refers to what the target audience needs to give up, but also what they can gain from the behaviour. The audience should be given information about the costs (both monetary and non-monetary) of the current and any alternative behaviour. For example antismoking campaigns focus on the cost of smoking which are not just monetary (the cost of a box of cigarettes) but health (87% of lung cancer deaths linked to smoking). If benefits outweigh costs then the person is likely to adopt the new behaviour. This can also include adding incentives to help guide the behaviour, for example deposits on products, charge for the use of plastic bags and special lanes on roads for cars with more than 2 people inside.

5. ***Place.*** The place is where the message is communicated to the target audience. This could be where the desired, or not desired, behaviour takes place. If the product is tangible like an energy efficient light bulb, the place also relates to where these products are available and should be easily accessible.

6. ***Promotion.*** The promotion is how the message is communicated to the target audience. This usually means using an appropriate mix of advertising, public relations, promotions, media advocacy, etc.

People need to hear a message over and over again (often more than 10 times) before it starts to sink in.

7. *Monitor and evaluate results.* Social marketing campaigns will also often include working on laws or regulations that influence the desired behaviour. Monitoring the campaign allows you to learn how the message changed your target audience, whether it had an impact and revise it as needed. Use prompts such as stickers and commitments to motivate people to continue to change. Let people know how the campaign went.

UNEP and Futerra, Communicating Sustainability – How to produce effective public campaigns (www.unep.fr/pc/sustain/reports/advertising/Communication_Guide/webEN2.pdf). Health Canada has a Social Marketing E-Learning Tool (www.hc-sc.gc.ca/ahc-asc/activit/marketsoc/tools-outils/index-eng.php) and (www.orau.gov/cdcynergy/soc2web/). Social Marketing Institute (www.social-marketing.org) (socialmarketingcollaborative.org), Social Marketing Wiki has a range of information and resources on the topic (socialmarketing.wetpaint.com). For more also see the box on managing change in the Organizational Behaviour chapter. **Read:** *Social Marketing* by Philip Kotler, which provides a good introduction.

Cause-related marketing

Cause-related marketing differs from social marketing in that it focuses on raising awareness and concern for a social issue (e.g. global warming), but it typically stops short of trying to change the behaviour itself. Companies explore cause-related marketing as a way of differentiating themselves, or of enhancing their reputation, and also to increase sales and contribute to a cause that is important to their stakeholders. Cause-related marketing usually involves a partnership between a for profit company, and a not for profit organization promoting the product to raise money for the not for profit. Cause-related marketing can take several different forms:

- *Sales based:* donation programmes where a company donates a percentage of its sales to a particular charity over a certain period of time;
- *support for customer aligned charities:* provide funds to charities that support causes that are important to your stakeholders; and
- *support causes aligned with business purpose:* endorse a cause that is a natural extension of the company's own business.

The phrase 'cause-related marketing' was first used by American Express in 1983 to describe its campaign to raise money for the restoration of the Statue of Liberty. American Express made a 1 cent donation to the Statue of Liberty every time someone used its charge card. As a result at the time the number of new card holders soon grew by 45% and card usage increased by 28%.[74]

Today there are many examples of cause-related marketing. The RED campaign, created to raise awareness and money to help women and children affected by HIV/AIDS in Africa. Companies involved in the RED campaign include Motorola red phones, American Express red card, Apple's red Ipod, the Gap's red t-shirts, Emporio Armani's red collection and red Converse shoes. A percentage of each RED product sold is given to AIDS programmes through the Global Fund. Innocent drinks organize a 'super gran woolly hats' promotion every year in the UK, where individuals around the country raise money for AgeConcern (over 25 000 older people die of cold related illnesses every winter in the UK). Individuals are taught, through their website or different in store knitting sessions at grocery stores and sandwich shops, to knit miniature hats which are sent into the company. Innocent put the hats on top of Innocent bottles around Christmas time and, in 2008, 50 pence of every bottle sold was given to AgeConcern. Through this campaign, in 2008 alone over 500 000 hats were mailed in by the community, put on bottles and sold to generate over £ 250 000.[75]

Over 700 businesses worldwide make up the group One Percent for the Planet where members of the business community contribute 1% of sales to environmental groups around the world (www.onepercentfortheplanet.org). Mountain Equipment Co-op joined One Percent for the Planet in 2007 and contributed $2.5 million towards conservation. They also launched with Canadian Parks and Wilderness Society the bigwild.org with the ambitious vision of keeping at least half of Canada's public land and water wild forever.

The success of a cause-related marketing campaign depends on finding the balance between doing something that benefits your company with what your customers perceive as being good for the community. Some tips:

> Cause Marketing Forum offers several resources (www.causemarketingforum.com.). Product Red campaign can be found at www.joinred.com.

- Make sure the not-for-profit that you are working with means something to your target market.
- Consider your options for scaling up. Local charities are good, but how do you go national or international?
- Place emphasis on behaviour change and action, as opposed to just increasing awareness.
- Recognize the importance of fairness. Everyone needs to be seen to be doing their bit, including government and industry.
- It has to make sense to the brand.

Challenges?

- *Green fatigue:* Customers are being bombarded with so many different kinds of sustainability messages that they often do not know which are real and which aren't. The growing prominence of eco-labels is helping, but also adding to the confusion.
- *Choice fatigue:* Consumers are offered so many different choices, with so much information, that it has become a more stressful experience to make choices and be happy with the outcomes.
- *Increased risk either way:* There is a risk of not moving into green marketing but also a risk when a company does. Sometimes the media is more inclined to question and attack relatively good companies attempting to move forward on sustainability, rather than highlighting the poor environmental performance of companies who have

not become involved in sustainability. Even with a well thought out campaign there is always the risk that consumers and other stakeholders will not respond favourably. Stakeholder engagement is key to help minimize this, as is having the substance to back up your claims.

- *Lack of overarching standards:* There are a lack of standards for determining exactly what makes a green product or a green company. Increased regulations and public awareness is needed to help educate consumers how to understand the increasing number of standards.
- *Confusing messages:* Marketers can work to promote more sustainable products, but this only works if consumers are able to accurately and effectively interpret the information they give and claims they make on their packaging.
- *Change:* Individuals generally do not like change and find change difficult. Promoting more sustainable products includes asking consumers to make lots of changes to their day-to-day lives, often involving switching from trusted brands to new ones.

Trends and new ideas

–Green = inexpensive	–Communicating with the customer virtually
–Eco-iconic to eco-embedded	
–Being authentic	–The barcode reinvented

Green = inexpensive Green products are generally seen as being more expensive than conventional choices. This may be true now, but the future is likely to see a dramatic shift. In fact, the same reasons that explain why green products have historically been priced higher could become the reasons why they are more affordable. For example:

- *Full costs across the life-cycle:* Green products often already include many of the costs that other products don't (such as the cost of disposal), making them more expensive. When comparing traditional costs of manufacture, many green products actually cost less to produce and to use. They also cost society less in terms of other direct costs and indirect costs such as pollution and health effects. As more companies begin to analyse and incorporate the true full cost of production, we may actually see a complete flip, where unsustainable products become much more expensive.

- *Economies of scale:* Pricing often comes down to simple supply and demand. Many of the materials used in these products have been more expensive because there has been less of a demand for them. As the demand goes up for more sustainable alternatives and they are produced in larger quantities, the price of these products could go down. At the same time, the cost of unsustainable options is going up, for example products produced using petroleum products.
- *Provide certain guarantees:* These types of products are often providing a set of guarantees regarding safety, sourcing, health and environmental impact that may cost a little bit more to ensure. As regulations and industry standards start requiring all products to uphold certain standards, other non-green products may also start to bear these costs, creating a more even playing field.

From eco-iconic to eco-embedded According to trendwatching. com, green products and services have moved from eco-ugly (ugly, over-priced, low-performance, unsavoury yet eco-friendly versions of the 'real thing') to eco-chic (eco-friendly stuff that actually looks as nice and cool as the less sustainable originals) to eco-iconic. Eco-iconic is defined as 'eco-friendly goods and services sporting bold, iconic markets and design, helping their eco-conscious owners show off their eco-credentials to their peers.' Eco-iconic is not about all green products. It is about those that from their appearance or stories actually show that they are green and in doing so attract recognition from their peers, in the same way as traditional status symbols do. The best-known examples are cars such as the Toyota Prius. A *New York Times* article answered the question 'Why are Prius sales surging when other hybrids are slumping? Because buyers want everyone to know they are driving a hybrid.' In fact research done showed that 57% of buyers in 2007 cited the main reason for buying the car as it 'makes a statement about me'. Another perhaps more important trend that is slowly overtaking it is eco-embedding, 'making products and processes more sustainable without consumers even noticing it, and, if necessary, not leaving much room for consumers and companies to opt for less sustainable alternatives.'

Understanding how people think One way of bringing out change, fast, is to make it normal. The Sacramento Municipal Utility District in the US began sending out statements in 2008 to 35 000 randomly selected customers, rating them on their energy use compared with that of neighbours in 100 homes of similar size. Customers who scored high earned two smiley faces on their statement. Good conservation got one smiley face. The utility found that customers who got the personalized energy report cut by 2% more than those who didn't, a number which seems small, but has a big impact.[76] In the book *Yes!*, the authors write of how they were able to boost participating in the towel recycling programme by 26% just by rewording the card to suggest that the majority of hotel guests reused their towels suggesting it was the social norm to participate rather than something to save the environment.[77] (www.neurosciencemarketing.com)

Communicating with the customer . . . virtually One of the oldest adages in marketing is that 'word-of-mouth is the best advertising'. Customers have always gotten information and made choices based on word of mouth. But the level of information has exploded with the Internet and social media. The amount of information overwhelms—stories, opinions and facts highlighting both good and bad practices are constantly shared through blogs, wikis and other social networks where people with the same interests come together to discuss those interests. These networks are not only being used by consumers interested in learning more about sustainability, but increasingly by companies as a way to connect directly with their current or potential customers. Product developers are tapping into them to gather intelligence and ideas, directly from the customer, on what kind of products they should

For a list of social networks relating to sustainability see the resource section at the end of this book.

provide and how to make their current products better. Starbucks at mystarbucksidea.force.com is a space where users can post and vote on ideas from everything from new products to store design.

The barcode reinvented Labels are taking on a life of their own. Recently, marketers have been exploring opportunities to tap into the potential of the single most ubiquitous product around—the one thing that billions of people have with them all the time and use the most throughout the day: their cell phones. How? Through the use of a barcode called the Quick Response (QR) Code that has already taken Japan by storm. These special barcodes are designed to be read by mobile phones with built-in cameras, a feature now standard on cell phones. The idea is both simple and ingenious. Companies put a special bar code on posters, magazines, interactive billboards even lawns. Once scanned by the cell phone camera, a message or set of instructions (such as a website or phone number) embedded in the QR code is revealed automatically on the phone's display. In Japan, senior citizens use the QR Code to check bus times. Others are printed on t-shirts, directing interested people to visit the website of the wearer. It is used by Starbucks to get a discount voucher and a map showing their 10 nearest locations.[78] Just imagine all the sustainability uses, such as being able to access instant information about the life-cycle of a product or where to buy a particular green product.

What you can do . . .

❑ Question assumptions about what a product is and how it must be made. Does it have to be disposed of? Does it have to be designed for obsolescence to be profitable?

- ❑ Don't rely too much on surveys. Although it is important to do proper market research, sustainability can be a little bit of a chicken and egg: Consumers don't know they want something until it is presented to them
- ❑ Listen to your customers. Put in place mechanisms for customers to tell you what they want. Not only is this a way to open communication with them, but you can get some really fantastic ideas.
- ❑ Approach the creation of a marketing strategy for sustainable products in the same way as for other products. Start as early on in the process as you can.
- ❑ Understand the full impact your product or service is having throughout its life-cycle.
- ❑ Be Consistent. It is important that the brand or the product is communicating what it is doing in terms of sustainability. It is equally important that it actually follows through and does what it claims to be doing. Be consistent with your messages across your organization's activities.
- ❑ Be proactive and demonstrate leadership.
- ❑ Develop a responsible marketing code and make it known to employees and stakeholders.
- ❑ Tell companies you buy from what you want.
- ❑ Report greenwashing and irresponsible marketing to the relevant national authorities.

Want more?

WBCSD Driving Success: Marketing and Sustainable Development (www.wbcsd.org/web/publications/marketing.pdf) and UNEP's Sustainable Consumption and Production Advertising section has several documents on communications, advertising and marketing including a toolkit called 'Sustainable Communications: A toolkit for marketing and advertising courses' (www.uneptie.org). NESTA also has an interesting report from 2008 on Selling Sustainability (www.nesta.org.uk/selling-sustainability-report/). Smart: Know-Net The Sustainable Marketing Knowledge Network is an online resource that brings together the worlds of marketing and sustainability (www.cfsd.org.uk/smart-know-net/index.htm).

Read: *The Green Marketing Manifesto* by John Grant (2007), which provides a roadmap on how to organize green marketing effectively and sustainably. *Green Marketing: Opportunities for Innovation in the New Marketing Age* by Jacquelyn A. Ottman (2004) looks at how simply 'greening' conventional marketing doesn't work and demonstrates how businesses that take the lead now while industry standards are forming can gain a competitive edge in the market.

Sustainable Marketing: Managerial-Ecological Issues (1999) by Donald A. Fuller explores the four Ps of marketing (product, price, place and promotion) to show how companies can craft 'win-win-win' solutions, where customers obtain genuine benefits, organizations achieve financial objectives and ecosystems are preserved or enhanced.

Advertising dos and don'ts

How not to communicate . . . Greenwashing

Although there is clearly a rise in sustainability leaders, it seems that there is also a parallel rise in greenwashing. According to TerraChoice, greenwashing is 'the act of misleading consumers regarding the environmental practices of a company or the environmental benefits of a product or service' (note that companies will also 'greenwash' social issues). It is believed that the term comes from a journalist who, in 1986, was covering the hotel schemes where you choose to keep your towel rather than washing it 'for the good of the environment'. The journalist examined the record of companies who promoted these schemes and concluded that since they did almost nothing else for the environment (at the time) and since towel schemes increased their profits by reducing washing costs, guests had to be cynical of their motives.

So why do people greenwash? Some say it is because of ignorance and/or sloppiness, some do it for quick wins. According to John Grant, 'the best reason for avoiding greenwashing is that you should be spending your money on something better, something which helps people change behaviour, to adopt a greener way of life.'[79] Ultimately it is your credibility and reputation that are on the line, and once lost, these are very difficult to regain. Consumers and marketers should think twice about:

1. *Green and social imagery:* Just because something is packaged green and has trees on it or has pictures of children and farmers, it doesn't mean that it is actually environmentally or socially friendly.
2. *Using general statements:* The same thing goes for products that use statements such as 'socially friendly', 'natural', 'bio', 'hypoallergenic', etc. When checked, many of these fail to live up to their promises unless accompanied by a recognized eco-label or regulated by government. Surprisingly many of these, such as the word 'nature', are not regulated by national legislation even though they can be very misleading.
3. *Missing the point:* A product that is water efficient could be very energy inefficient. Beware of companies using one claim to distract from the key sustainability issues of a particular product.
4. *When a label is not all it claims to be:* Having an environmental management system in place, or an environmental or social policy, or being part of a voluntary network, does not automatically make a company, or a particular product, more sustainable. Make sure these are backed up with policies and practices that are auditable, quantifiable and have targets and objectives.
5. *Giving options consumers can't act on:* Saying that a product has an environmental or social feature that consumers not only can't check, but also can't follow up on is misleading. This includes products that are recyclable but no facilities currently exist to recycle them. The recent push for biodegradable bags could be another example, as many of these are only biodegradable in certain environments, not when buried in landfills.
6. *When it isn't really as good as it seems:* This relates to claims that may sound good but that aren't really doing what they say. For example, organizations which claim to be carbon neutral or have carbon

(continued)

neutral services when neutral was achieved by buying offsets rather than through actual energy efficiencies.

7. *The product may be good, but the company definitely is not:* It is hard to take claims made about environmentally and socially friendly products seriously when the company producing the product has been shown to be anything but environmentally and socially friendly. This includes companies that, according to Greenpeace are, 'Advertising or speaking about corporate "green" commitments while lobbying against pending or current environmental laws and regulations.'

8. *Baby steps:* When a product makes tiny improvements and makes a big fuss about it. For example, an international magazine claiming to have turned green because one issue was made of 10% recycled paper, leaving you wondering about the other 90%.

There are several NGOs and online groups working to bring out examples of greenwash including the CorpWatch Greenwash awards (*www. corpwatch.org*) and Greenpeace (stopgreenwash.org). Greenwashing index allows people to submit company ads and judge for themselves whether they are greenwashing or not (*www.greenwashingindex.com*).

How to communicate . . . Responsible Marketing

There are an increasing number of advertising and marketing codes, both mandatory and voluntary, which outline responsible marketing practices on the international, national and company-specific level. These include regulations dealing with misleading or deceitful advertising, voluntary codes, professional association codes. A few such ideas include:

1. *Be good:* Do not market to groups by creating unnecessary pressure or concerns. For example companies who use awareness campaigns to scare people about a supposed illness and then sell the medicine. Unilever's Marketing Principles require that marketing practices do not convey misleading messages, do not undermine parental influence, do not suggest time or price pressure and do not encourage unhealthy dietary habits.

2. *Be honest:* Be transparent about what you are doing and share your successes and your challenges. Don't just make stuff up, make sure whatever you do say or claim is backed up and easy for the reader to understand. Seventh Generation reports on all the things that are wrong with its product and that it is still working on those

areas. Innocent included on its fruit juice bottles how much of the content was recycled and that they were working on the rest (a year later they were at 100%). Avoid abusing consumers' concern for the environment or taking advantage of their possible lack of knowledge in this area.

3. *Be creative:* It seems that all ads for green business use trees and flowers. Look at different ways of getting your message out. The Creative Gallery on Sustainability Communications includes around 1000 campaigns produced by companies, public authorities and NGOs from all over the world (http://www.unep.fr/scp/communications/ads.htm).

4. *Be positive:* Stay away from doom and gloom and instead surprise the customer with a positive message. Keep the message simple and easy to remember.

5. *Be consistent:* Consistency should exist between your engagement or initiatives and your image and product lines. It should be reinforced across your marketing messages as well as between your internal and external operations.

6. *Make the connection:* Communicate how products are relevant to people's lives and needs. Empower your customers by giving them something they can do. Get your customers involved.

7. *Focus on what is important to your audience:* Toyota Prius focused on fuel economy and quiet ride more than saving the planet. Link environmental and social benefits to things that concern customers in their daily lives and of which you can measure the impact.

Consumers are bombarded with messages everyday from supposedly green companies. A lot of the information makes it seem that no matter what a company says, nothing is changing. There are lots of companies out there that are truly working on these issues. For the consumer here are some tips on how to do your part:

- *Don't assume that everyone is lying or telling the truth,* just pay attention to what they are claiming (for example on their labels and packaging) and use your common sense to see if it looks right.
- *Don't blindly believe all the bad things or good things you read,* check the sources of the information and where possible check more than one source.

(continued)

- *Question companies who aren't doing anything at all ... or who seem to be doing too much*. Don't hesitate to contact those companies and request that they do something or find information to back up what they say they are doing. You are one of their stakeholders, they need to listen.
- *Report misleading messages*. Many countries, including at the international and company levels, have guidelines for environmental and social marketing claims. In many instances, customers who feel that a company is not telling the full truth can report them to relevant authorities who will investigate. Following a complaint to the Council of Better Business Bureau, Clorox was told to make changes to some of the claims it made on how its green products work.
- *Reward companies who you feel are doing it right*. Either through buying their products, telling the company or telling others.

Want more?

For more on responsible marketing and different advertising codes see ISO 14020 standard for information on the environmental properties of products (www.iso.org) and the International Chamber of Commerce consolidated codes of advertising and marketing communication (www. iccwbo.org/policy/marketing/id8532/index.html). Also see professional associations such as the European Advertising Standards Alliance (www. easa-alliance.org). At the national level different groups are set up, for example UK Committee of Advertising Practice (www.cap.org.uk) (www. ipa.co.uk), US National Advertising Review Council (www.narcpartners. org) and the Better Business Bureau (www.bbb.org). Companies themselves also have marketing and advertising codes.

12 Operations

Chefs around the world are exploring molecular gastronomy, mixing science with cooking. Forward-thinking chefs such as Chef Blumenthal bring food to a whole new level by questioning the assumptions about what food is and redefining what food could be. One of his treats is a candied beetroot and grapefruit lollipop with edible wrappers which looks like plastic but melts in your mouth. Edible packaging may not take off anytime soon in the world of business, but it does reflect an increasing number of innovative ideas to make the life-cycle of products and processes more sustainable that can, and will, help businesses flourish.

Increasingly, successful businesses share three characteristics with chefs like Blumenthal: (1) they question assumptions; (2) they think across disciplines; and (3) they are creative about the way that products are made. And these characteristics underlie modern operations management. Operations management is all about a company's supply chain and product life-cycles: its products and services; how they are designed, how they are made, how they are used and how they are disposed of. Obviously, operations management is the area that has the biggest direct impact on sustainability, since all the things we make and the way we make them affects our natural and social resources. Sustainability brings innovation into the supply chain, challenging our assumptions about the way things have always been done, and creating products and processes that are not only better for business, but better for society as well.

Until recently, management in many companies believed that what happened in parts of their supply chain, from design choices to overseas contractors, was not their responsibility. Today, organizations are realizing that not only is it their responsibility, but that proper management can bring about competitive advantages. As we continue to move into the 21st century, sustainability and operations management will increasingly go hand in hand.

Why is it important?

- *There's a lot of room for improvement:* Considering that on average, 80% of a product's overall cost is a consequence of its design, 93% of product materials do not end up in saleable products, 80% of products are discarded after first use and 99% of materials used in the production of or contained within goods are discarded in the first six weeks, there is obviously a lot of room for improvement and innovative ideas.[80]
- *Responsibility is shifting up the supply chain:* Not long ago, it was up to the consumer to choose to be greener, but today, consumer demand is shifting this responsibility to the retailer to provide these products. In some countries, (e.g. France) it will soon be mandatory to display the environmental performance of some products either on the product labels or the shelves. As more retailers decide to engage in more sustainable procurement strategies, the companies making the products will also have to uphold those standards in design and production.
- *Reduce costs and improve operational efficiency:* By using fewer and safer source materials and less energy, transportation and water resources, and by making processes more efficient, a company can significantly reduce production and labour costs. Creating simpler products that are easier to disassemble and recycle reduces waste and disposal costs and gives a company the potential to reuse products. It can also reduce labour costs through reduced need for training.
- *Compliance with existing and future legislation:* Steady increases in legislation and regulations drive operations management

decisions on many fronts. Regulations are being enacted to increase transparency in supply chains and standards, such as the European Union 'take back' laws which require manufacturers to take back all vehicles and electronic equipment sold in a particular country and recycle or dispose of them safely after use. Increasingly, we are seeing product taxes put in place to discourage people from buying certain products; banned materials lists are covering more and more substances (i.e. chemicals); and packaging waste and pollution prevention regulations are on the rise.

- *Increased risk of bad press:* Organizational stakeholders, the media, and others, no longer hesitate to expose and report on any questionable aspects of a company's supply chain, including incidents of child labour, forced labour, illegal waste dumping, and product recalls. This can result in significant losses not only to sales, but also to a company's hard earned reputation.
- *Improved quality and customer satisfaction:* Many consumers are looking for products that allow them to save money but also make them feel they have made a positive impact on society and the environment. Delivering and promoting simpler, more efficient products that have reduced operational costs and result in reduced environmental impact can mean improved customer satisfaction and increased market share. Eco-labelling schemes, 'design for' products and other environmental awareness programmes are creating an increasingly educated consumer who is not only willing to buy products designed for the environment and society, but may even boycott those that are not.

The key concepts

The Operations Management approach to sustainability involves analysing products and processes throughout their whole life-cycle and ultimately aims to have zero impact. However, products and services are produced and distributed through complex supply chains, where to reach zero impact one needs to:

• Design the product smartly upfront	→ *Eco-design*
• Use non harmful materials and components	→ *Green chemistry*
• Create more efficient processes	→ *Doing more with less*
• Use sustainable technologies to support these processes	→ *Sustainable technologies*
• Source them through optimized supply chains	→ *Suppliers and contractors*
• Moving products and services from point A to point B	→ *Transportation*
• Move from waste treatment to waste prevention	→ *Waste management*
• Consider sustainability aspects across all stages	→ *Box: Life-cycle Analysis*

Eco-design

Eco-design, also known as Design for the Environment, concerns designing or redesigning a product or service to take into account the environmental (and social) impacts throughout its life-cycle. Best practices in eco-design involve:

- *Re-thinking* the product and its functions from raw materials on up in order to make it more efficient, thereby reducing use of energy and other natural resources.
- *Re-ducing* energy and material consumption throughout a product's life-cycle.
- *Re-placing* harmful substances with more environmentally friendly alternatives.
- Selecting materials that can be *Re-cycled*, and build the product so that it disassembles easily to allow recycling.
- Designing the product so parts can be *Re-used*.
- Improving the product durability and ease of *Re-pair* so that the product does not need to be replaced as often.

Products that follow some or all of the above mentioned eco-design concepts often state that they are a 'design for' product (i.e. design for water conservation, design for disassembly, etc.). Eco-design principles can be applied to a single product or service, or a production process. HP for example has been working to design products that are easier to recycle by integrating clear design guidelines and checklists to assess and improve the recyclability of its products. They do his by using modular design to allow components to be removed, upgraded or replaced, eliminating glues and adhesives by using snap-in features, reducing the number and types of materials used, using single plastic polymers and using moulded in colours and finishes instead of paint, coating or plating.[81]

Some things to keep in mind ...

- *Understand your existing products:* When redesigning an existing product, a good way to understand eco-design and how it can relate to your project involves physically taking apart the product, looking at the different components and identifying excessive use of materials as well as opportunities to make improvements in packaging, product use, production, materials and disposal.
- *Understand what people really want or need:* The key to successful design is to observe what people do and understand how people feel and think and to use these observations as inspiration for designing or redesigning a product. Often there is a disconnect between what people say and what they actually do, which is why the insights cannot simply come out of market surveys or focus groups: people often don't say what they think or do what they say.
- *Create designs that engage the customer:* The key is to create products and services that inspire engagement and encourage positive behaviour. Many people buy the Toyota Prius not for the return on investment, but for the experience. One of the features drivers like is the constant information displayed about the fuel economy drivers are getting and how they can get more. Drivers can then take this information and compare it with other users through an online forum on the Toyota website.

For more on eco-design, look at the Design for Sustainability manual on the topic (www.d4s-de.org). There are several networks for designers interested in this area including O2 (www.o2.org) and the Designer Accord (www.designeraccord.org). For a good read see *EcoDesign: The Sourcebook* by Alastair Faud-Luke (2002) which provides hundreds of examples of innovative eco design. 'Aligned for Sustainable Design, An ABCD Approach to Making Better Products' by IDEO and BSR. Clean Production Action is an NGO that works on solutions for green chemicals, sustainable materials and environmentally preferable products (www.cleanproduction.org).

'Green' chemistry

Internationally, a number of regulations and laws govern use or prohibition of chemicals' transportation and disposal, including the Rotterdam Convention on the Prior Informed Consent Procedure for Certain Hazardous Chemicals and Pesticides in International Trade (www.pic.int) and the Stockholm Convention on Persistent Organic Pollutants (www.pops.int). In Europe REACH (Registration, Evaluation, Authorization and Restriction of Chemical Substances) gives greater responsibility to industry to manage the risks from chemicals and provide safety information on the thousands of substances in use. Companies such as Target, Microsoft and Johnson and Johnson are phasing out PVCs and other chemicals considered harmful.

As the international community enacts more and more legislation that limits the use of certain chemicals in products or bans them altogether, companies are looking to green chemistry for alternatives. Green, or sustainable, chemistry is about designing, developing and implementing chemical products and processes that reduce or eliminate the use and generation of substances that are hazardous to people and the environment. It involves rethinking the chemicals themselves, and how they are being used, as well as searching for greener, more environmentally and socially acceptable alternatives. Considering that chemistry—chemicals and chemical processes—delivers over 95 % of all the products used in society, green chemistry is a key area in sustainability. Green chemistry involves:

- Designing safer chemicals with little or no human or environmental toxicity
- Designing less hazardous chemical syntheses
- Using renewable materials such as wastes or by-products from other processes
- Using safer solvents or avoiding their use altogether
- Increasing energy efficiency by running reactions at room temperature and pressure
- Designing chemicals that degrade after use rather than accumulating in the environment
- Providing real time information during syntheses to minimize or eliminate by-products
- Minimizing the potential for accidents [82]

Legislation is not the only driver. Many organizations are using green chemistry as a way to produce unique and innovative products in the market, often to fill a demand by the consumer for more natural products. German carpet producer Donau-Tufting decided to remove heavy metal colourings and vulcanization chemicals from the carpets they make. The company gained an advantage in the market over its competitors, when the new carpet rapidly achieved an additional 25 % turnover.[83]

Reducing or eliminating the need for hazardous chemicals means a company does not need to invest in training and systems to manage and dispose of the waste. Dow Chemical Company, an international company which has a focus on exploring sustainable chemistry options, leases the use of its organic solvents rather than selling them through SAFECHEM. Once the customer is finished with them, rather than being left with the responsibility to dispose of them, Dow recovers them and, where possible, recycles them for future use.

There are also a growing number of initiatives from companies who are releasing more information on the ingredients used in their products, in particular the chemicals. SC Johnson has put together a website which provides a closer look at the ingredients it uses in its products (www.whatsinsidescjohnson.com).

The main green chemistry initiative is Responsible Care, the industry's global voluntary initiative (www.responsiblecare.org), which is coordinated by the International Council of Chemical Associations (www.icca-chem.org).

Other programmes with national or regional perspectives include the Royal Society of Chemistry's Green Chemistry Network (www.rsc.org/chemsoc/gcm), SETAC (www.setac.org), EPA's Green Chemistry Program (www.epa.gov/greenchemistry) and the ACS's green chemistry Institute (www.acs.org/greenchemistry). International and global programmes of interest include the UNEP Strategic Approach to International Chemical Management (www.chem.unep.ch/saicm) and the Inter-Organization Programme for the Sound Management of Chemicals (www.who.int/iomc). The ICIS has a blog on green chemistry (www.icis.com/blogs/green-chemicals). Finally, Greener Industry is an excellent resource on the range of chemicals out there, their applications and the issues with them (www.greener-industry.org and www.sustain-ed.org).

Doing more with less

Enter an appliance store in Europe or the US and you will see energy labels showing the energy usage of the different products. Consumers, whether to cut bills or be more responsible, are looking for products that use less energy and water. Businesses are also interested in cutting their energy and water use for the same reasons. The growing international movement focused on sustainable consumption and production has roots in both the private and public sectors. The idea is that natural resources can be used more efficiently—it's not just about consuming and producing less, but also consuming and producing differently.

Two concepts that put this idea into practice are gaining momentum:

- **Eco-efficiency**, developed by the WBCSD, 'is a management philosophy that encourages business to search for environmental improvements which yield parallel economic benefits'. It is not simply about making incremental efficiency improvements; it is about stimulating creativity and innovation in search of new ways of doing things throughout the full value chain. The philosophy encompasses three broad objectives:

  - *Reducing the consumption of resources:* including energy, materials, water and land while also enhancing the recyclability and durability of products and closing material loops.

  - *Reducing the impact on nature:* including air emissions, water discharges, waste disposal and dispersion of toxic substances while focusing on the sustainable use of renewable resources.

  - *Increasing product or service value:* providing more benefits to customers through product functionality, flexibility and modularity plus additional services, focusing on selling the functional need that customers want.

- **Cleaner production** is a preventative approach to environmental management where environmental impact is minimized. UNEP, who introduced the concept in 1989, defines it as 'the continuous application of an integrated preventive environmental strategy to processes, products and services to increase overall efficiency, reduce risks to humans and the environment. Cleaner production can be applied to the processes used in any industry, to products themselves and to various services provided in society.'

For more, see the WBCSD Eco-Efficiency Learning Module at www.wbcsd.org. For Cleaner Production see UNEP Cleaner Production and the International Declaration on Cleaner Production (www.uneptie.org/pc/cp).

In 1994, UNIDO started setting up Cleaner Production Centres to help SMEs, large enterprises, industry associations, universities, consultants and policy makers in developing and transition countries that now number over 40. UNIDO also has a cleaner production toolkit (www.unido.org/doc/5133).

Sustainable technology

Technological innovation is an important part of finding solutions to our economic, social and environmental problems. These technologies are generally categorized into four areas:

- *Remediation Technologies* treat environmental problems after they have occurred and attempt to repair or remediate the damage. These include soil and water cleanup methods, and are typically very expensive.
- *Abatement Technologies* capture or treat pollutants before they escape into the environment using physical, chemical or biological mechanisms to reduce emissions, like clean coal or sewage treatment systems. Abatement technologies are usually capital intensive, require lots of energy and resources to operate, and generate their own waste.
- *Pollution Prevention Technologies* include improved or alternative industrial and agricultural processes that avoid the production of pollutants (i.e. paper making that eliminates chlorine bleaching) as well as alternative products that result in less pollution through their use and disposal (i.e. lead-free petrol, biodegradable detergents, mercury free batteries and water based paints).
- *Sustainable Technologies* are the ultimate goal, and focus on achieving low or no ecological impact (100% recyclable and non toxic) and using resources efficiently. Examples include daylight sensitive lighting, bicycles, cost effective non-polluting renewable energy technologies and non bleached recycled paper.[84]

A recent trend has been towards what is being called 'cleantech', or clean technology, considered by many to be the largest economic opportunity of the 21st century. The venture capital industry invested $ 8.4 billion in cleantech in 2008. According to Forum for the Future, 'clean technologies are technologies—including products, services and processes—that reduce or eliminate the environmental impact of currently available technology through increasing resource efficiency, improving performance and reducing waste.'[85] A lot of the work we hear about is in renewable energies such as solar, wind and alternative fuels, as well as in agriculture, infrastructure, recycling, efficiency, transportation and storage. Initiatives are abundant, at all levels and in all industries in this area. For example:

- Devices that collect energy to generate electricity are being fitted to bicycles in Times Square, revolving doors in the Netherlands and even dance floors in night clubs.
- Xerox research concludes that 40% of paper printed in the office is discarded after one use, so the company is developing reusable paper where the image disappears after 24 hours and is reusable 10 times.
- A scientist in Taiwan invented an organic chlorophyll battery which can supply electricity within 10 seconds of being made wet with water or any kind of beverage.
- The Soil Lamp is an LED light that takes advantage of the electricity generated by the chemical reaction between metallic strips of zinc and the minerals and organisms in damp soil.
- Smog-eating cement was invented in Italy, and in the presence of light breaks down air pollutants like carbon monoxide, nitrogen oxide and benzene through a natural process called photocatalysis. It is now being used in buildings across Europe, as well as North America.
- Kites are being explored instead of wind mills as power generators. Kites eliminate the need for expensive infrastructures such as towers, and have the potential to supply energy at a fraction of the current cost of electricity in Europe today.[86]

Technology hype cycle www.psfk.com/2008/08/ charting-the-technology-hype-cycle.html.   www.greentechmedia.com   offers up to date news on cleantech companies   and   investment activities and insights.

Innovation in existing technologies goes beyond alternative energies; it can also be applied to bring about social change. Social change innovations are occurring in the information and telecommunication area in particular. For example, Vodafone's mobile payment service could allow customers without bank accounts to use mobile phones for financial transactions. Citi's biometric ATM allows customers in developing countries to access services using fingerprints.

Suppliers

Why is a close relationship with your suppliers important? One reason: the failure of supplier relationships can have a catastrophic effect on company brand and image. This is clearly illustrated by the example of Nike in the 1990s. The company was held accountable by the global public for the child labour practices of their suppliers in Asia, which in turn had a long standing detrimental effect on its reputation. Today, companies are realizing that they are accountable to their stakeholders and the public for activities throughout their whole supply chain, including the actions of their suppliers. By working closely with suppliers, companies of any size can minimize the risk of unknowingly being exposed to negative impacts, and can also understand the environmental and social impacts their products and services have throughout their full life-cycle, while exploring ways of creating a better product, at a better price. Suppliers usually know the products better than the buyer, putting them in the best position to help maximize efficiencies and minimize waste. At the end of the day, their business is your business as well.

PepsiCo works closely with their suppliers to ensure that they are working with like-minded companies, and to see what they can learn from suppliers who are further ahead in this journey than they are. As their sustainability strategies evolve, they expect their suppliers to evolve with them. According to John C. Scott, PepsiCo Director of Responsible and Sustainable Sourcing, 'Setting expectations for performance with suppliers is good for PepsiCo because it results in suppliers running their businesses more effectively and reducing costs, which ultimately translates into having a better economic relationship with the supplier. While we recognize we still have a lot to learn in this area, we're working with them while we continue to refine our approach'.

As you execute your supplier selection strategy and build supplier relationships, keep the following points in mind:

- *Create a policy for improving the economic, environmental and social sustainability performance of suppliers:* Integrate sustainability criteria into supplier contracts, i.e. minimum performance standards, code of conduct, performance against targets. Ford Motor Company is requiring ISO 14001 certification from 5000 of its suppliers with manufacturing facilities. To help suppliers meet these goals, Ford developed and provided ISO 14001 Awareness Training and created Environmental Recognition awards that recognize suppliers for outstanding environmental achievement and innovation.
- *Work with suppliers to help them craft their sustainability strategies:* Consider hosting a forum where suppliers and buyers can discuss and question decisions, and can move forward with real action items. You are likely to find that many suppliers don't know where to start and such a forum allows them to learn from the buyer and other suppliers who have already started the journey. Because of a desire to certify its suppliers that are using forestry products, PepsiCo brought nearly 200 of its largest suppliers together with leading not-for-profits, NGOs and government organizations to explain PepsiCo's approach and commitment to work with credible organizations that promote responsible business practices, and how those programmes tie into expectations for PepsiCo's suppliers. Through their supplier outreach programmes, PepsiCo also empowers employees to work with suppliers to set goals and monitor improvement in resource conservation programmes such as Energy Star and carbon disclosure.

- *Conduct a baseline assessment of suppliers' current sustainability performance:* HP's Supplier Environmental Performance Review Questionnaire aims to provide a tool to gather consistent information on supplier environmental practices, and to optimize the transfer of environmental performance information between purchasers and suppliers. The Body Shop, Canon and Sony have all instituted rating systems to evaluate existing and potential suppliers on a number of sustainability criteria. Vendors with higher ratings receive a larger percentage of business and are rewarded for improvements.

- *Don't ignore the suppliers of suppliers:* Many suppliers are themselves managing other suppliers, an area where problems can easily arise if not managed carefully. Companies need to work to make sure their values spread throughout the supply chain. Novo Nordisk's sustainable supply chain management programme, launched in 2002, works with their main suppliers as well as their second tier suppliers (those that supply to main suppliers) to support human rights and labour standards, as well as to ensure that sound environmental practices are in place. It provides information and tools for them to use via a website (www.suppliertoolbox.novonordisk.com).

- *Send consistent messages:* Many suppliers work with different companies at the same time. Thus, one of the major challenges for suppliers is keeping track of each company's individual sustainability programmes and targets that it must meet. In order to ensure that suppliers are receiving consistent messages in terms of minimum standards from the different companies they work with, several international initiatives have also been put into place to help. AIM-PROGRESS is a group of large international companies working together to develop common guidelines on responsible sourcing (www.aim.be). Sedex connects businesses and their global suppliers to share ethical data. They can translate information to people all over the world (www.sedex.org.uk).

IKEA uses a lot of wood based materials in its products. In recognition that their suppliers are at different levels when it comes to sustainability, the company created a staircase model applicable to suppliers delivering or producing IKEA articles that contain solid wood, veneer, plywood or layer-glued wood.

- Level 1. Start-up conditions: The origin of the wood must be known, it must not originate from intact natural forests or high conservation value forests. High value tropical tree species must be certified FSC.
- Level 2. Minimum requirements: Wood must be produced in accordance to national and regional forest legislation and laws and it must not originate from certain plantations in tropical and subtropical regions.
- Level 3. 4Wood to ease transition: emphasis on the use of wood-tracking procedures and other routines to better control wood from procurement through production.
- Level 4. Forest certified as responsibly managed: suppliers are recognized through Forest Stewardship Council as coming from forests that are managed sustainably.

IKEA aims to have 100% of its suppliers be at minimum level 2 in 2009 and 30% at level 4. This has brought multiple benefits. For example the number of wood supply chain audits conducted in FY07 decreased from 90 to 50 due in part to the increased documentation requirements for full FSC chain of custody certification.

Fair Factories Clearinghouse provides information on labour practices in factories around the world (www.fairfactories.org). In the US, the Green Suppliers Network is a collaborative venture between industry, the US Environmental Protection Agency and the US Department of Commerce (www.greensuppliers.gov).

Transportation

Transportation systems move goods and people around the globe. However, our increasing reliance upon traditional transportation systems brings its own set of problems to bear: air and noise pollution, traffic congestion and road accidents, over-reliance on non-renewable resources, as well as land use to name a few. Companies today must look at not just how their products are created and packaged, but also at the impact that transportation has on the life-cycle of a product. Across the sector many initiatives are taking place to positively impact fuel efficiency, and environmental and personnel safety.

- *Cars and trucks:* Companies are choosing to buy more fuel-efficient vehicles including hybrids and electric cars, and are filling up with alternative fuels where they are available (www.greenfuels.org). Driver training programmes result in better driving practices that not only reduce fuel consumption, but also improve road safety (www. greener-driving.net). In order to reduce the incidence of chemical transport highway accidents, Dow Chemicals and DuPont jointly introduced a Behaviour-Based Safety programme to influence the behaviour of drivers through observation, coaching and communi- cation. Wal-Mart, which owns the second largest private truck fleet in the US, has committed to doubling its fleet's fuel efficiency by 2015. SC Johnson saved $1.6 million annually through its Truckload Utilization Project, which combines multiple customer orders and different products to send out the most fully loaded and best configured trucks in order to maximize each truck's carrying capacity and ship- ping routes. Shipping companies such as UPS, FedEx and DHL have similar policies.

- *Maritime shipping:* Transportation by sea underpins global trade and, while not without its own problems, generally has a lower environmental impact than air or road transport. Companies that cannot source locally should investigate using sea transport, as it is often more cost effective. One example of vessel operators and port authorities working together to reduce pollution is the Los Angeles port in the US, who now provide clean electrical hook ups shore side to avoid cruise and containerships from having to operate generators and engines while docked. Shipping company Bremen introduced the world's first cargo vessel with the innova- tive SkySails towing kite system. This wind propulsion system har- nesses wind energy to assist in propelling the ship, and depending on wind conditions, can lower fuel costs by between 10 and 35%.

A small freighter could save over $250 000 in fuel costs per year using this system.[87] The Global Industry Alliance, will encourage the shipping industry to share approaches on limiting the number of invasive species transferred in ballast water, the leading cause of introducing a marine alien species (globallast.imo.org).

- *Air transport:* The volume of passenger and freight transport by air is expected to continue to grow, as are demands by stakeholders to make air travel more sustainable. At the current rate of growth in air travel and transportation, the UK's Royal Commission on Environmental Pollution calculates that, by 2050, emissions of greenhouse gases from aviation will account for more than half of the UK's impact on global warming. To combat this, the International Air Transportation Association (www.iata.org) as well as The Clean Sky initiative in Europe aims to cut the industry's emissions by 40% of present levels by 2015 (www.cleansky.eu). One way to achieve this is through advances in aircraft technology that improve fuel efficiency, while simultaneously reducing both operating cost and pollution. The use of composite materials to reduce weight, were recently introduced in the Airbus A380. The industry is also researching ideas like aircraft with blended wing bodies that would make less noise and use up to 25% less fuel than conventionally shaped aircraft.[88]

Operations managers reviewing transportation strategy should keep in mind the importance of sourcing raw materials locally where possible as this can not only reduce transportation costs, but also help support the local industries that supply them.

Scania, a leading manufacturer of heavy trucks and buses as well as industrial and marine engines based in Sweden has a recipe for sustainable transportation.

It isn't just about getting goods and services across the globe but also people, see the International Association of Public Transportation (www. uitp.org). For more on transportation in general see the WBCSD's Sustainable Mobility Project (www.wbcsd.org).

1. Transitioning now to renewable fuels
2. Increased investments in developing hybrid technology
3. Driver training can improve fuel efficiency by 10–15% and results in lower damage and maintenance costs
4. Correct tyre pressure, rolling resistance accounts for about 30% of a vehicle's fuel consumption
5. Improved efficiency of transport system by eliminating empty or near empty runs
6. Greater cargo capacity through longer vehicles and maximized cargo space
7. Reduced air resistance by correctly fitting objects mounted on the truck
8. Better fuel economy with the latest technology (www.scania.com)

Waste management

Believe it or not, waste has become exciting. We may have once thought of waste as dirty, uninteresting, expensive and useless, but today, numerous pressures are combining to make waste management a focal point in sustainability. Faced with increasing regulations, public pressure, raw material and landfill shortages and the need for increased resource efficiency, companies are moving away from the waste treatment approach and towards waste prevention and reuse.

Apart from obvious environmental and societal benefits, cost remains the most serious driver for improving waste management. Treatment, handling, transportation and disposal of waste all add significant costs to a business, especially when the waste is hazardous. Hidden costs, such as the loss of raw materials, cost of treatment, time and energy, are often ignored and can increase the true price tag of waste as much as five to twenty times.

From a business point of view, pollution and waste represent incomplete, ineffective or inefficient use of raw materials. Since waste does not enhance customer or stakeholder value it has no place in business. According to the New Zealand Business Council for Sustainable Development, 'Zero

Waste means a 100% resource efficient economy where, as in nature, material flows are cyclical and everything is re-used or recycled harmlessly back into society or nature. "Waste" as we think of it today will cease to exist because everything will be viewed as a resource." Today many global companies such as DuPont and Xerox are aiming for zero waste (www. zerowaste.org, www.zeri.org and www.nzbcsd.org.nz/zerowaste).

In rethinking waste management, companies should first and foremost identify what the waste streams are, and how much waste is being generated throughout the life-cycle and supply chain from raw materials to packaging. Then a company should look at the waste hierarchy:

1. *Preventing the waste altogether:* By considering product design to avoid producing waste in the first place.
2. *Reducing waste:* Minimizing the amount of waste you produce through design, procurement and less packaging.
3. *Recycling and reusing:* Where waste cannot be prevented, as many of the materials as possible should be recovered through recycling or reuse.
4. *Improving disposal and monitoring:* Where there is no other choice, waste should be disposed of safely and appropriately.

Several waste management strategies are rapidly gaining popularity that address one or more levels of the waste hierarchy:

Extended Producer Responsibility: The EU has several directives that oblige member states and EU producers to set up and participate in product take-back schemes for electronic goods and automobiles. These schemes, also called EPRs, have been established to push for changes at the source that reduce the environmental impacts of products throughout the life-cycle. EPRs place the physical and financial responsibility on producers to recover and then dispose, recycle or reuse their products. These schemes can also be extended to include the responsibility to provide information on the environmental and social properties of the products manufactured. Overall, the EPR strategy not only encourages companies to follow principles such as eco-design and minimization of hazardous materials, but also shifts the cost of waste collection away from municipalities. It also forces producers to better internalize the full costs of waste.

Turning a product into a service: Schindler, an elevator company, determined that, rather than selling its high quality elevators as a product, it would rent out a 'vertical transportation system' to its customers. The decision benefits everyone. The company keeps the asset on its books and remains responsible for all service and repairs. Schindler also can invest in providing the most up to date, quality product they can and provide more tailored solutions to the needs of their customers, which helps them attain their profit objectives. Xerox's leasing programme recovers and reuses materials and components from copiers, including toner. Both Schindler and Xerox represent a new trend—companies are exploring what is known as Product Service Systems, moving from selling a product to renting the service that the product provided. Actually, the idea of PSS is nothing new; launderettes, movie theatres and libraries are all based on the same principle. What is new is the way that increasing numbers and types of businesses are exploring these opportunities by re-examining the original assumptions behind an existing product, material or service decision. Instead of traditional product decisions based on resources available, and ability to sell, these companies are focusing on the original need the product fulfils and providing that service instead.

> For more see the Product/service design network (www.suspronet.org) and UNEP's PSS resources (www.uneptie.org/scp/design/pss). For some other examples see www.treehugger.com and search for PSS.

By-product synergies (also known as industrial ecology or industrial symbiosis) involves a range of organizations, such as companies, offices and government, acting together as a single ecosystem, taking one company's by-products and waste and selling or sharing them as primary inputs to another company. The idea behind by-product synergies is to design and operate industrial systems as living systems.

- *Within a company:* BASF's Verbund is an integrated system within its manufacturing plants that allows by-products and waste from one plant to serve as the raw materials in another plant. Calculations show that this saves the company about € 500 million each year at the company's Ludwigshafen site alone.

- *Between two companies:* The Carlton United Brewery in Australia sells the extra yeast produced in its brewery to Kraft, which uses it to make Vegemite, a yeast based spread.
- *On a small scale:* Green Zone in Sweden combines a Ford car service centre, a Statoil fuel station and a McDonalds, all of which are heated using a central heat pump and ground source technology. Surplus heat generated by the McDonalds grills as well as the heated coolant water from Statoil's refrigeration system is transported to the central heat pump, thus allowing the buildings to benefit from the energy surplus (www.greenzone.nu).
- *On a large scale:* In the Danish industrial town of Kalundborg, six main partners share waste and other materials including Asnacs (the largest coal-fired plant in Denmark), Statoil (an oil refinery), Novo Nordisk (a large biotechnology company), a plasterboard company and the town of Kalunborg (www.symbiosis.dk).

Ensuring quality: A number of corporations are looking at preventing waste from occurring in the first place, in part by ensuring quality and minimizing waste. Many quality-focused approaches originate from Japanese business mentality. *Hoshin Kanri* says that the success of the product or process development is directly linked to the ability of an organization to put into practice its strategic goals. *Kaizen* is ongoing, continuous improvement. It can be implemented in corporations by improving every aspect of a business process in a step-by-step approach, while gradually developing employee skills through training and increased involvement. *Poka-Yoke* is designed either to prevent an error from happening or to make an error obvious at a glance. This approach aggressively seeks to eliminate the possibility of errors and waste and to increase resource efficiency in the entire product lifecycle. Lean manufacturing, based on the methods pioneered in the Toyota production system, focuses on eliminating waste, enhancing quality and delivering value to customers while achieving environmental performance goals at the lowest cost. Lean manufacturing derives specific strategies and actions from the idea that environmental waste does not add value to the customer, is a sign of inefficient production and that it affects production flow, time, quality and cost. Lean typically targets seven kinds of wastes: overproduction, inventory, transportation, motion, defects, over processing and waiting.

Tapping into garbage dumps: There are several threads of thought that now involve how garbage that has already been disposed of in landfills can be mined for resources. Methane gas produced by decomposing garbage in dumps in New Jersey is captured and used as fuel to generate electricity. There are 21 landfills being used like this in the state and 445 across the US. Dumps are also being mined for materials. For example, in the US about 680 000 tonnes of aluminium cans are thrown out every year totalling about $1.83 billion worth of metal per year. The world throws away 18 million tonnes of electronic waste each year and one tonne of scrap from discarded computers can contain more gold than can be produced from 16 tonnes of ore. So why aren't more companies tapping into this? As mining garbage is costly and often hazardous, many are finding that the best use of their resources is to stop products from reaching the landfill to begin with.[89]

There is no lack of websites and resources on waste for example at the national level (www.environment.nsw.gov.au/waste), regional level (www.europa.eu/scadplus/leg/en/s15002.htm) and international level (www.uneptie.org/pc/hazardouswaste). For information on recycling symbols see www.thedailygreen.com/green-homes/latest/recycling-symbols-plastics-460321.

Challenges?

- *Gathering information:* The transparency of supplier information is not always available and accurate especially when you are looking beyond just a company's suppliers to also look at the suppliers of those suppliers.

- *Misalignment between companies and their suppliers:* Often there is a lack of effective communication between companies and their suppliers. Suppliers do not have financial incentives, such as increased orders or preferential contracts and are not given any support for putting in place sustainability systems. Also, each company has different requirements for its suppliers making it complicated and expensive for suppliers to engage.
- *Large number of standards:* The increasing number of regulatory and industry codes with different requirements is generating confusion, and often results in multiple audits all with different recommendations.
- *These efforts take time:* Sometimes it is unrealistic to look at the whole supply chain. Changes are often easier to make incrementally, or one step at a time. Companies should adopt a process of continuous improvement.
- *Ideas:* The biggest challenge often lies in just learning how to tap into your creativity and to imagine the possibilities.

Trends and new ideas

– Inspiration from nature	– Instant Feedback
– Products that do more	– Exploring new materials
– Traceability	

Inspiration from nature Tapping into nature for inspiration is nothing new. What is gaining momentum is the use of nature as inspiration for new and better technologies, an idea made popular through the concept of biomimicry. Biomimicry 'studies nature's best ideas and then imitates these designs and processes to solve human problems'. Nature is the source of 'technologies' that have been used by the natural world successfully and sustainably for the past 3.8 billion years. Increasingly, biologists, engineers, architects and business leaders are coming together to learn how to tap into and use nature as inspiration for the development of new products or to completely redesign existing ones.

www.biomimicryinstitute.org and www.AskNature.org
Read: *Biomimicry: Innovation Inspired by Nature* by Janine Benyus (1997), which is all about this concept.

So how does it work? The Shinkansen bullet train in Japan, which travels at 200 miles per hour used to make lots of noise as it emerged from tunnels. The chief engineer, an avid bird-watcher, tried modelling the front of the train after the Kingfisher bird's long pointed beak which enables the bird to dive from air into water with very little splash. The result was a train that was not only quieter but used 15 % less energy even when the train travelled 10 % faster. One does not need to be a biologist to explore these opportunities as they surround all of us.

Some tips to get started in product design through biomimicry:

1. Don't ask 'What do I want to design?'. Instead ask 'What do I want my design to do?' and 'Why do I want my design to do that?'
2. Ask 'Does nature do this function, and if so, how?'
3. Explore natural models by going outside and doing first-hand research.
4. Brainstorm multiple solutions.

Products that do more We are starting to see the beginnings of a new era, in which both companies and consumers are not just content with 'doing no harm', but actually look for ways to 'do more good'. Already we see homes installed with solar panels 'selling' excess energy back into the power grid. What's next on the horizon? Perhaps, cars that not only generate enough energy to run themselves but also put extra energy into the electrical grid and engines that filter the air, releasing it cleaner than it came in. The next time you are waiting in line, keep an eye out for floors that use the footsteps of pedestrians to generate power, a great way to provide the energy needs of supermarkets and railways stations. The Spinnaker Tower in Portsmouth, UK will be using this technology on the stairs that visitors go up to reach the 560 ft high viewing platform.[90] The next wave of global consumerism will focus more on selling products that make it easy for people to 'go green' and on allowing consumers to save money . . . or even make money by being green.

Traceability Throughout this chapter, we have talked about how companies are looking at environmental and social issues across their supply chains. How they make their supply chain more sustainable is often communicated to the consumer through eco-labels (see the marketing chapter). But eco-labels are merely a starting point for some companies and consumers. In the past consumers got information about the positive and negative aspects of product life-cycles from consumer websites, but increasingly the producers themselves are providing that information via the 'backstory' as it is called. Icebreaker, an outdoor clothing company based in New Zealand, has tagged its garments made from merino wool with a code that customers can enter on the website to check out the products history—known as a 'Baacode'. In Japan, grocery shoppers can use cell phones to scan RFID tags on food items to find out more details about the origins. The luxury food court at Harrods in the UK provides live video feed of the farm from which their chickens are sourced.

Instant feedback focused on better use People are being asked on a day-to-day basis to make decisions about changes to their life-styles in order to prevent something bad from happening in the future, a future their children will see, but they themselves may never see. Many sustainability messages focus on issues that are not tangible for the consumers, either because they are occurring far away, will not occur during this life time, or are difficult to observe on a daily basis. The solution is to focus on those things that do impact consumers, and communicate this to them. According to the UNEP/Wuppertal Institute Collaborating Centre on Sustainable Consumption and Production 80% of data currently collected focuses on impacts from manufacturing; however 80% of the impacts themselves occur during end use. More and more we will see companies providing information to customers to enable them to use and dispose of the products sustainably. This includes monitors that show how much energy, gasoline and water is being used in real time and how this translates to money saved and environmental impact.

Exploring new materials Many eco-friendly raw material alternatives are being explored for use in everything from textiles to building materials including algae, soya, bamboo, organic cotton and hemp. For example, Patagonia makes fleece sweaters using recycled plastic bottles. Websites such as Ecolect (www.ecolect.net), Materia (www.materia.nl) and Material Connexion (www.materialconnexion.com) provide searchable databases and information on a variety of sustainable materials options.

What you can do . . .

- ❑ Look at your own organization before you start working with others within the supply chain.
- ❑ Find projects that get your company and employees as well as your customers involved.
- ❑ Test out ideas through pilot projects.
- ❑ Implement codes and guidelines for suppliers.
- ❑ Put in place internal and supply-chain guidelines for packaging, ingredients and so on, as they relate to your product design and procurement activities.
- ❑ Offer tours of your office. If you are proud of how you have embedded sustainability into the way you work tell people about it by offering tours of the facilities.

Want more?

Global Environmental Management Initiative (www.gemi.org/supplychain/) is one of many organizations with guidelines and resources on supply chain management.

The Green Grid has taken up the challenge of developing standards to measure data centre efficiency, which includes both the facility and the IT equipment inside of it. Members include Intel, Microsoft, Dell, IBM and Google (www.thegreengrid.org). The Electronic Industry Citizenship Coalition is a group of companies working together to create a code of best practice for the world's major electronic brands and their suppliers (www.eicc.info).

Read: *Cradle to Cradle* by William McDonough and Michael Braugart (2002 and 2009), which calls for a new industrial revolution where waste is eliminated as a concept altogether and companies make money not by doing less harm but by actually doing some good and making money in the process. *Factor Four: Doubling Wealth – Halving Resource Use* by Ernst Ulrich Weizsacker, Amory Lovins and L. Hunter Lovins (1997) shows a new form of resource productivity where at least four times as much wealth can be extracted from the resources we use (www.wupperinst.org/FactorFour).

Life-cycle analysis

The life-cycle approach looks at the environmental and social aspects and impacts of a product or a service across all stages of production and consumption, from design to disposal. Life-cycle thinking can be applied at several different levels; a whole product, one part of a system, or simply a part of the product such as the material used. Companies then choose to either make changes across the whole life-cycle, or just those with the biggest impact, or a combination that represents incremental improvements. For example, when P&G conducted a life-cycle assessment of its laundry detergents it found that 85% of greenhouse

(continued)

gas emissions were coming from customers heating the water to do the laundry. In response to this new information, it developed cold-water detergents that both saved customers money on energy bills and reduced their emissions. It was the first company to launch cold-water detergent in both the US and Europe.

According to the UNEP/SETAC Life-cycle Initiative, a life-cycle approach promotes:

- *Awareness that our selections are not isolated but are part of a larger system.* For example the decision to purchase office paper. It takes 24 trees to create 50 000 sheets of paper and 2.3 cubic metres of landfill space to dispose of it. Thus, the choice to procure recycled paper and paper products from sustainably managed forests and to reuse and recycle paper after use impacts multiple points in the system.
- *Making choices for the longer term and considering all environmental and social issues associated with those.* Thinking about the whole life-cycle of a product helps avoid making short-term decisions that can have a lasting negative influence, such as over-fishing or releasing pollutants into the air.
- *Improving entire systems, not single parts of systems.* Life-cycle thinking was initially designed to prevent decisions, for example, that fix one environmental problem but cause another unexpected or costly problem to arise. This approach helps prevent shifting problems from one life-cycle stage to another, from one region of the world to another and from one environmental or social issue to another.
- *Informed selections but not necessarily 'right' or 'wrong' ones.* Life-cycle thinking helps put the decisions that are made about products and processes into context to look at the unintentional impacts of our actions, such as damaging nature or supporting unfair labour conditions. If one fully understood the impacts of their actions they might choose to act differently, in the best interests of people and planet.[91]

For businesses, this approach also helps to understand products, processes and services better and the impacts these can have on the environment, on society and on the company at every step. Companies can make better decisions and find opportunities to improve products and processes and ultimately, their bottom line. Companies such as Johnson and Johnson track the life-cycle costs avoided as a result of sustainability projects have helped them to build a strong business case for its environmental goals and programmes.

Tips in conducting life-cycle analysis

* Understand what your goal is before starting. This includes why you are looking at your product's life-cycle, what kind of information you need to know in order to make the necessary decisions.
* Determine how much information you need. There are so many different elements of a product that you can gather information on that it can very quickly become overwhelming. Understand before you start what level of information you need to make decisions.
* Understand what you are getting into before you start. A full life-cycle assessment can be a very resource- and time-intensive activity. Businesses often apply streamlined LCAs or quick LCAs with much less information based on the experience gained and on a previous hotspot analysis.
* Retain the findings of the life-cycle analyses for future efforts on product enhancements and new product designs.
* Understanding that the life-cycle will not give you all the answers, it should be used as one component of a decision-making process.

The life-cycle analysis checklist

Virtually all the products that one uses have a life-cycle that incorporates the same steps. The following checklist provides a range of topics and issues to address in analysing the life-cycle of a product.

Design: The Life-cycle begins at the design table where designers of products or services decide on what the product or service will produce, the need it fulfils, the resources to produce it.

❑ Follow the principles of eco-design to select raw materials; create simpler designs with fewer components that are easy to separate for repair and recycling, and are modular to permit easy repair, recycling, upgrades or service; and create efficient production processes that aim for zero impact.

(continued)

❏ Uphold labour standards and human rights throughout the life-cycle.

Sourcing material: Once the materials have been selected, they need to be sourced (i.e. wood, minerals, water, etc.).

❏ Use materials with less environmental impact, for example timber from sustainable forests.
❏ Work with suppliers that use sustainable processes to extract raw materials.
❏ Use fewer materials, energy and water resources.
❏ Develop an eco-efficient production strategy: Increase bio-degradable products, renewable materials and recyclables.
❏ Source locally available materials and resources.
❏ Purchase materials with eco-labels, recycled material to improve transparency throughout the supply chain.
❏ Apply green chemistry to production processes, and minimize and phase out purchase, use, handling and disposal of materials and substances that are hazardous or toxic.
❏ Work with suppliers to increase supply chain efficiency.
❏ Use by-products or wastes from one process in another product or process.

Production and Manufacturing: Raw materials are transformed into the product through a series of processes.

❏ Use eco-efficiency and clean production concepts in production processes.
❏ Reduce material variety and weight.
❏ Aim for sustainable technologies first.
❏ Meet all applicable environmental regulations, safety and performance standards, and labour and human rights standards.
❏ Sell by-products to others as primary inputs.

Packaging and Transportation: Once created, a product is then packaged and transported to distribution centres and to the customer.

❏ Use minimal, robust, reusable, returnable, recyclable packaging.

❑ Look at innovative solutions such as labelling the product instead of the packaging, and consumable packaging.

❑ Design products that are easier to transport and to store.

❑ Use reusable or recyclable shipping containers, pallets, skids or packaging.

❑ Use fleet management tools, techniques and technologies to optimize distribution and shipping efficiency.

Use: How the product or service is actually used has quite an impact on the overall life-cycle of a product.

❑ Use fewer resources and cause less pollution and waste during use.

❑ Optimize functionality and service life by communicating multifunctional, modular features, part load operations, upgrade-ability, energy efficiency, simplicity, increased durability, reliability, reusability, easy maintenance.

❑ Educate users about how to best use and dispose of product.

❑ Look at other inputs needed for use (such as for cleaning or maintenance).

❑ Increase the service intensity and/or leasing options of your products.

❑ Encourage customer sharing, swapping.

Disposal and End of Life: Finally, the end of the life-cycle is how the product is disposed of after use.

❑ Reduce environmental impact of disposal by allowing easy reuse, recycling, ease of disassembly, ability to remanufacture.

❑ Find innovative uses for waste.

❑ Label reusable and recyclable content.

❑ Educate consumers about how to dispose of product.

❑ Provide product refurbishment, remanufacturing, refilling or other services.

❑ Offer exchange or take-back programme for old or used products.

(*continued*)

Want more?

- For a basic but very informative introduction to product life-cycles see the 20 minute video on http://www.storyofstuff.com/.
- Several international networks exist to help users put this thinking into practice including UNEP Life-cycle Initiative (lcinitiative.unep.fr/) and European Platform on LCA (lca.jrc.ec.europa.eu/EPLCA). The US EPA's site has a good resource section (www.epa.gov/ord/NRMRL/lcaccess/resources.html).
- There are some alternatives to LCA. See Input/Output tool developed by CarnegieMellon (www.eiolca.net).
- The life-cycle approach can also be used for decisions we make on a daily basis as consumers. Websites have examples of the life-cycle of consumer goods such as Good stuff: Behind the Scene Guide to things we buy (www.worldwatch.org/taxonomy/term/44) and Behind the Label (www.behindthelabel.org).

13   Organizational Behaviour

'CSR-HR = PR. If employees are not engaged, Corporate Social Responsibility becomes an exercise in public relations. The credibility of an organization will become damaged when it becomes evident that a company is not "walking the talk".'
Adine Mees And Jamie Bunham, Canadian Business For
Social Responsibility [92]

At a recent sustainability conference, the keynote speaker addressing one of the challenges of sustainable development said: 'Money is not the issue, it's people!' They had a point. Companies everywhere are putting in place sustainability programmes but are not always seeing the benefits and impacts that they expect. This is because the success of a sustainability strategy depends on being able to integrate these issues into the company's culture and the way a business operates on a day-to-day basis. To do this you need to align the key systems and processes on which delivery of an organization's sustainability programmes depends (i.e. managing change, developing competencies, supporting engagement, managing talent and diversity, recruiting, etc). All managers within an organization play a role in embedding sustainability into the culture of that organization.

The Human Resources department generally has constant links with all groups within a company, and a finger on the pulse of the whole organization. The people in this department play a key role in promoting positive behaviour, in creating an engaging work force and in creating an environment where sustainability is embedded in every aspect of the employee's life-cycle, from recruitment to retirement. Once a strategy has been decided by upper management, HR's role is to help management implement that strategy by embedding it into the way the organization works, making sure that what a company says they are doing is consistent with what they are actually doing.

Why is it important?

- *Highly strategic issue:* Of the 79 Global Reporting Initiative indicators, 24 can be considered to be related to organizational behaviour and HR. There is a growing international consensus that human capital management will become the biggest strategic issue for business. A survey by the Economist Intelligence Unit found risk mangers consider poor human capital management as the biggest threat to the long-term success of global business.[93]
- *Changing labour markets:* Taking sustainability issues seriously will help companies recruit and retain top talent. Graduates and potential employees at all levels are increasingly asking to work for companies with serious commitments to environmental, social and ethical responsibility and know how to identify empty corporate 'greenwashing' rhetoric.
- *Saves money:* It is a myth that HR represents the 'soft' side of business. In fact, HR is a costly business if not taken seriously. Replacing an employee often costs two or three times his or her salary. Keeping employees happy and motivated reduces recruiting and attrition costs and reduces absenteeism.
- *Increased Productivity:* Organizations with an internal commitment to sustainability experience happier employees. Not only do they give employees reasons to come into work in the morning and get involved in meaningful activities, they bring employees together and teach them new skills and networks. Studies show that 75% of employees who consider their employers to be sustainable exhibit high levels of commitment and that employees with high levels of

commitment perform 20% better than their peers and are 87% less likely to leave the organization.[94]

- ***Reputation:*** No matter how slick the web and media presentations, a company's sustainability policy may be perceived merely as green-washing if its employees are not informed and actively engaged in carrying out this policy through their relationships with customers and stakeholders.

The key concepts

Embedding sustainability thinking into a company's organization involves integrating it into the underlying systems and processes that govern behaviour within that organization.

- Systems and processes to embed sustainability thinking → ***Creating a culture of sustainability***
- Sending consistent messages about sustainability across the company → ***Communication***
- Attracting and hiring the right people to carry out that strategy → ***Recruiting***
- Retaining those employees in the organization → ***Employee engagement***
- Providing incentives and rewards that are in line with sustainability → ***Motivation and Rewards***
- Providing employees with the right tools → ***Talent development and training***
- Advice for ensuring successful change programmes → ***Box: Managing Change***

Creating a 'sustainability' culture

The story often goes like this: XYZ company decides to jump on the sustainability wagon, puts together a sustainability strategy with goals, sends an internal memo around the organization saying they are now going to be more sustainable, but neither implements the strategy nor achieves the goals. What went wrong?

Putting in place systems and processes related to sustainability within an organization is not always enough. Few managers understand that in order to be successful and really reap the full benefits, they must be committed to mainstreaming sustainability into the values and belief systems already present in the organization. Organizational habits— the way in which people work and make decisions, on a day-to-day basis—must be understood and moulded to accept the necessary changes, move forward and make sustainability goals possible. Sustainability isn't just something you do it is a way of thinking that can be applied to everything you do, a sort of lens through which to see the world in a more environmentally, socially and economically profitable way. If all employees see through this lens then the necessary changes are embraced and new opportunities emerge.

Of course embedding sustainability into the culture of an organization is easier said than done. A company's culture is made up of the values, beliefs, underlying assumptions, attitudes and behaviours shared by a group of people. It is a set of rules that govern how employees work together, some written but mostly unwritten rules. A culture is not just something you create, or that you can simply change. It is formed over time by the people, processes and systems that a company follows, and is a result of taking action and being consistent. Every organization has its own unique culture, so not surprisingly some cultures will make it more challenging to embed sustainability thinking than others.

- *The founder:* The basis of a company's culture is usually formed by the founder of the company and the values that she or he based the company on. If the founder built the company upon values that are intricately linked to sustainability or that support sustainability, it will be easier to embed sustainability into the culture.
- *The CEO:* The individual at the top of the organization has a tremendous influence over how an organization operates. People take action based on her or his words and actions. A consistent message from the

top will help to push change across the company. An inspired leader will play a key role in motivating and inspiring others to action.

- *Management:* A large part of culture is also driven by the managers of a company, what they pay attention to, how they react to situations, how they communicate with others, what they reward and which issues they consistently support.

- *Mission, value statements:* Many organizations have a set of written rules such as mission statements or formal declarations that attempt to explain what the company stands for. It is not enough to just have these, they must really represent what the company is and where it wants to go and be part of the culture. Many companies make changes to these to reflect their focus on sustainability.

- *Codes of conduct:* Codes of conduct throughout the organization guide the behaviour of people by telling them what behaviour is and what is not acceptable in the workplace. These take the form of both written and unwritten codes (i.e. culturally or historically accepted ways of behaving). These should be understood and practiced by the organization.

- *What is rewarded:* How employees are judged, rewarded and the criteria for promotion and firing tells a lot about what is expected of employees and how seriously sustainability is taken by the company.

- *How people interact:* How people interact within the organization. Do they work together, do they share information or is there competition within. Not just those in the company, but the perceptions of potential employees, business partners, customers, etc. that can be even harder to change. How the office space is organized and used can often say a lot about the culture of an organization.

Communicating sustainability internally

Everyone agrees that communication is important. Nevertheless, many companies are not communicating their sustainability strategies effectively to their employees in a way that allows them to become actively engaged and involved.

Different companies have chosen different ways in communicating their sustainability strategies to employees. Shell produced a biodiversity management primer brochure for their employees that brings together the information that employees need to know about the company's position in relation to biodiversity. It explains what biodiversity is, why it is important for the company, what the company's commitments are and, most importantly, what managers at Shell can and should do to manage their impacts and help conserve biodiversity. The CEO of carpet company Interface meets with senior management for one day every year just to discuss sustainability issues. Those senior managers then go on to spend a day talking about these issues to their staff. This continues until all members of staff have been informed.[95]

Communication on sustainability should answer the following three questions:

1. ***Why is sustainability important to the company?*** Why are these issues important to the company? How do they affect the company? Why have leaders of the company chosen to act? Once an individual understands the why, most of the battle is already won.

2. ***What is the company doing about it?*** Information should be given relating to how the company is reacting to this risk or/and opportunity. Is there a new partnership, a new code of conduct, new goal? If an issue is truly important to the company and there is a strong reason why, employees will see that message delivered consistently through the different levels and processes of the company.

3. ***What can employees do?*** Communications should not only be about raising awareness about the direction of a company and the sustainability strategy. A major part of the communication needs to be aimed at how this affects the employee and what their role is in it.

> Institute for Sustainable Communication (www.sustainablecommunication.org/). For more on communicating sustainability externally see the marketing chapter.

Recruiting—who is interviewing whom?

Recruiting is a two way process. A company's engagement in sustainability depends in large part on the kind of people it has working for it. The company needs to adjust recruiting processes to attract employees with the necessary skills. To be competitive in recruiting, companies can no longer ignore sustainability, because graduates and new employees are asking for it and are often pre-assessing the social and environmental performance of companies before choosing an employer. Potential employees are increasingly looking to work for companies that have a good reputation, are ethical, provide a good work environment and share the same beliefs as they do.

When looking at embedding sustainability into your recruitment processes, consider the following:

- *Recruiting strategy:* The first step of HR in supporting the company's sustainability strategy is to align its recruitment strategy with it. This means aligning recruitment processes (including job descriptions) to that sustainability strategy based on identifying the skills, experience, knowledge and aptitudes of potential staff members. A clear strategy makes people want to work for you and ensures that you get very strong applicants who know why they want to work for you.
- *External communication:* Candidates for recruitment should be sent consistent messages about what the company represents through the company website, the recruiting website, and all other recruiting communications. Information on what the company is doing in sustainability should be consistent across all communications and should be easily accessible.
- *The interviewer:* Interviewers should be armed with knowledge about the company's sustainability policies not just so they ask the right questions, but also so they can answer those that interviewees may ask them. If the individual giving the interview cannot answer simple questions made by the interviewee about the company's sustainability direction, then this can send the message that it is not everyone's business, and that the company isn't serious about it.

- *The employment package:* When putting together a package to recruit employees into the company look at all the different elements of that package from pension funds (green of course) to opportunities for employees to take paid or unpaid time off to do community service.

- *Job description:* An individual's job description sets out what they will be expected to do and what their roles and responsibilities are.

- *First messages:* Once you have the right people you need to set their expectation of how things work in the company. If it really is important, these messages will be delivered consistently and from the start. Employees arrive at a company fresh and open to learn, so take the opportunity to inform them as soon as they enter the door. This involves not just training (explained further on) but also the way new employees are introduced to the company. Are office greening projects emphasized during the tour of the buildings and facilities? Are these issues introduced to new employees from day one?

- *Current employee recommendations:* Current and past employees can be very effective ambassadors, spreading the message about what a company stands for to the public, potential customers and also to potential employees. According to a survey by KPMG only 20% of workers who feel that their bosses lack integrity would recommend the workplace to recruits. In comparison, 80% of the respondents who believed their company managers had strong ethics would recommend their organization.

The University of Cambridge Programme for Industry has developed a Competency Map displaying the core competencies required by people to integrate a sustainable development perspective into their work. This includes knowing how to identify and prioritize issues in terms of risks and opportunities, identifying and engaging with stakeholders, and demonstrating personal commitment to the principles and values of sustainable development (www.cpi.cam.ac.uk/pdf/FHR_briefing.pdf).

Employee engagement in sustainability

Organizations are looking for employees that will give 100% to the organization, who will go above and beyond what is expected. Employees are looking to work for companies with a stimulating environment. Employee engagement is when both meet: when an employee is committed to the organization and pushes forward its missions and goals. Engaged workers are much more likely to be committed and productive. Studies done by PwC show that, employees who are more committed to their employer perform 20% better than their peers and are 87% less likely to leave the organization.

However, engagement is an attitude that is nurtured over time. Some of the drivers of engagement include:

- A sense of feeling valued and involved, with the potential to make a positive difference to the company.
- Freedom to voice ideas that managers not only listen to but respond to.
- Opportunities to develop on the job.
- A sense that the leaders of the organization care about the wellbeing of employees and the planet.
- A feeling by employees that they are well-informed about what is happening in their organization.
- The belief that managers and the CEO are walking the talk.

Companies that engage employees on issues of sustainability find the benefits diffused throughout the organizational hierarchy. Involved employees feedback a wide range of knowledge and ideas to management about ways to create strategies to move forward. Employees want to understand the contribution that they can make. There are countless ways to engage employees in your sustainability efforts, in a way that benefits the employees, the company as a whole and often the environment and the community:

- ***In defining the strategy . . .*** IBM's Big Green Innovations programme includes environmentally-focused initiatives focused on advancing water management, alternative energy and carbon management.

The idea came out of the IBM innovation jam in 2006 which involved 150 000 employees blogging for two to three days, and resulted in 30–40 000 new ideas. These were narrowed down to 10 which the company decided to adopt, of which Big Green Innovations was one.

- *In identifying problems . . .* Employees can be useful sensors in identifying problems before they occur. One company has a programme in place that involves all of its employees in identifying health, safety and environmental risks. Every employee is required to report at least one potential environmental hazard into the system each year.

- *In coming up with solutions . . .* Employees are often best placed to identify ways that their jobs could be done better. In order to take advantage of this, many companies have systems in place so that when employees are asked for their ideas and suggestions they can be processed, assessed, acted on and feedback given. The 3M Corporation has been doing this since 1975 when they set up their 3P programme (Pollution Prevention Pays). This programme depends directly on the voluntary participation of 3M employees. Innovative ideas are recognized with 3P Awards. Worldwide employees have completed over 7 400 suggestions through 3P. By the early 2000s they had over $896 million worth of employee-suggested improvements (nearly $92 million in 2008 alone). Projects must meet three criteria:

  - Eliminate or reduce a pollutant.

  - Benefit the environment through reduced energy use or more efficient use of manufacturing materials and resources.

  - Save money – through avoidance or deferral of pollution control equipment costs, reduced operating and materials expenses, or increased sales of an existing or new product.

- *In the local community:* Employees are increasingly asking for opportunities to get involved in the communities in which their businesses are working and are looking to work for companies that provide those opportunities. Employees who are active in community projects through their company are more likely to feel a stronger sense of belonging to the company, increasing employee morale, motivation and commitment. Intel Corporation is an example of a company that embraces the volunteerism philosophy. Among its many programmes, its Intel Involved Program enables employees to volunteer thousands of hours in the communities where they work.

- ***By giving them time to explore these issues:*** Bill Gates in his speech at the Davos Summit in 2008 called on corporations to 'dedicate a percentage of their top innovators' time to issues that could help people left out of the global economy. This kind of contribution is even more powerful than giving cash or offering employees time off to volunteer'. Companies such as 3M and Google dedicate 15–20% of employees' work time to projects of their choosing.

- ***By encouraging healthier lifestyles:*** Wal-Mart's Personal Sustainability Project (PSP) is a voluntary project that helps the company's 1.3 million US employees integrate sustainability into their own lives by making small changes to everyday habits. PSP Captains are trained in each office to educate other employees about the programme. Every employee then chooses a goal to improve their own health and wellness or the health of the planet over the next four to seven weeks to monitor progress. As part of their PSP 18 000 stopped smoking. Dow Chemical's Sustainable Living campaign promotes ways that its 46 000 global employees and their families can reduce energy use and live more sustainably. Unilever's Personal Vitality campaign launched in 2005 is focused on promoting wellbeing of employees in terms of fitness of body, heart, mind and spirit.

> Many companies have employee engagement strategies. Check their websites for more information.

Aligning incentives

Once an overall strategy and direction for the company is decided upon and goals and targets have been set, the next step is to rally the full organization around reaching those goals. Sustainability targets will not be reached simply by telling people that they exist. To be truly effective, incentives need to be put in place to ensure that sustainability targets and goals are met. Rewards should focus on promoting and reinforcing the desired behaviours; they should be promoted within the organization and easily understood by all. Here are some pointers:

- *Be clear on the objective:* Decide what kind of behaviour you want to promote and reinforce and clearly align incentive programmes to reward that behaviour. Objectives need to be inspiring and not be seen as merely an extra burden for employees.
- *Identifying and eliminating de-motivating factors that undermine the achievement of sustainability goals:* If individuals who are in a position to make sustainability changes but do not have sufficient authority or financial and human resources necessary to achieve the sustainability goals.
- *Performance appraisal:* Employees are often given individual and team targets on a yearly basis on which they are appraised at the end of the year. If measurable long-term sustainability goals and targets are important to the organization they should be incorporated into these appraisals and it should be clear that employees will be judged on their success at moving forward in this area. On the other hand, a manager who is compensated for maximizing short-term accounting earnings is less likely to be committed to long-term projects.
- *Promotion and bonus eligibility:* With sustainability tied into job descriptions and performance appraisals, bonuses and promotions can therefore be tied to reaching set sustainability goals. SC Johnson has a company Greenlist that provides environmental ratings for all ingredients used in its products. Annual Greenlist goals are tied to the bonuses of people at officer and management level. Further bonuses are set within the relevant R&D groups and linked to annual merit increases.[96]

Understanding what motivates people is key to providing an incentive structure that will motivate a company's employees to achieve its sustainability goals. Employees are motivated by a wide range of factors, everything from feeling a sense of achievement, advancement and a sense of belonging to something else (e.g. challenge, contribution to society, sense of ownership and involvement in a project, financial rewards, intellectual interest, job security, pride in organization, recognition and respect, responsibility and a sense of wellbeing of the work environment).[97]

Talent development and training

In order to be successful, a company's sustainability strategy must be understood and practiced throughout the organization and not just by a few managers or specialists. Employees need to be given the tools to be able to implement sustainability in their jobs. Therefore, sustainability should be part of the initial training from day one until the day the employee leaves the company. There are different ways to do this:

- *General awareness:* Make sure that there is a common understanding within the organization of what the company sees as sustainability, and what its priorities are. Every individual employee needs to receive basic information about the sustainability strategy, how it affects him or her, and what his or her role is in implementing the strategy.
- *Specific training:* Specific sustainability training should be given to employees when it is relevant to their job function. It should also be embedded into already existing training that is required for specific jobs.

There are several delivery methods for the training:

- *In class training:* These courses should be used to raise the general awareness about these issues as well as provide specific tools and knowledge. One way is to identify key personnel and in a sense 'train the trainers' who will help spread the messages. PWC sent its top 400 employees to a sustainability executive leadership programme.
- *Web based:* Web based training is a simple and cost effective way to get information out to employees. It should not be used as a way of getting key messages across but can be used when they have already bought into the process and need to help develop new skills. Some companies have developed simple online modules that are compulsory for employees to complete, and which allow managers to

track their progress online in order to ensure that their employees are fulfilling these requirements. Companies such as Shell and Dow Chemicals use Chronos, an e-learning tutorial presenting the business case for sustainable development, as pre-work for a range of courses and management training programmes (www.sdchronos.org).

Some elements of sustainability are not easy to learn through web modules or in-class lectures, but need to be experienced in order for the employees to learn both the knowledge and the skills required. These include certain skills that are critical for all aspects of the company including exploring and implementing new ideas, questioning the standard 'business as usual' practices, multidisciplinary thinking, creativity and innovation, leadership and networking to name but a few.

- *Basic Skills:* Marks and Spencer, a British retailer, has been providing free literacy and numeracy classes to workers in their supply chain in Morocco. The factories have rearranged their work schedules to allow the employees to take the three hour classes on the premises. This literacy training programme has involved more than 1000 supply chain workers in Morocco, increasing productivity by 15% as workers read instructions themselves and need less supervision.
- *Secondments:* A growing number of companies send some of their employees to international organizations and NGOs. The individuals learn a set of skills and leadership capabilities and the organization benefits from their application when the employee returns. The WBCSD and its member companies regularly second employees to the IUCN and vice versa.
- *Job rotation:* Some companies aim to integrate sustainability principles into everything they do. After a stint in a sustainability position an employee goes on to a new department where he or she can share the experience and knowledge with a new team in a new work context.
- *Placements:* Top employees at Accenture have the opportunity to work on non-profit consulting projects in developing countries with the Accenture Development Partnership. Employees learn many skills and experiences that are important to them, and also to the company as it looks to expand its services into those regions.

It started off as an activity to recruit and train staff by exposing them to new opportunities and giving them first hand exposure. Today it is part of the strategic direction of the company to provide a new range of services to customers in developing markets.

- **Community engagement:** The prime objective of community involvement has always been and will continue to be to benefit charities and communities. However, increasingly volunteer programmes are proving to be not just good for the communities, but also good for the companies involved. Volunteer opportunities can also develop certain skills for employees including communication, teamwork, managerial, professional and technical skills to name a few.

Often companies will raise the awareness of employees and then wait for miracles to happen. Most employees and in particular managers have a series of big folders sitting in their office shelves from past training sessions that they rarely look at again. Post-training follow up is just as important as the training to support newly trained employees who are motivated to apply their ideas and skills about sustainability to their work. There is no point sending them off to training if there is no way for them to incorporate this new knowledge into their regular jobs.

> A range of NGOs, private businesses and universities offer sustainable business courses at different levels and for different durations. The University of Cambridge for example provides executive sustainability leadership programmes. Consulting firms such as Futureye in Australia and Forum for the Future in the UK also provide training.

Challenges?

- **Raising the importance of HR in general:** Most do not fully understand the crucial role of HR in an organization, let alone the role that HR plays in sustainability. HR is often seen simply as a support function rather than a strategic piece of the puzzle. The fact that titles usually seen around the executive table are CEO, CFO, CIO, COO but typically no CHRO, serves as a reminder that HR is not seen in the same way as other support functions. Things are changing though; for example Boliden, a leading European metals company, appointed an SVP of Human Resources and Sustainability, thereby recognizing the importance of HR, environmental and social matters.

- *Bringing it all together:* Many companies will have many different employee engagement activities happening throughout the organization but not one overarching strategy to bring them all together in a strong, clear, consistent message.

- *Building capacity:* Employees in HR themselves are often not equipped with the skills and tools to play a part in contributing and implementing sustainability strategies. There is the need to build their knowledge as key players in influencing others in the organization. Also leaders must make sure that the organization is ready for the changes and that this isn't seen as adding work to people's jobs.

- *Joint role of management and HR:* HR's role is to implement management decisions and without top management working with HR none of the corporate goals and targets can succeed. Neither can do it without the other but often there is little communication between the two.

- *A question of priorities:* Many companies have examples of HR related sustainability projects diffused throughout the company but lack global structures and strategies.

- *Cost versus asset:* Employee and related programmes are often seen as a cost to be controlled rather than an important asset in an organization. Community engagement programmes, training and personnel development are seen as costs without looking at the benefits to the overall profitability of the organization.

- *Measuring effectiveness as well as efficiency:* HR can play a vital role in measuring the impact that its programmes have and on the state of implementation of the company's sustainability strategy. Often the correlation is difficult to see. A CSR Pilot survey by SHRM in 2007 found that the main reasons for not pursuing different sustainability strategies are costs and unproven benefits. Furthermore less than one half of respondents calculated return on investment for CSR programmes.

* ***Benefits are often intangible:*** A key challenge is that many of the benefits of sustainability practices at an employee level are often difficult to measure. For this reason they are often ignored.

Trends and new ideas

– Sustainability balanced scorecards	– Creating great workplaces
– Diversity	– Changing the way we talk

Sustainability balanced scorecard One of the tools being explored as a means of mainstreaming sustainability issues into appraisal systems is the Sustainability Balanced Scorecard. The balanced scorecard is a tool that is already being used by many companies. According to the Balanced Scorecard Institute it is a performance measurement framework that adds non-financial performance measures to traditional financial metrics to give managers and executives a more 'balanced' view of organizational performance. A sustainability balanced scorecard, as the name suggests, incorporates the sustainability measures and targets of an organization into performance metrics. These new expanded versions are being used to integrate sustainability into operations. For example McDonalds uses a scorecard that links performance indicators to relevant environmental guidelines for suppliers. The scorecard is intended as a tool for suppliers to measure and report upon performance related to a particular guideline (www.cleanerproduction.com/SBS/scorecards.htm).

Diversity In the past companies sought to increase diversity for many reasons, but increasingly there are clearer business reasons for implementing a diversity plan. As companies expand geographically, they will encounter greater diversity of customer base. Having employees from a variety of socio-economic, ethnic, linguistic and religious backgrounds will give companies an edge in predicting and understanding consumer preferences, and allow them to communicate more effectively with their customers. Diversity of educational and skill backgrounds also brings different ways of viewing and solving problems to an organization. Look at the innovative work being done through the biomimicry movement (see operations chapter) where biologists are sitting at the table with business to find profitable business solutions inspired by nature. Investors say that the strength of some companies is their cultural diversity. Schlumberger is a leading service company in the Oil and Gas sector operating in over 80 countries. It employs over 80 000 employees from more than 100 countries, and investment companies consider one of its major competitive advantages to be the diversity of its international workforce.

Diversity also means thinking outside the box when hiring. In 1989 B&Q, a UK hardware store, opened a store entirely staffed by workers over the age of 50 as an attempt to tackle the problem of high average annual staff turnover. There were 7000 applications for 55 jobs. The store was a success; staff turnover was reduced by about 80%, absenteeism 33% lower, profitability 18% higher, stock leakage was cut by more than half while productivity and costs remained the same compared to similar stores. Today 25% of its 35 000 workforce is aged 50 or over (in 2006 the oldest employee was 92 and 20% of employees were under the age of 24). This policy is based on the belief that its customers, stores and offices benefit from new ideas and expertise from a mix of both younger and older employees.[98]

Creating great workplaces Creating a work environment where employees can succeed goes beyond upholding basic labour standards. It is about creating an environment where innovation is both encouraged and expected. It is about creating a work environment that people want to be in.

Good places to work tend to receive more qualified job applications, have lower levels of turnover, higher levels of customer satisfaction, greater creativity and innovation, and benefit from higher productivity and profitability. The publicly traded companies on the list consistently outperform the S&P 500 by a wide margin.[99] According to the Great Place to Work Institute, the quality of a great workplace is measured by three interconnected relationships; the relationship between employees and management, between employees and their jobs/company and the relationship between employees and other employees. Some things that can make a great place to work include:

- *Work environment:* noise, lighting, colour, safety and food.
- *Flexibility:* job sharing, sabbaticals, telecommuting, flexible working hours.
- *Work-family benefits:* domestic partner benefits, adoption assistance, eldercare services, childcare services.
- *Work/Life Balance:* gym memberships, professional training or educational support, medical checkups, language courses, resting rooms, washers and dryers.
- *Profit sharing:* Companies are finding more ways to share their profits with employees through programmes such as stock options and deferred profit sharing.
- *Unusual:* scuba diving certification, relaxation rooms, dance classes, you name it, some company is trying it.

Changing the way we talk If you want to change the way your organization approaches sustainability, it may be as simple as

Many organizations around the world release lists of the best places to work yearly. Fortune 100 Best Companies to Work for (money.cnn.com/magazines/fortune/bestcompanies) and 'World's Most Admired Companies' (money.cnn.com/magazines/fortune/mostadmired). The Great Places to Work Institute (www.greatplacetowork.com). See *Greening the Office* for more on creating a better, greener work environment.

changing the way that you talk and the language that you use. Changing the kind of language you use to refer to sustainability can raise awareness about the issues and get people excited about it. For example:

- Moving away from blaming and complaining to taking responsibility and doing something.
- Moving away from vague, dull terminology to words that are clear and that inspire.
- Moving away from making people feel guilty to inspiring people to get involved.
- Moving away from wishes and hopes to making strong commitments to action.
- Moving away from ignoring to getting informed.
- Moving away from seeing all the reasons why not to looking at all the reasons it could.
- Moving away from seeing it as a problem, a risk or a cost to seeing it as an opportunity.
- Moving away from it being someone else's responsibility to taking responsibility.
- Moving away from you the individual to us the team, the organization, the community, the country, the planet.
- Moving away from being told or telling people what to do to working together to determine what needs to be done.
- Moving away from one time events to continuous progress.
- Moving away from boring to fun.
- Moving away from saving the planet to language that speaks more to individuals and business.

For some interesting insights into language and how we use it read *Seven Languages for Transformation: How the way we talk can change the way we work* by Robert Kegan and Lisa Laskow Lahey 2001.

What you can do . . .

- ❏ Get rid of unsustainable rules: Keep a look out for rules in your organization that limit you from exploring and putting in place more sustainable options.
- ❏ Get involved in activities organized by your company: Many companies have events organized to get employees involved in sustainability either within the company or in the community. Get involved in these activities. If there are none that interest you, organize one.
- ❏ Identify the sustainability change agents: Identify those people who influence others, who can get things done, and give them the tools and space to do it.
- ❏ Have a job review session: Spend some time with your team, your boss, to evaluate how sustainability could be incorporated into your current job description.
- ❏ Employees benefiting from sustainability success: Sustainability suggestions from employees are saving some companies a lot of money. Why not tie some of the savings from employee suggestions or overall sustainability programmes back to the employees? Some companies are starting to explore this. At KPMG UK, 50% of the savings made through responsible consumption programmes have been donated to staff-selected charities, over £ 340 000 since 2004.[100]

Want more?

World Business Council for Sustainable Development has published an introductory Guide on Human Resources and Sustainable Development (www.wbcsd.org).

Read: *Leading Change Towards Sustainability* by Bob Doppelt (2003), a change management guide for business, government and civil society. *Organizational Change for corporate Sustainability* by Dexter Dunphy (2003) is a practical guide for students and practitioners for change agents in bringing about sustainability in a systematic way. *Get them on your Side* by Samuel Bacharach (2005) looks at how to overcome resistance in the workforce.

Managing change

Sustainability, no matter what you are trying to do, all comes down to change: changing the way something works, the way that people think, the way that people act, behaviours, assumptions, etc. However, some 50–70% of all major programmes of change fail to meet their objectives, including many change programmes relating to sustainability. So, understanding and taking change seriously is key to sustainability.

There are many reasons why initiatives fail but ultimately change programmes often do because they fail to engage the very people they are trying to change including the underlying thought patterns, outlooks and behaviours of employees. Whether change is a major one (like a merger) or a minor one (like a recycling programme) here are some tips:

- *Get to the root cause of the problem:* Be clear of what you are trying to change and why. Change the right things for the right reasons. Focus on the causes not the symptoms.
- *Create a vision:* Know where you want to go. Set audacious targets that inspire debate and that unite people. Be flexible.
- *Gather information:* Take time to observe how people do their jobs every day. Ask people how they think things should change. Understand what makes people tick and why people might resist change.
- *Get support:* Unless the change process is coming from and supported from upper management it will go nowhere. Identify those who support and those who do not support the change. Build a coalition of people who will help bring about the change. Understand the nature and culture of the organization, the relationship networks.

Understand who the key people in your organization are that can influence the desired outcome.

- *Create ownership:* Involve people in creating the vision and the plan. If they feel they are part of the change they are more likely to implement the change.
- *Identify change champions:* Identify and train key people that are aware, motivated and seeking to take action to act as champions and be a point of communication and motivation in the group.
- *Empower people:* Survey after survey show that people are interested in these issues but there is a gap between interest and action. This is in part because of information overload. Make the change relevant to people and their job. Give them the knowledge, tools and opportunities.
- *Take different approaches:* Recognize that behaviour change does not take place in the same way for all people and that different people may be at different points along the change curve (awareness, motivation, action).
- *Recognize people's emotional response to change:* Ignorance (not knowing), shock (the first response), denial (pretending it isn't important or true), anger (blaming yourself or others), depression (feeling as if nothing I do can make a difference), resignation (letting go of old ways), exploration (explore benefits of change), integration (taking ownership of the change).
- *Lead by example:* Ensure that senior managers are leading by example. Employees will have a hard time changing their behaviour if they do not see those above them doing so.
- *Manage expectations:* Don't get employees too excited about sustainability and then not deliver – focus on keeping energy levels up, but not so high that they will tire people.
- *Choose your fights wisely:* You will not be able to change everything, or everyone.
- *Communication:* Focus your messages. Be clear and consistent. Use stories and best practice. Be honest.
- *Create a sense of urgency:* Change does not necessarily fail because of resistance, rather because of inertia within the organization. Creating a sense of urgency can provide that push for an organization to really get on top of things.

(continued)

- *Be patient:* Often there is a delayed response to changes in an organization.
- *Celebrate wins and learn from failures:* Failure allows you a chance to understand where you went wrong and to learn from your mistakes. Celebrate wins to keep momentum and positive energy levels up.
- *Institutionalizing new approaches:* Change should become a part of the way people operate.
- *Just get started:* Don't worry about all the details before getting started, just get started. Having pilot projects can be a good way to learn lessons and test out approaches.
- *Keep it light:* People find change hard enough as it is so make it as easy as possible for them. Don't use guilt or make people feel like it is going to increase their workload.

We tend to remember 10% of what we read, 20% of what we hear, 30% of what we see, 50% of what we read, hear and see, 70% of what we say, 90% of what we both say and do.

14 Strategy

'The fact is, the prevailing approaches to CSR are so fragmented and so disconnected from business and strategy as to obscure many of the greatest opportunities for companies to benefit society. If, instead, corporations were to analyze their prospects for social responsibility using the same frameworks that guide their core business choices, they would discover that CSR can be much more than a cost, a constraint, or a charitable deed—it can be a source of opportunity, innovation, and competitive advantage.'

MICHAEL PORTER

Until recently the management of social and environmental issues was largely driven by external factors and the response by business mostly tactical and communications driven. Today these issues have ascended to the corporate agenda as issues that are becoming increasingly 'real'. With this increased awareness and acceptance is coming a slow, but necessary shift to mainstream these issues into the overall strategy of a company.

If sustainability is a puzzle, strategy is the centrepiece which keeps everything together. Incorporating sustainability into strategy not only shows that a company is taking these issues seriously, more importantly it ensures a real organized effort rather than small, unconnected activities. It inspires employees and mobilizes the whole company and often its supply chain, towards common goals that benefit both the company and society at large. The goal: that sustainability is so integrated it becomes hard to distinguish from the day-to-day business of the company.

Why is it important?

- *Take full advantage of opportunities:* Partial or bolt-on approaches don't work. Although individual projects across the organization can have limited success, an organization will not truly see the benefits of sustainability unless it is integrated into a company's strategy at all levels.
- *Mobilize the whole company:* A strong, clear and inspiring sustainability strategy can guide the actions of employees and get them motivated and excited. A company can better understand its business and maximize the indirect benefits which a coordinated approach to sustainability can bring.
- *Stakeholders are asking for it:* Stakeholders, shareholders, regulators, customers, employees and business partners are increasingly expecting companies to explore these issues and can tell the difference between a company that takes these issues seriously and one that does not.
- *Risk is changing:* Business is being confronted with an increasing variety and number of risks. A business's ability to achieve its objectives depends on being able to recognize and deal with these. Recognize that not all risk is downside, and that some risks also present opportunities.
- *No longer just for 'high risk' companies:* Sustainability has moved beyond being an issue just for companies in sectors like oil and gas, who have an obvious impact on the environment and society. Today, companies in virtually all industries are affected by sustainability issues.
- *Differentiation:* In today's business reality you can't just do what everyone else is doing, you need to be different, unique. In addition, companies can shape their industries. There is a lot of room for

companies to become leaders locally, nationally, regionally and internationally in these issues.

> *'You can't be remarkable by following someone else who's remarkable...The thing that all great companies have in common is that they have nothing in common'*
>
> SETH GODIN, AUTHOR

The key concepts

Embedding sustainability into a company's strategy involves developing an understanding for what the issues are, and how they are and will affect the business and its ability to continue to do business in the future.

- Understand the wider business context you are working in → ***The wider business environment***
- Understand how sustainability affects your industry → ***Understanding where you stand***
- Understanding the sources and magnitude of risks → ***Understanding risks***
- Exploring a wide range of sustainability strategic options → ***Sustainability strategies***
- Setting the direction for the company → ***Goals and targets***
- Working and learning from others → ***Working with others***
- Companies active in influencing wider change → ***Influencing change***
- Getting things right the first time → ***Box: Why initiatives fail***
- Identifying and involving stakeholders in strategic decisions → ***Box: Stakeholder engagement***

Understanding the wider business environment

An organization needs to understand the broader environment in which it operates and how this environment can and will affect their operations. Several tools already used by managers are being expanded to include relevant sustainability issues. These tools are being used not just to see the big picture, but also to explore what the future may bring and how this may affect the way they do business. Based on this information, an organization can decide whether they are interested in just keeping up with the change, or playing a key role in shaping their industry.

ESTMPLE: PEST (political, economic, social and technological trends) is a process technique that outlines how forces in the larger business environment will change over time. This process has been expanded further to include other trends.[101]

- *Economic:* Health and direction of the economy (or economies) in which the firm competes. Variables include GDP levels, inflation, interest rates, money supply, unemployment and disposable income.
- *Social:* This can include demographic variables such as population size, age structure, geographic distribution, ethnic mix, income distribution as well as tastes, fashions, attitudes and values.
- *Technological:* This can include understanding current technologies (e.g. products, processes, materials, etc.), as well as emerging or undeveloped technologies.
- *Ecological:* This can include concerns for sustainability of the physical environment, greenhouse gases, waste disposal, environmental policies and energy consumption.
- *Media:* The increasingly important influence of media on business, politics and society, as an opinion former and shaper and its power to affect outcomes.
- *Political:* This can include government stability, alignment at the international level, taxation and fiscal policy, foreign trade regulation, social welfare policies.
- *Legal:* This can include employment law, health and safety and product safety.

- *Ethical:* This includes the rising number of codes affecting the ways a business should operate, which increasingly have a financial impact on the company's performance.

Sources of info for ESTEMPLE include Economist Intelligence Unit (www.eiu.com), World Bank (www.worldbank.org) and Business Environment Risk Intelligence (www.beri.com). International Futures is an integrated global modelling system which represents demographic, economic, energy, agricultural, socio-political and environmental subsystems for 183 countries. (ifsmodel.org). Gapminder provides time series of development statistics for all countries (www.gapminder.org). World Values Survey is a world-wide network of social scientists studying changing values and their impact on social and political life (www.worldvaluessurvey.org).

Understanding where you stand

A range of widely used management tools can be applied to help guide your thinking on sustainability, whether it be for a whole company or for a particular activity. 'Five forces' is a tool widely taught in MBA courses used to analyse the competitive forces that shape an industry and that can influence business profitability. The five elements it considers are:

- *How hard is it for new companies to enter this industry?* The threat of new entrants is usually based on the entry barriers for that market, or in other words, when it is too time consuming or expensive to enter easily. This can include, for example, patents for green technology. While usually new entrants to a market are considered a threat, some-times this can turn out to be a good thing. For example when Clorox entered the green cleaning product market with green works, rather than taking away market share from other smaller brands such as Seventh Generation, it actually played a role in growing the overall market.
- *Threat of substitute products or services:* As with competitors, today new innovative products and services are not just affecting their own sectors, but can also have a huge impact across sectors.

New forms of service delivery are bringing in greater profits while also enabling companies to build customer loyalty and long-term competitive advantage. Many consumers, as introduced in the marketing chapter, are looking to switch to more sustainable options once they become available.

- ***Rivalry among established firms:*** Who are the existing competitors in the industry and what is the level of competition? In the past new innovations and companies usually only affected specific sectors, however, today innovations in sustainability are impacting across sectors regardless of the size, or location of the company. Many companies are choosing to work together to further sustainability issues, for example through initiatives such as the Sustainable Agriculture initiative or different labelling schemes.

- ***The power of buyers:*** Who is buying the industry's products and how easy is it to negotiate with them? Many organizations that have made a commitment to sustainability are now also looking at the products and services they are buying. One example is The Warehouse, New Zealand's largest mixed retailer, who in 1999 declared a national corporate goal of zero waste. In order to reach this goal, the companies it buys from, its suppliers, have been given radical packaging reduction targets.

- ***The power of suppliers:*** Who supplies the industry's inputs and how hard is it to negotiate with them? This includes raw materials, labour and expertise. For example some suppliers of green products and services charge a premium for the products, not just because of higher costs associated with them, but also because there is a higher demand for these products, but not a lot of suppliers offering them.

SWOT is another strategic planning tool used to evaluate the strengths, weaknesses, opportunities, and threats involved in a project or in a business venture. It is also used once objectives have been identified to help in pursuing that objective. For example, a SWOT analysis conducted on labour issues within the supply chain of a company could look like this:

- ***Strengths:*** These are attributes of the organization that help in achieving the objective. For example the company has partnerships with some NGOs who specialize in this area. Some of their suppliers are certified.

- **Weaknesses:** These are attributes of the organization that are harmful to achieving the objective. For example, the labour practices of some of the company's suppliers are not known and could be very bad.
- **Opportunities:** These are external conditions that are helpful to achieving the objective. The company could have access to new customers if all of their suppliers meet minimum or high labour standards. Suppliers themselves will also benefit as higher labour standards can create a more stable and productive workforce.
- **Threats:** These are external conditions that are harmful to achieving the objective. Poor labour standards could become known by the media or stakeholders and have a serious effect on our reputation and our ability to keep customers.

Understanding risk

According to the WBCSD, 'The challenge for the corporate sector is to understand how different sources and magnitude of risk are likely to affect them over the long term. In order to gain that understanding, companies need to take a genuinely holistic approach that includes a consideration of sustainability as well as commercial political, and societal risks'.

A business's ability to achieve its objectives depends on it being able to recognize and deal with risks. Not managing these risks properly can have a major impact on business reputation and also on financial performance, as many so called non financial risks can rapidly become material. Business is being confronted with an increasing variety and number of risks relating to sustainability. Global population increases are leading to increased demand, and scarcity of necessities like clean water. With increased interconnectedness related to growing population densities comes greater levels of international trade and significantly improved information sharing across the globe. Increased globalization of markets has led to increased complexity in the way business operates. A threat may build slowly from a number of small events, but one of those events can be the catalyst that sets off an uncontrollable reaction. A relatively minor incident in one country can have a bigger impact elsewhere.[102]

The WBCSD in its publication 'Running the Risk, Risk and Sustainable Development: a business perspective' identified a list of mega-risks, part of the ever increasing variety of risks that companies are confronted with, that present unprecedented challenges to companies and governments alike. These include:

- **Energy and climate:** The environmental impacts of rising energy production and consumption are introducing uncertainties to industries, such as oil and gas, reinsurance and agriculture.
- **Demography:** As the population continues to grow, population dynamics are at the root of almost every trend shaping tomorrow's business climate.
- **Intangibles:** The value of corporations is increasingly made up, not of tangible assets such as property and land, but intangible assets such as reputation, brand, trust and credibility, up to 75 %.
- **Globalization:** Globalization is creating increasing interdependence, making it all the easier for dangerous viruses, pollutants and technical failures to spread. The legal framework in which companies do business remains local even though the world has 'gone global'.
- **Political risk and terrorism:** Political risk is by no means a new threat, but changing political realities have amplified its magnitude and thereby its capability to disrupt critical systems.
- **Ecological risk:** The world economy depends on a base of natural resources that is showing signs of severe degradation. Without improved environmental performance, future business operations will be exposed to additional risks such as rising prices for water, materials and for waste disposal.
- **Litigation risk:** There has been an exponential increase in society's willingness to get involved in litigation, primarily driven from the US.

- *Infrastructure and security:* Health services, transport, energy, food and water supplies, information and telecommunications are examples of sectors with vital systems that can be severely damaged by a single catastrophic event or chain of events.
- *Pandemic and /health risks:* Despite a century of rapid progress in improving human health, many people still do not have access to basic healthcare or hygiene to protect them from infectious agents in the environment, and many new and serious risks continue to grow.
- *Innovation and technology:* New technologies offer substantial benefits, but are seldom risk-free. In some cases the risks are not always obvious at the time of introducing a new technology, for example with freons and the ozone hole.

For business, these mega risks translate into:

- *Market risks:* such as regulatory bans, reduced market demand for products, degradation of product quality by environmental factors, customer boycotts.
- *Balance-sheet risks:* such as remediation liabilities, insurance underwriting losses, impairment of real property values, damage assessments, toxic torts.
- *Operating risks:* such as costs of cleaning up spills and accidents, risks to workers, safety from handling hazardous materials, rise in prices of material and energy.
- *Capital cost risks:* such as product redesign to meet new industry standards or regulations, costly input substitutions to meet new industry standards or regulations.
- *Sustainability risks:* such as competitive disadvantage from energy or material inefficiencies, impact of mandatory take back rules, future taxes and regulatory restrictions.[103]
- *Legal risks:* such as companies being held responsible for actions that were legal at the time but later determined to be harmful.
- *Liabilities risks:* such as penalties and fines, higher insurance premiums, product liability costs, site remediation costs.
- *Reputation risks:* such as attacks on your image, bad-mouthing of your product, boycotts.

Running the Risk, Risk and Sustainable Development: a business perspective World Business Council for Sustainable Development (www.wbcsd.org). A Sustainability Lens for Capital Decisions, A Corporate Sustainability Approach to Reduce Business Risk, EXCEL Partnership A Guide to Risk Assessment and Risk Management for Environmental Protection (www.defra.gov.uk/environment/risk/eramguide). Environmental Risk Assessment—Approaches, Experiences and Information Sources (reports.eea.europa.eu). CSFI and PwC 'Banking Banana Skins' reports on top 30 risks financial institutions face. (www.pwc.com).

For many, sustainability begins as an exercise in identifying and mitigating risks to the business. Risk is often defined as those things that stop or limit a company from achieving its objectives. However, this is only half the story. As the WBCSD puts it, 'the traditional approach to risk has been fragmented, largely reactive and focused on the short term. Because risk is multi-dimensional managers tend to associate it with loss, rather than weighing up the downsides against the upsides.' It is crucial for companies to understand the risks posed by sustainability issues and decisions facing an organization, where they are coming from and how to mitigate them. It is also important that companies go beyond just identifying risks to also exploring the opportunity presented by taking risks, for example in terms of new products and services.

Exploring different strategies

Companies have taken a wide range of different approaches when it comes to their sustainability strategies. Some companies take a whole company approach while others approach it separately. Some examples include:

- *Sustainability at the heart of how a company does business:* For some companies, sustainability is an integral part of how the company chooses to do business and is at the core of their business model from the start. Ben and Jerry's ice cream company is focused on making business decisions based on their values, as well as the power of their business to change the world for the better. They have been making all natural ice cream since 1978 and are focused on what they call 'Values-Led Sourcing', supporting suppliers who are also trying to make the world a better place with, for example, fair trade chocolate, cage free eggs, and strawberries from leading edge sustainable agricultural practices.

- *Companies who have re-invented themselves through sustainability:* Other companies such as Interface carpet manufacturer did not start out as being focused on sustainability. The founder became committed to industrial ecology after reading Paul Hawken's *The Ecology of Commerce* in 1994. Their vision today: To be the first company that, by its deeds, shows the entire industrial world what sustainability is in all its dimensions: people, process, product, place and profits, by 2020, and in doing so will become restorative through the power of influence. They aim to do this through a whole company approach, integrating sustainability into everything they do. Based on its experiences over the past 14 years in this area, the company now provides peer-to-peer advisory service for business through InterfaceRAISE.

- *Staying ahead of the pack:* While some companies start with a focus on values and doing the right thing, others quickly identify the incredible range of business opportunities sustainability can present. The CEO of GE recognized this in 2004 and launched 'ecomagination' in 2005, a business initiative to help meet customers' demand for more energy-efficient products and to drive reliable growth for GE. 'While we had investigated other corporate socio-environmental programs, we knew they didn't make cultural sense for GE. Metrics and accountability are major reasons why GE continues to flourish after 130 years, and the building blocks for the initiative could be no different . . . Simply put: ecomagination had to make money for our investors'. Since then the company has increased its ecomagination portfolio from 17 to 60 products and ecomagination is mainstreamed across the business. In 2007 revenue for these products reached $ 14 billion, and GE raised its annual revenue target for this product line in 2010 from $ 20 billion to $ 25 billion.[104]

- *Companies testing out the success of sustainability brands:* These are companies that do not necessarily have a sustainability strategy, but are experimenting with sustainability through acquisitions or new product lines. This is done either to try new things out before committing the whole organization, or sometimes just as an 'add on' that has no impact on the company as a whole. Clorox, a company known for its bleach and other cleaning products moved into the area of sustainability with the acquisition of natural personal care company Burt's Bees. Burt's Bees, a leader in the field of business and sustainability, chose Clorox because they found a partner with a shared vision who allows them to continue to work independently. They will be part of the Clorox platform for the next 100 years, and Burt's Bees provides a business model for Clorox to learn from.

- *Companies adopting different shades of sustainability:* Many leaders in this area have not changed what they do; they are now using sustainability as a tool to do it better. Sustainability is an extension of what the company already does. Companies such as IKEA and Marks and Spencer haven't necessarily changed their products, but they have changed how those products are sourced, the ingredients, their packaging, etc.

- *Companies expanding their focus:* Some companies are adopting sustainability practices by expanding the range of products and services they provide as a response to increasing and changing consumer demands. Several traditional oil and gas companies such as BP and Shell have expanded the focus of their operations to include new forms of renewable energy such as wind, solar and biofuels.

> There are a growing number of companies around the world that have a sustainability story to tell. Pick the companies you buy from and look at their websites and annual reports to see what they are doing.

Setting objectives and goals

Companies that are taking sustainability seriously are setting goals and objectives to guide their actions. Having a clear set of goals focuses the organization in a common direction. More importantly perhaps, having clear and inspiring goals will motivate employees. Goals should:

- *Be clear:* Goals should be clearly understood. Have objectives framed so that all members of the team know whether or not they have been achieved. There should not be so many that they are difficult to follow.
- *Be credible:* Goals should be realistic and believable. They should be put in place for the short, medium and long-term and you should show the steps needed to reach those goals. In addition, don't have too many. Be absolutely certain that your organization can and will live up to the standards you set.
- *Be consistent:* Goals should be visibly supported by management and be incorporated into the way employees are rewarded. They should be used in making business decisions and should not contradict with goals that teams already have.
- *Be challenging:* Have elevating objectives that are personally challenging, inspiring and important. Sometimes more progressive goals are easier to reach than smaller ones. Clothing manufacturer Patagonia is working to meet its goal of recycling 100 % of its products by 2010 through its Common Threads Garment Recycling Program where customers can return used clothing which is then turned into new products.
- *Be communicated:* Systems should be in place to actually collect, compile and report on these goals. Progress towards goals should be reported on frequently, internally and where relevant, externally.
- *Be celebrated:* Build enthusiasm for goals and celebrate reaching those goals.
- *Be continuously evolving:* Goals should be revaluated on a regular basis. P&G provides information on their sustainability goals for 2012 along with the progress that has been made. In early 2009 they

announced significantly increased targets for 2012 reflecting the company's continued commitment and progress in sustainability.

- *Be catchy:* Package your goals in a story that it is easy to remember and which inspires employees and stakeholders. Herman Miller's 'Perfect Vision' initiative is a strategy to achieve a wide range of corporate sustainability targets including zero waste to landfills, zero hazardous waste generation and a carbon neutral operational footprint by the year 2020.

Companies aren't just creating goals, in many cases they are choosing to make these public and once they go public there is no turning back. The Clinton Global Initiative, for example, is an initiative which is focused on turning ideas into action. Through its 'Commitments to Action' initiative, members translate practical goals into meaningful and measurable results aimed at addressing global challenges (www.clintonglobalinitiative.org).

> See the accounting section for more on indicators. To see different companies goals look at their sustainability reports or annual reports and websites.

Working with others

In the area of sustainability, no company is expected to figure it all out alone. Businesses are coming together in networks at the local, national and international level to share best practices and lessons learnt, to create minimum standards and to push the agenda forward. It seems that everyday there is a new network which brings business together to work on common projects. Joining a network can provide many benefits:

- *Working with like-minded companies:* The opportunity to work with like-minded companies within the same industry or across industries. It allows individuals from the business to network and collaborate with others on the issues that are important to their business.
- *Provides tools and resources:* Networks often develop their own resources with the help of member companies and provide a space

for organizations to share their own research. Networks provide a platform to share best practices, challenges, guidance and seek advice.

- ***Being part of a bigger change:*** Working with other organizations who have similar goals and are working on similar issues to you provides the opportunity to be part of a bigger change and help to move the larger sustainability agenda forward.

With so many options, how can an organization choose which groups to work with? Here are some things to look at:

- ***What themes or issues do they cover?*** Networks will either pick a few issues and focus exclusively on those or, in some cases, operate at a much broader level and explore the issues that are important to their members. The Rainforest Alliance works to conserve biodiversity and ensure sustainable livelihoods by transforming land-use practices, business practices and consumer behaviour. They work with many companies and organizations around the world on sustainable agriculture and forestry (www.rainforest-alliance.org).

- ***Who coordinates them?*** Networks can be coordinated by any number of groups, for example government, NGOs, the UN or businesses themselves. Most organizations are already part of a professional or local network of some sort. Many of these networks have started to work on sustainability and provide resources for their members. For example, the national and international professional accounting bodies such as the IFAC and ACCA are working on sustainability issues now.

- ***Where do they operate?*** There are networks operating at local, national, regional and international levels. Some groups operate at a national or local level but are themselves part of a larger, sometimes international network. The WBCSD is a global network of companies committed to improving the long-term 'sustainability' of their own operations. The network brings together over 200 international companies from more than 35 countries and 20 major industrial sectors with a shared commitment to sustainable development. The Council also benefits from a global network of more than 55 national and regional business councils and partners (www.wbcsd.org).

- ***Who are they aimed at?*** Is the network aimed at organizations working in a particular sector or is it aimed at businesses at a broader level? Is it mainly for large companies or for small ones or both? Who are the other members? Is this a group of organizations you are interested in working with? ICLEI is a network for local governments around the world working on sustainability issues. Over 1071 cities, towns, counties are members (www.iclei.org).

- ***How do they work in practice?*** Being part of a network takes time and resources from a company therefore the decision to join should be taken seriously. Different networks will require different commitments from members; signing onto a code of conduct and upholding certain minimum standards, some have mandatory sustainability reporting requirements. The Sustainable Business Network in New Zealand has a membership fee structure based on the turnover of the company so that small companies pay smaller membership fees (www.sustainable.org.nz).

IKEA recognizes that by co-operating with companies, trade unions and organizations, they are able to learn, share experiences and accomplish more than they could have done by working on their own. Cotton is one of the most important raw materials for the company, however conventional cotton growing and processing consumes large amounts of water and chemicals. In order to help guide their strategy they have chosen to work with different networks.

- Work with WWF focuses on better management practices in India and Pakistan, environmental practices that enable farmers to reduce environmental impact, improve e-efficiency, maintain crop yields and increase their gross margins (www.panda.org search IKEA).
- Work with the Better Cotton Initiative aims to promote measurable improvements in the key environmental and social impacts of cotton cultivation worldwide to make it more sustainable (www. bettercotton.org).
- Work with UNICEF aims to prevent young girls from working on cotton seed farms in southern India and instead make sure these children gain access to quality education.

IKEA also provides, as do many other companies, a list of the organizations they work with in their annual reports.

> The Partnership Initiative has several resources including a Communication Manual for partnership practitioners and a Partnering Toolbook (thepartneringinitiative.org). The UN Global Compact website has a whole section on partnerships (www.unglobalcompact.org/Issues/partnerships) including a Partnership Assessment Tool. Guide to Successful Corporate–NGO Partnerships by GEMI and Environmental Defence Fund (www.gemi.org/resources/GEMI-EDF%20Guide.pdf) for many examples of best practice.

Influencing change

One of the most important roles that a company can have in society is influencing and driving change at the highest level. Much of the emphasis when it comes to sustainability has been focused on a company's own direct impacts, things like tonnes of emissions or the amount of raw material used. However, increasingly there is a much wider recognition of the influence companies have and could have on other parts of the business environment, the way they and their peers will do business in the future. Although traditionally companies have pushed for less regulation, there are a growing number that are pushing for tougher regulation. Companies are recognizing that if they invest the time and resources in becoming more sustainable and being beyond compliant, then they can benefit from this and also stay ahead of their competition when the standards are raised. There are countless ways that companies can influence larger changes:

- **Creating an even playing field:** According to personal care company Burt's Bees in the US, '78% of people think that natural personal care products are regulated—97% of people think they should be ... the fact is, it's not'. The company pushed efforts for a clearer definition of what 'natural' is, and is not, in the US market. The result was the Natural Standard for Personal Care Products launched on 1st May 2008, which required products labelled or branded as 'natural' to be made of at least 95 % all-natural ingredients and contain only those synthetic ingredients allowed under the standard. Prior to this, companies could label a product as 'natural' when they had as little as 1 % natural ingredients. This helps Burt's Bees as over half of their products are 100 % natural and they are working on the rest.

- **Companies influencing other companies:** Companies are not only using their influence to bring about change at a policy level, but also in other companies. In 2007 the Aspen Ski Company removed Kimberly-Clark Products from all of its facilities. It even renamed one of its ski runs, which for over 40 years had been called 'Kleenex Corner'. According to Matthew Hamilton, the manager of Community and Environmental Responsibility at the resort, 'We will not consider using any Kimberly-Clark products until the company has committed to not source from endangered forests, dramatically increase its use of recycled fibre, and source from certified sustainable logging operations'. As a result, they have been able to enter into an environmental dialogue with a company 160 times its size.[105]

- **Companies influencing decisions made by government by lobbying:** The Mary Kay cosmetic company which has always focused on giving women the chance to succeed, took their founders passion one step further to try and stem violence against women. The company actively lobbied the US government to reauthorize the Violence Against Women Act, and the saleswomen from the company spoke to legislators about the importance of renewing it. In 2006 they succeeded, as the act was reauthorized into law. Levi relies on Guatemala for materials, so when the US government in 2001 was looking at whether Guatemala should continue to enjoy duty free exporting to the US, they found that they had not adequately enforced labour laws. So instead of lobbying the US government, Levi went to Guatemala to lobby the Guatemalan government to strengthen labour laws.[106]

Views on lobbying relating to government are mixed. Some say companies need to take an active role in pushing sustainability while others argue that because of their power, they can push for changes that may not be in the best interests of society as a whole. There are a few challenges. First, corporate lobbying is often not aligned with sustainability policies, and in some cases can even be against those policies and positions. Second, although some companies do the lobbying themselves, others are taking part in lobbying through other means, such as by funding other groups who do the lobbying for them (in some cases NGOs) or by being members of groups who are lobbying on different issues. Third, because there is a relative lack of transparency about a company's lobbying efforts, it is very difficult to know what they are actually lobbying for. Some countries do require companies to disclose certain information about lobbying, however, this rarely includes the positions they are lobbying about, but rather just the amount of money being put into lobbying and these regulations are often poorly regulated.

'Influencing Power: Reviewing the conduct and content of corporate lobbying' by SustainAbility and the WWF outlines the results of a research project which reviews how 100 of the world's largest companies report on their lobbying practices in order to assess corporate transparency (www.sustainability.com). Worst EU Lobbying Awards are organized by several EU NGOs with the aim to discourage controversial lobbying practices by exposing them to the public (www.worstlobby.eu). The Alliance for Lobbying Transparency and Ethics Regulations in the EU is a group of 160 civil society groups concerned with the increasing influence exerted by corporate lobbyists (www.alter-eu.org).

There is also some work starting to happen on the voluntary front. The Global Reporting initiative has two reporting indicators on lobbying that reporting organizations are asked to report on: S05 public policy positions and participation in public policy development and lobbying; and S06 total value of financial ad in-kind contributions to political parties, politicians and related institutions by country. GlaxoKleinSmith, for example, in their annual report lists all the trade associations they are part of, what other groups they are working with and what their positions are.

Challenges?

- *Bringing it all together:* Many companies work on lots of initiatives independently across the company, but will increasingly need to bring these together into a more coordinated effort in order to maximize the benefits.

- *Taking it beyond the specialists:* Sustainability is not just the job of people with the word in their job title. A sustainability strategy is not much use if employees themselves who want to get engaged have no role to play in it.

- *Having a clear message:* More often than not, employees seem unaware of the strategic directions and priorities that their company has put in place. The goal is not only to communicate the strategy clearly, but also to get people involved and excited about carrying it out.

- *Understanding the risks:* Pursuing sustainability strategies can also bring with it certain risks. If sustainability isn't taken seriously within the organization it can be viewed as greenwashing. It can also raise unrealistic expectations by stakeholders.

- *No one size fits all:* Many organizations are looking for a standard that specifically outlines what a green company looks like in the same way that the LEED certification outlines what a green building looks like. Companies need to determine the strategy that works best for them, as no one strategy will work for all.

- *Silo thinking:* For some businesses the challenge is to not focus too much on one issue without putting in the time to properly explore other issues, which could potentially be more material to the business.

- *Boundaries of responsibility:* Where do one organization's responsibilities end and another's begin? How can we consider an organization's individual responsibility when it is participating in a socio-economic system which only rewards certain sorts of behaviour?[107]

Trends and new ideas

– Reinventing the business model	– Dashboards
– Zero and 100 %	– Strategic philanthropy

Reinventing the business model Whether it is for environmental or social reasons, some companies are exploring completely new ways of doing business, and succeeding in both impacting society positively and profiting from it.

Some companies, like TerraCycle, are turning the business model upside down by taking waste and transforming it into product. TerraCycle creates its products for the garden, home and office by using the product packaging from other products recovered via the customer. For example, they work with Capri Sun and Honest Kids to collect drink pouches from these companies and convert them into fashion bags and pencil cases. The two drink companies collect drink pouches from anyone who signs up to the programme and donate 2 cents per Capri Sun, KoolAid and Honest Kids drink pouches, and 1 cent per other drink pouch collected, to the charity of the customer's choice. In return, the companies are preventing their waste from ending up in landfills across America and TerraCycle gains raw materials for its products. Similar programmes exist for other non-recyclable packaging such as yogurt containers and cookie wrappers (www.terracycle.com).

Zero and 100 % It is one thing to aim to reduce energy use by 20 %. Even 50 % seems impressive. But when companies make goals to reduce energy use or waste by 100 % one stops to listen. And this is exactly what many organizations are doing. We are also increasingly seeing zero and 100 % as targets when it comes to products being made with 100 % natural ingredients, 100 % organic, zero chemicals, zero emissions, etc. Some have been at this level for years, such as Xerox who set up a waste free factory in the mid 1990s. Coca Cola has set a goal to recycle or reuse

Look at www.bsr.org/reports/BSR_Carbon-Neutral-Chart.pdf to see who has gone or is committed to going carbon neutral.

all of the plastic bottles it uses in the US market so that zero bottles go to landfills. Over 30 companies have committed to carbon-neutral status including HSBC, Nike and Interface. IKEA is looking to be 100% fully powered by renewable energy. It does make one wonder why it hasn't all been done before, and makes you realize what is possible.

Instant Information Increasingly, the focus is on having the right information available instantly. The dashboard in a car gives the driver accurate, up to date information that the driver needs to make decisions and to know what the car is doing. This is most noticeable in the new generation of hybrid cars, which provide feedback to the driver on how efficiently they are driving. Many managers are frustrated by the lack of this sort of information, which would enable them to make wise decisions on a day-to-day basis. By taking advantage of the power of modern information technology, various organizations, such as IISD, have developed what they call Dashboards of Sustainability, which illustrate in real time the complex relationships among different issues by combining evaluation of social, economic and environmental performance within countries or regions. Other dashboards can be posted in a common area where building users can see and track their ability to reduce energy consumption, such as water and electricity. Dashboard projects have been implemented in several college dormitories where students hold contests to see which dorm can cut energy consumption the most.

The IISD Dashboard of Sustainability which illustrates the complex relationships among the different issues (www.iisd.org/cgsdi/intro_dashboard.htm), The Environmental Sustainability Index which aims to shift environmental decision-making to firmer analytic foundations using environmental indicators and statistics (www.yale.edu/esi/). For a whole range of different dashboards, including one on the MDGs, visit the European's Joint Research Centre at esl.jrc.it/envind/dashbrds.htm.

Strategic philanthropy Philanthropy, when companies donate resources, whether that be money, time or goods, to charitable causes, is changing with the times. Companies are increasingly applying rigorous procedures and are looking to finance genuine solutions with clear impact targets, and also ensure that every dollar spent is spent furthering community and business objectives. They are looking to donate resources to causes that are in line with their own material issues. According to a global survey in 2008 by consulting firm McKinsey, 30% of responses indicate that some companies are trying to reach very concrete goals, such as building knowledge about potential new markets and informing areas of innovation through their giving. Companies such as Cisco (through its Network Academies) have learned how to create foundation strategies that complement both community needs for high-tech training and company interests in supporting the creation of a highly technically skilled and more valuable work force.

> The Centre for Effective Philanthropy (www. effectivephilanthropy.com), The State of Corporate Philanthropy: A McKinsey Global Survey, February 2008 (www.mckinseyquarterly. com).

Transformation of partners As companies are increasingly looking to explore more of the sustainability tools and options explored throughout this book, they are looking for NGOs and partnerships with other organizations that will help them. Therefore, NGOs can play a role not just in influencing business to change, but in being part of that change. According to Gib Bulloch from Accenture, 'international NGOs will have to go through a fairly transformative change process if they are to operate effectively with, influence and engage the private sector in a new breed of development coalitions. And it's imperative that they fulfill this important role. We believe the required transformation is already underway, but the impact and nature of the change varies quite significantly across different organizations.'[108] Furthermore, as business relies increasingly on partnerships with NGOs to do work on the ground, there will be a need to ensure the transparency and accountability of the NGOs themselves to ensure that companies are actually doing what they say they are doing and that the NGOs are too.

What you can do . . .

- ❑ Does it make sense? Use common sense when developing your strategy. Does the story make sense? Don't try to do everything, focus on what is important to your company.
- ❑ Look into networks: Networks are not just for businesses to join, there are just as many networks for individuals. These range from professional networks for lawyers, accountants etc., networks for sustainability professionals such as the Institute of environmental Management and Assessment in the UK (www. iema.net) or Net Impact, a global network of leaders who are changing the world through business (www.netimpact.org).
- ❑ Go work for an NGO: Bring your business skills and your talent to work or volunteer for an NGO working directly with companies in this area.

Want more?

Business for Social Responsibility works with its global network of more than 250 member companies to develop sustainable business strategies and solutions through consulting, research and cross-sector collaboration (www.bsr.org).

Read: There are many books out there on sustainability and strategy. A few include *Green to Gold* by Daniel C. Esty and Andrew S. Winston (2006) which provides executives with knowledge on how to manage environmental challenges facing society and business. *Getting Green Done* by Auden Schendler (2009) is an honest look at what it really takes to make a company more sustainable.

Also take a look at Michael Porter and Mark R. Kramer's article on 'Strategy and Society: The Link between competitive advantage and corporate social responsibility'.

Why do initiatives fail?

1. *Organizations don't clearly understand what sustainability means:* They interpret it as being philanthropy, giving money to community groups and generally about giving money rather than saving or making it.
2. *They don't set clear priorities:* It is one thing to have a mission statement saying you are sustainable, but unless you have clear priorities and goals, and ways to reach these, you aren't really moving forward. Make sure these are realistic.
3. *Information overload:* Some organizations try to do everything at once and get overwhelmed by the amount of work required and all the roadblocks and challenges they encounter. Take things at a pace your organization can handle. Don't try to do everything at once.
4. *Doing it alone:* Great things are almost never done alone. You can still be competitive and share information with your peers to help you all move forward.
5. *No leadership:* If senior management, the CEO, or managers in general are not supporting the initiative actively, they will never have the pull they could.
6. *Making assumptions:* Don't create a more expensive green product and assume that someone will buy it just because it is better for society. Use sound business judgement.
7. *Incentives:* You could have a fantastic vision, plans in place, targets and a great management structure, but unless employee and company

(continued)

incentives match up with what you are trying to do you will encounter problems.

8. ***Burnout:*** Employees care and want to get involved in supporting a company's sustainability strategies, however, a company needs to allow involvement without burning employees out by overwhelming them with too much work. Channel employee enthusiasm with clear project goals and assign roles and responsibilities.

9. ***Auditing:*** Nothing in business is a one off thing. Sustainability is not just a box you can check once you put up a website and send out a press release. Be clear of where you stand when you start and continuously check to see how you are doing and what you could do better.

10. ***Lack of resources:*** Make sure sustainability projects have resources attached to them, whether that be people, time or money. Without these, they won't be able to explore their full potential.

Stakeholder engagement

'The old, adversarial model of business-NGO relations is being eroded; companies that learn to build constructive cross-sector partnerships gain competitive advantage in new markets, as well as make an active contribution to development. For their part, many development actors recognize that partnering with the private sector can bring benefits, such as innovative technology, scale, and a sustainable model to finance their efforts.'

WBCSD

The environment in which organizations operate is becoming increasingly complex due to everything from regulatory and voluntary requirements, environmental and social issues, to the increased expectations of stakeholders for transparency and accountability. Organizations are finding that engaging with stakeholders is providing them with opportunities to better understand the challenges they face, to understand and mitigate the risks, and also to explore new opportunities including innovations to products, processes and strategy. Engaging with stakeholders is nothing new, but the level of engagement is becoming more sophisticated, as diverse groups continue to learn how to leverage and maximize the outcomes of these relationships. Although in the past engagement started in response to a negative issue, companies are increasingly being proactive in this area.

Stakeholders are those groups who impact and/or are impacted by the company and its activities. This can include but is not limited to:

- employees and their families;
- customers;
- shareholders/investors;
- communities;
- suppliers/business partners;
- academia
- NGOs/international organizations;
- environmental NGOs;
- government/regulators;
- trade unions;
- media;
- advocacy groups.

Why is stakeholder engagement important?

- *Better informed decision-making:* Stakeholder engagement gives an organization a clearer picture of external and internal threats and opportunities. Management can get better information and therefore can make better decisions. For example, the Norwegian company Statoil worked with Amnesty Norway to train its employees to identify and solve business dilemmas in connection with human rights issues, thus reducing the company's exposure to human rights related risks. [109]
- *Spot problems before they occur:* Engagement can help organizations spot trends and issues that may impact their activities as well as possible solutions. It also allows them to assess and manage risks by identifying problems before they occur. The mining industry uses stakeholder engagement tools to engage communities and their representatives prior to breaking ground.
- *Legal and voluntary obligations:* At a basic level, organizations are required to engage stakeholders in different activities and disclose information through different legal requirements (e.g. US Sarbanes Oxley Act, Japanese law of promotion of environmentally conscious business activations) as well as part of voluntary obligations (e.g. GRI, the Global Compact, SA8000 and the Equator Principles).

(*continued*)

- *Increased transparency and credibility:* Companies such as Nike have multi-stakeholder review committees which work with them on the development of their CSR report. As a result of stakeholder dialogue and subsequent feedback, Nike disclosed an unprecedented wealth of information in 2005 about its operations and in doing so raised the benchmark of corporate transparency.
- *Access to resources:* Benefit from a wealth of experience, expertise and resource sharing. Resources can be technical, human, knowledge, physical and financial and can include better access to information and networks, greater reach, improved operational efficiency, more appropriate and effective products and services etc.
- *Identify opportunities:* Engagement allows organizations to better understand their customers and their needs in order to develop new products, processes and services, as well as enter new markets. Working with different partners allows a company to see issues through a different lens and come up with creative and innovative solutions. FedEx partnered with the Alliance for Environmental Innovation to reduce the environmental impact of their vehicle fleet hoping that the new hybrid electric vehicles will replace the company's 30 000 fleet leading to significant reductions in environmental emissions.
- *Making an impact:* According to the IBLF, 'working separately different sectors have developed activities in isolation—sometimes competing with each other and/or duplicating efforts and wasting valuable resources'. Because partners have similar goals, the idea is that they can accomplish more by working together.

How to engage with stakeholders

Determine who the stakeholders are: Engagement goes beyond identifying those groups that could have an adverse effect on a company's activities to actively engaging with those that could also be helpful. Engagement may focus on one group of stakeholders or several and may involve a different group of stakeholders depending on the issue or project. Stakeholders can be determined:

- *By responsibility:* people for whom you have legal, financial or operational responsibility.

- *By influence:* people who are able to influence the ability of your organization to meet its goals and influence others.
- *By proximity:* people that your organization interacts with most.
- *By dependency:* people who are dependent on your organization such as employees, their families and customers.
- *By representation:* people such as heads of local communities, trade union representatives, councillors etc.[110]

A company must also consider a stakeholder's capacity for and willingness to engage:

- *Power and reach of the representative:* Not all NGOs are the same. There is a huge variety of global and local NGOs: broad versus narrow scope, some work alone and others work as part of networks, some are campaign focused while others are more collaborative.
- *Knowledge of the issue:* Be clear about the representative's knowledge of the issue, they may know as much, more or much less than you do. Different stakeholders will use different vocabulary to express ideas of sustainability. Spend the time to make sure that everyone is on the same page before discussions begin.
- *Experience working with business:* While business may have little or a lot of experience working with different stakeholders, the stakeholders themselves will also have different levels of experience. Some, such as World Wildlife Federation (www.wwf.org.uk/business/) and The World Conservation Union (www.iucn.org/themes/business/), have specific divisions that focus on working with business. Others, in particular small scale ones, may not have experience and may not have sufficient capacity to engage. This does not mean that engagement should not be attempted but capacity issues should be accounted for.

What level of engagement? Low levels are adequate for solving or addressing minor challenges but engaging more deeply has the potential to enable more sustained changes and transformation. At earlier levels of engagement, you are able to engage more stakeholders while higher levels (e.g. partnership) require more resources. The level of engagement will depend on your strategic engagement objectives and may be different for different stakeholders.

(continued)

- *Ignore or monitor:* An organization chooses not to engage or communicate with stakeholders and hears their concerns through letters, protests and websites.
- *Communicate:* An organization puts together messages targeted to particular stakeholder groups such as brochures, reports and websites, speeches, conferences, and so on, and gets involved in transactional relationships, for example, grant making.
- *Consult:* An organization collects information from stakeholder groups directly through surveys, focus groups, workplace assessments, one-to-one meetings, etc.
- *Dialogue:* An organization works with the stakeholder to gather information and advice but goes a step further by exploring different perspectives, needs and alternatives.
- *Collaborate:* An organization gets involved in two way dialogues such as advisory panels, forums, participatory decision-making processes, joint projects, voluntary two-party or multi-stakeholder initiatives, driven by both the company and the stakeholder (e.g. global stakeholders on Dow Chemical's Corporate Environmental Advisory Council have been meeting since 1991; Chiquita joining Social Accountability International, a multi-stakeholder initiative that includes companies, NGOs and trade unions as part of its governance structure).
- *Partnerships:* Both organizations share both the risks and the benefits of engagement. They look for synergies between competencies and resources; these can be between companies, companies and NGOs, joint ventures, alliances (i.e. Lafarge worked with CARE to develop its health policy in Africa).

How to Engage? A company seeking to engage with stakeholders should consider:

1. *Why does it want to engage?* Engagement should not be an add-on or one off activity. A company needs to strategically think about why they want to engage.
2. *What should be engaged in?* Engagement can be focused on a particular issue, a process, a product or a decision. It could be related to new policy, where to build a new site or help in entering a new market. Sometimes there is no specific subject for engagement and the engagement is focused on developing a dialogue between groups.

Be clear about how this is going to benefit the business and what changes you are willing to make based on the engagement process.

3. ***What are the strategic engagement objectives?*** Think strategically about what you want to get out of the engagement. This can be anything from developing a new approach or managing risks, to just gathering more information. Agree on the rules of engagement. The most important indicator of success is clearly tying the stakeholder engagement to a strong business need. This means that there is a clear link to core strategy, resources to support the engagement and genuine business interest in the outcome.

4. ***Spend time getting to know each other:*** The success of engagement is often based on the degree of respect in the relationship that has been built over time. Spend time building the relationship, understanding the strengths and weaknesses of both organizations. Minimize uncertainty by agreeing on clear goals and policies and providing the information to act on them.

5. ***Build internal capacity:*** Assess your organizations internal capacity for engagement and understanding of the issue. Engagement is part art and part science and different skill sets are needed, as well as new forms of leadership.

6. ***Embed it into the organization:*** Engagement should be managed like a business function, it should have a clear strategy, objectives, timetable, budget and allocation of responsibilities. Engagement should be part of performance evaluations for leadership. It should also focus on strengthening the company's ability to respond to the issues and opportunities brought up by the engagement process.

7. ***How can success be measured?*** Ensure that goals and milestones are established and that mechanisms exist for monitoring performance and tracking achievements. Continually revise engagement performance and make needed adjustments. Ensure that there are mechanisms in place to take the learnings and put them into improving your business. Share learning and follow up.

Tips?

• ***Manage expectations:*** Some stakeholders want to open a dialogue while others will expect specific operational changes or adherence

(continued)

to certain performance standards. Be clear about what yours and their expectations are.

- **Understand the potential obstacles to participation:** Consider the specific cultural circumstances of the engagement e.g. language, customs regarding social interaction, gender issues, scale at which the representative operates – global or local – understanding that stakeholders often have limited financial means and staffing capabilities.
- **Be transparent:** Provide the stakeholders with enough information so that they can contribute to the process. Be open and honest during the process.
- **If you aren't prepared to be influenced by what stakeholders have to say, don't do it:** You are wasting time and resources, both yours and theirs. You are also taking a greater risk by engaging. Stakeholder engagement is different from a public relations strategy and your credibility will be judged more on your actions than your words.
- **Get in early:** Relationship building takes time. Stakeholder dialogue should not be hurried: start early, invest in planning and preparation and allow people time to learn from and with each other. Allow for sufficient resources to support the engagement.
- **Don't wait until there is a problem to engage:** Often interacting with stakeholders is viewed as a low priority but when a conflict or crisis does arise the absence of an established relationship can challenge communications. Stakeholders are less likely to give a company they don't know the benefit of the doubt and making contact with stakeholders in a reactive mode can create lasting negative perceptions as well as question if a company is being genuine.
- **You don't have to be perfect:** Stakeholder dialogue can be often messy, disjointed and even chaotic at times. Remember to be transparent, open to new ideas, empathetic, listen and reflect. Focus on quality, not quantity. Take it seriously.
- **Be aware of language and cultural differences:** These actors who were traditionally critical of business are now looking at ways of

working together. But there are still a lot of cultural differences that need to be considered.

• **Be Patient:** Partnerships take time.

'The vehemence of a stakeholder group does not necessarily signify the importance of an issue—either to the company or to the world'

Michael Porter [111]

Want more?

• The AA1000 Stakeholder Engagement Standard is a generally applicable framework for improving the quality of design, implementation, assessment, communication and assurance of stakeholder engagement (www.accountability21.net). Building Partnerships by UN and IBLF 2002 has a comprehensive overview of co-operation between the UN and the private sector.

• Several organizations have publications on *stakeholder engagement* including: IFC's Stakeholder Engagement: A good practice handbook for companies doing business in emerging markets (www.ifc.org). Stakeholder dialogue from the WBSCD (www.wbcsd.org), The 21st Century NGO by SustainAbility and Practices and Principles for Successful Stakeholder Engagement (www.sustainability.com). From Words to Action The Stakeholder Engagement Manual volume 1 and 2 UNEP (www.unep.fr).

• For resources on *community engagement* see: Participation works! 21 Techniques of Community Participation for the 21st Century New Economics Foundation (www.neweconomics.org), Participation Learning and Action series IIED (www.iied.org), Participatory methods toolkit (www.viwta.be), World Bank on Participation and Civic Engagement (www.worldbank.org).

'The reason why we have two ears and only one mouth is that we may listen the more and talk the less'.

Zeno of Citium

PART 3

TOOLS

Monitoring, Managing and Improving Performance
Greening Offices and Buildings

15 Tools for Monitoring, Managing and Improving Performance

Many tools have been developed to assist businesses, both big and small, in managing, monitoring and improving their sustainability performance at all stages of the decision-making process. These include (but are not limited to):

• Gather sustainability information to assist in decision-making	→ *Assessments*
• Benchmark and monitor how an organization is doing	→ *Audits*
• Create a system to manage your environmental performance	→ *Environmental Management Systems*
• Use sustainability standards as a tool to guide your efforts	→ *Standards*

Assessments

An environmental or social assessment is a means of gathering information to ensure that environmental and social implications of decisions are taken into account before those decisions are made. Assessments are usually taken before moving forward with a proposal or an individual project. An assessment is an important tool to:

- Identify the significant social and environmental impacts of a project.
- Incorporate environmental factors into decision-making.
- Identify the potential benefits and disadvantages of the project.
- Identify critical problems which require further studies and/or monitoring.
- Minimize or avoid adverse environmental and social effects before they occur.
- Examine and select from possible alternatives.

There are many different kinds of assessments including:

- *Life-cycle Assessment* looks at understanding the full life-cycle of a product. ISO 14040:2006 describes the principles and framework for life-cycle assessment (www.iso.org).
- *Technology assessment* is carried out in order to determine which technology to use. It looks at the proposed technology, any alternatives, the requirements of the technology and the pressures the technology places on the environment (http://www.unep.fr/en/branches/ietc.htm).
- *Opportunity assessment* looks at recognizing potential opportunities that could lead to gain (i.e. reduction of energy and resource consumption and therefore cost of production).
- *Risk assessments* explore the likelihood of an event occurring and the resulting severity of loss if that event occurred (risk = likelihood $\times$ severity). Where there is a high risk involved in a project, the risk assessment will define how to mitigate or prevent it through proper controls to make the risk acceptable.
- *Environmental and social impact assessments* (EIA, SIA) were introduced because of concerns regarding the effects that major development projects were having on society and the environment. The benefits were quickly recognized and it has now become established as an internationally recognized decision-making tool.

Assessments should be conducted as early as possible in the planning and proposal stages. Many of the major decisions about the location of a project, the scale, layout or design, for example, are made at the very beginning and many of these can have a significant impact on the environment and society. Identifying these issues right from the start can allow an organization to prevent many problems before they occur. The commonly accepted steps include:

1. *Screening:* To decide whether or not a proposal needs an EIA and if it does at what level of detail.
2. *Scoping:* To identify the key issues and impacts that are likely to require further investigation.
3. *Impact analysis:* To identify and predict the likely environmental and social effects of the proposal and evaluate their significance.
4. *Mitigation and impact management:* To develop measures to avoid, reduce or compensate for impacts, making good any environmental damage.
5. *Reporting:* To describe the results to decision makers and other interested parties.
6. *Implementation and monitoring:* To put in place the plans agreed upon and continue to monitor them through audits.

When doing assessments keep in mind:

> There are many resources on environmental impact assessments including UNEP EIA (www.unep.fr/pc/pc/tools/eia.htm), the EU website on EIA (ec.europa.eu/environment/eia) and the International Association of Impact Assessment (www.iaia.org). The Environmental Impact Assessment Open Educational Resource has learning modules and resources on the topic (eia.unu.edu). The WBCSD also has some guidelines on Environmental and social impact assessment (www.wbcsd.com). The Convention on Environmental Impact Assessment in a Transboundary Context (www.unece.org/env/eia) sets out obligations for parties to assess the environmental impact at the early stages of planning and notify and consult each other on major projects under consideration that are likely to have a significant adverse environmental impact across borders.

- Many assessments fail because inadequate attention is given to identifying the effects that are most likely to be significant.
- Stakeholder involvement in the early stages will not only help throughout the assessment process but also in gaining acceptance

during the implementation phase after the assessment is completed.

- As the assessment proceeds, one often discovers new information that requires a revision of previous assumptions.

Example: Conducting an environmental or social risk assessment

Identifying risks: Identify which risks a company is facing and where they are coming from. Risk can be explored from the following angles:

- *Sector and company specific risks:* Start by considering the most obvious risks that are relevant to the organization. Look at the issues that organizations more advanced in sustainability are exploring.
- *Operational opportunities and risks:* Look at how an organization impacts on stakeholder groups and broader society through its operations. Look at risks and opportunities throughout the full life-cycle of the product.
- *Stakeholder related opportunities and risks:* Look at their perceptions of who your stakeholders are, and what their risks are; look at boundaries of responsibility the organization has for products and services.

Assessing and prioritizing risks: For each risk identified, what might happen, how it might happen and how large the consequences will be. When an organization is faced with a number of potential sustainability related risks, a matrix can be created to help prioritize the risks and establish their relative importance. The potential impact of the risks (high or low) and the likelihood of that impact (high or low).

Managing risks: Once identified and prioritized, companies need to proactively seek to reduce and manage these risks. Many risks cannot be eliminated but they can be minimized. Managing risks involves asking what can be done to manage any significant adverse occurrence, and who should be involved.

- See if you can tolerate the risk and work with it, through improved environmental management techniques.
- Work to reduce the risk through new technology, procedures, investments and stakeholder engagement.

- Eliminate the risk, for example, banning a particular chemical.
- Transfer the risk when it is felt that the business has no control over it (i.e. through insurance companies).

Risk analysis should not be overly complex, so don't ignore it because of inadequate understanding. Remember that many risks and opportunities are inter-related. Recognize the need to engage with stakeholders, and to sharing of information and responsibility for any risk. Your performance and the performance of your customers and suppliers are intrinsically linked and sharing risks is therefore beneficial.

Audits

A business may have internal requirements, policies, standards or procedures or even external rules, regulations or third party requirements that they are required to follow. An audit is simply a check of how well they are doing at meeting these internal or external requirements. Audits are used as a tool to help a business measure and improve the performance of a project, a site, a particular product or service. An audit can be a useful tool to:

- Monitor the sustainability practices of suppliers and contractors.
- Monitor the level of compliance with relevant regulatory and internal requirements.
- Monitor the amount of resources used or generated, such as water, energy, waste and pollutants.
- Explore improvement opportunities.
- Establish a performance baseline.

The following steps show one approach to setting up an audit:

1. ***Determine who will conduct the audit:*** Will it be performed internally, or by a third party auditor? For example, one that belongs to a commercial auditing firm.
2. ***Determine the scope:*** Will it be at a small level, such as an audit of recycling practices or waste at one location? Will it be of a particular product or service (design, performance, disposal), or of a process

(manufacturing, management, design, procurement)? Will it be done by geographic location or organizational unit (company, division)?

3. ***Determine what you are auditing:*** An organization can audit just about anything. It might sound obvious, but make sure it is clear what is being audited.

4. ***Select objectives:*** Whether the audit is to check for compliance, management assurance, stakeholder assurance or to provide information for decision-making, make sure the objectives are set and clear to all involved.

5. ***Choose indicators:*** Put in place indicators against which performance will be measured. This often includes legislative or regulatory and compliance requirements.

6. ***Conduct the audit:*** Conduct a quick self audit in order to understand where you stand, in particular if a third party is conducting the audit; this typically involves interviews with managers and personnel, detailed site inspections, etc.

7. ***Develop and implement an Action Plan:*** This should address shortcomings identified by the audit, by outlining specific actions required to meet the audit objectives, with appropriate budget allocation, programme implementation and monitoring.

8. ***Report:*** Write in non-technical language so that the information and questions are accessible to all, and the messages are clear and useful for those who need to use the information.

9. ***Focus on continuous improvement:*** Conduct the audits on a regular basis, and review and update the audit questions as progress is made in order to keep them focused and relevant.

Many companies conduct internal and external audits in order to verify the status of environmental initiatives. At Toyota, for example, internal audits consist of plant audits conducted by each plant's auditing team and Head Office audits of the whole company, plant by plant, by audit teams in which members are drawn from all the company's plants, so that no difference arises in the audits of the different plants. After the audit, study sessions are held for the staff of each plant on any issues raised. Plants try to improve their environmental track record.

Audits usually focus on compliance, however, compliance does not necessarily indicate operational effectiveness. Audits should go beyond reporting on compliance to covering effectiveness and provide managers with strategic information about how they compare to current best practice. They

'Environmental Audit, a simple guide' produced by the Environmental Protection Department of the Government of Hong Kong (www.epd. gov.hk/epd/english/how_ help/tools_ea/audit_1.html).

also need to look at behaviour and so called 'soft' issues, such as motivation, culture and teamwork in order to assess behaviours that provide evidence of how such factors affect the performance of a product.

Example: Waste audit

Audits can also be used to identify, for example, how much waste is being generated and how to manage it.

1. Identify all points at which waste is generated.
2. Identify the origin of each type of waste.
3. Measure the quantity of each type of waste and its environmental impact.
4. Establish a method for the continued monitoring of waste levels.
5. Identify the current costs of dealing with waste.
6. Look at opportunities to reduce, recycle or reuse the waste.
7. Set waste minimization targets.
8. Communicate the results to the company and get people involved in achieving the targets.

Environmental and social management systems

Organizations are adopting programmes to help manage their environmental impacts on a day-to-day basis. An environmental management system (EMS) is a set of policies and procedures that defines how a company evaluates, manages and tracks its overall environmental impacts. It is a voluntary management standard that helps managers to identify and prioritize their key environmental impacts. It also provides a framework for setting clear objectives and targets for managing those impacts.

An EMS is important as a tool to ensure a company is compliant with regulatory and company requirements and knowing the impacts it has on society. It helps focus an organization on priorities for actions and serves as a framework for putting ideas into practice. All EMS standards follow the same cycle:

- *PLAN:* Understand where the company currently stands (typically through an audit or assessment) in terms of legislative and regulatory requirements, existing environmental management practices, etc. This involves getting top management and employee support, setting objectives and targets, prioritizing actions and creating an action plan.
- *DO:* Ensure that there are established roles and responsibilities that are clearly communicated; and that members of staff are aware and trained to carry our responsibilities. Make sure they have the support they need to carry out their roles.
- *CHECK:* Formulate a measurement system, establish and define benchmarks, perform regular audits. Check to ensure that what you planned to do actually happened.
- *ACT:* An EMS is most effective when used to review progress towards the targets and objectives set by a company to protect the environment. The procedures set in place to meet these objectives should be constantly examined to see if they can be improved or if more effective systems can be introduced.

The key elements of an EMS include:

- *Creating a policy:* An environmental policy is a declaration of the organization's overall aims and principles. It includes compliance with environmental, legal and other requirements. The policy should recognize the impacts the organization has on the environment.

It should be supported by senior management and the CEO. Such a policy should be reviewed regularly (for many this is annually).

- *Identifying and evaluating your environmental impacts:* Evaluate the impacts of your activities, products and services. This allows the EMS to be focused on those environmental issues that are most significant so that resources and time are concentrated on these. Significance is often determined by considering the size, nature, frequency, likelihood and duration of the environmental impact, the importance to stakeholders and the sensitivity of the receiving environment.
- *Operational control, targets and objectives:* This information can then be used to identify control measures and to set objectives and targets for environmental improvements. An environmental programme is then put in place to turn objectives and targets into practical actions. People are then assigned the responsibility for completing the tasks.
- *Monitoring, evaluation and review:* The EMS process is documented and procedures are established to ensure that everyone knows how the system operates and what is required. Progress is tracked through regular monitoring and audits. Effective communication internally is vital to keep people up to date. An EMS is a cyclical process of identifying, improving and checking. Reviews are done periodically by management to ensure that the EMS is achieving the desired outcomes and that polices are being implemented.

This is a voluntary activity, however, increasingly companies are choosing to get certification for their EMS systems. Currently Japan leads the world in the number of ISO 14001 certified companies followed by China, Spain and Italy. These types of standards are becoming increasingly important, as many multinationals are requiring suppliers to have the standard. A company can seek official accreditation for its EMS under one of several schemes at the national level (i.e. BSI in the UK), regional level (EMAS in Europe) or international level (ISO4001). Others have developed their own specific national or international standards.

There is plenty of guidance on how to put in place EMS. EMAS Toolkit for Small Organizations provides step by step guidance and tools for implementing an environmental management system (according to ISO 14001) (www.epa.gov/owm/iso14001/ems2001final.pdf). Several self-assessment checklists are available for example from the Global Environmental Management Initiative (GEMI) (www.gemi.org). Another interesting resource is the Environmental Management Tools for SMEs, a handbook produced by the European Environment Agency (reports.eea.europa.eu/GH-14-98-065-EN-C/en/enviissu10.pdf) and Environmental Management Systems Toolkit for Small organizations produced by the EU and INEM (ec.europa.eu/environment/emas/toolkit/).

Choosing standards and codes

Many international standards and networks started as attempts to help guide organizations on how to improve the consistency of their products (such as ISO 9001), reduce their impact on the environment (ISO 14001) or to generally improve their environmental and social management. These programmes are voluntary and involve a range of activities, from a simple commitment to investigate sustainability issues to the adherence to strict protocols for environmental and social standards.

> *'Corporate responsibility standards, norms, principles and guidelines aim to provide generally accepted reference points for improving aspects of social and environmental performance. Although mostly voluntary, some are emerging as de facto industry standards that provide the desired legitimacy, consistency and comparability required by business and its stakeholders'.*
>
> ACCOUNTABILITY[112]

The rapidly growing number of overlapping codes, standards and guidelines being developed for and by business around the world can be confusing.

The International Organization of Standardization (ISO) coordinates standards at the international level. **ISO 14001** are a series of voluntary, auditable standards designed to provide customers with a reasonable assurance that the performance claims of a company are accurate. ISO reviews all of its standards at least every five years (www.iso.org).

- Environmental management systems: 14001, 14002, 14004.
- Environmental auditing: 14010, 14011, 14012.
- Evaluation of environmental performance: 14031.
- Environmental labelling: 14020, 14021, 14022, 14023, 14024, 14025.
- Life-cycle assessment: 14040, 14041, 14042, 14043.
- Greenhouse gas accounting and verification: 14064.
- Social responsibility ISO26000.

The ISO 19011:2002 standard was introduced with the aim of applying a common and consistent approach to the auditing of both the ISO9001 quality and ISO14001 environmental management systems standards. The benefits of integrated management systems are now widely recognized, where a combined approach is helpful in minimizing the resource demands of operating a certificated management system.

Standards are also being developed by NGOs at an international level. Two examples include:

- *AA1000:* Developed by Accountability, AA1000 is a set of standards based on principles for social and ethical accounting, auditing and reporting (www.accountability.org.uk/aa1000).
  AA1000 Purpose and Principles
  AA1000 Framework for Integration
  AA1000 Assurance Standard
  AA1000 Stakeholder Engagement Standard

- ***SA8000:*** Social Accountability International is a non-profit human rights organization dedicated to the ethical treatment of workers around the world. SAI's social standard, called SA8000, is an auditable certification standard based on international workplace norms of International Labour Organization conventions, the Universal Declaration of Human Rights and the UN Convention on the Rights of the Child. In order to qualify, a company must follow standards relating to child labour, forced labour, health and safety, freedom of association and right to collective bargaining, discrimination, discipline, working hours, compensation and management systems (www.sa-intl.org).

Industry and issue specific standards can be found within the different chapters and in the resources by industry section at the end of this book. ISEAL Code of Good Practice for Setting Social and Environmental Standards (www.isealalliance.org), ISO standardization documentation (www.iso.org). See WBCSD Accountability Codes (www.wbcsd.org/web/publications/accountability-codes. pdf). Sigma guide to guidelines and standards relevant to sustainable development (www.projectsigma.co.uk). There are also several national level standards such as SD21000 in France, AS8003 in Australia and SI0000 in Israel.

16 Tools for Greening Offices and Buildings

One of the easiest ways to introduce sustainable practices into a company and where most organizations start, is to consider ways of 'greening' the office, whether that be a small room, or a whole building. This can include changing the way that you buy products and services (procurement), the way that you build your operational headquarters, or simply the way that you use the office space on a daily basis. There are many benefits to office greening programmes.

- *Employees get engaged:* Many initiatives to green the office show results fast, giving employees successes to build on and motivation for their work.
- *Raising awareness:* Putting in place office greening programmes is not only a good way to get employees engaged, but is also an opportunity to educate them about the impact sustainability can have on an operation.
- *Reduced costs:* By increasing efficiency and minimizing waste, organizations are finding many opportunities to reduce costs in energy, water, maintenance and materials.
- *Increased employee retention and productivity:* Studies have shown that green building features can increase worker productivity and reduce absenteeism. Research performed by the Rocky Mountain Institute and the US department of Energy found it increased productivity by 3 to 16%.[113]

- **_Enhanced corporate reputation:_** Sustainability building and procurement shows a commitment by a company to the environment, society and to its workers.
- **_Tax and regulatory incentives:_** There are an increasing number of incentives for building green or for redeveloping brownfield properties for example.

Steps for setting up office greening programmes

The following steps can be used when designing and implementing any office greening programme.

1. **_Find out where you stand now:_** Audit your organization to see what you are currently using, where you are getting if from and how much you are paying for it. This information is useful in gathering information and establishing a baseline. Then, monitor how much energy and water you use and how much it is costing you so you can keep track of improvements.

2. **_Think about the business case:_** Understand the different direct and indirect benefits that can occur through office greening projects within your company.

3. **_Get everyone involved:_** No office greening programme can be a success without employees getting involved. In fact office greening is all about employees changing the way they work in the office. Seek employee suggestions on where more could be done.

4. **_Set goals and targets and develop a plan to achieve these:_** Set goals and targets of what you would like to achieve. If in doubt, run a pilot project to see how it works.

5. **_Monitor and review your plan:_** Regularly look at your plan to take into account new

> There are countless books and online resources on greening offices. National environmental protection agencies often have information on office greening such as the US EPA (www.usepa.org). The Sustainable Office Toolkit has resources on how to set up an office greening programme (www.p2ad.org/toolkit/guidebook.html).

products, technologies or opportunities that may arise. Quantifying savings and benefits will also come in handy when looking at expanding office greening programmes.

6. ***Communicate your successes and progress:*** Keep the whole organization informed and continue to renew their enthusiasm and involvement in the programme. Let your employees know what is changing and how they can get involved.

Buildings

Whether your company is building a whole new building, doing major renovations or even minor changes, green buildings have moved from being the exception to becoming the norm. An extra incentive is that the price premium for green buildings is shrinking according to the WBCSD. Furthermore, even if there is an additional upfront cost, green buildings are typically less expensive to operate and maintain, provide work environments that boost productivity, decrease the environmental impacts of construction and operations, reduce worker health and safety liabilities, and improve corporate image. All of these have potentially high financial and reputational benefits associated with them, especially if you consider that a 1% increase in productivity can easily result in savings that exceed the entire energy bill for many companies.

Design

- ❏ Select your site carefully (i.e. avoid contributing to sprawl, focus on redevelopment of sites).
- ❏ Work with the surrounding environment (i.e. the sun and wind direction).
- ❏ Incorporate health and safety concerns, including indoor air quality.
- ❏ Optimize energy and water efficiency.
- ❏ Redesign the interior work spaces.
- ❏ Use daylight when possible and design spaces that use daylight.
- ❏ Insulate properly.
- ❏ Integrate solar hot water heating into the design to minimize hot water heating bills.

Materials

❑ Minimizing the use of materials in the construction of the building.
❑ As far as possible use recycled, certified and locally produced materials and eliminate waste.
❑ Choose building products that are sustainable for example paints, etc.

Gardens

❑ Landscape using local species that need little maintenance and water.
❑ Use compost and other organic techniques in maintaining gardens (International Federation of Organic Agricultural Movements www.ifoam.org).
❑ Put in a green roof which can significantly reduce indoor temperatures. This can either be by using materials that absorb less heat or by putting plants and grass on the roof (www.greenroofs.com).

There are several different standards in place for green building. From the US, the Leadership in Energy and Environmental Design (LEED) Green Building Rating System is an accepted benchmark for the design, construction and operation of high performance green buildings (www.usgbc.org/leed). The Hannover Principles aim to provide a platform upon which designers can consider how to adapt their work toward sustainable ends (www.mcdonough.com/principles.pdf). Also look at US EPA green building (epa.gov/greenbuilding/), Greener Buildings (www.greenerbuildings.com) and UNEP's Sustainable Building and Constructive Initiative (www.unepsbci.org). For examples of green buildings, check out the Editt Tower in Singapore, BedZed in the UK, the Reichstag in Germany and the Bank of America Tower in the US.

The ING Bank headquarters, which uses one tenth the energy of its predecessor, has also lowered absenteeism by 15%.[114]

Energy

Energy bills are an easily reduced cost for most businesses, yet many ignore this opportunity for an easy win. An assessment of the 'electric productivity' in the US indicated that improvements in energy efficiency could not only cut consumption by 30%, but also eliminate the need for more than 60% of coal-fired generation, according to a new study by the Rocky Mountain Institute.[115]

- ❏ Start by installing energy-efficient light bulbs, which can use up to 80% less energy than regular incandescent ones.
- ❏ Use dimmers, automatic timers and motion detection sensors to ensure optimal lighting throughout the building.
- ❏ Consider retrofitting your office lighting – a well designed lighting system using more energy efficient lights can result not only in a reduction in your energy bill, but also in productivity gains that far outweigh the cost of the upgrade.
- ❏ Regulate heating and air conditioning to be more energy efficient. If the air conditioning has ever left you feeling cold in summer, then it's wasting energy. Simply increase its setting by a few degrees to save significant amounts of energy.
- ❏ Change electricity suppliers to one that produces energy from renewable sources.
- ❏ Look at generating your own power by installing your own solar panels or wind generators. Increasingly, governments are offering subsidies or other incentives to encourage this.
- ❏ Turn things off when they are not being used, like the lights, computers and other appliances.
- ❏ Buy energy efficient appliances, look for labels for recognized programmes that provide a guarantee about lower energy use such as energy star in the US or the EU energy label.
- ❏ Open windows instead of using air conditioning.
- ❏ Turn down your heating, don't heat empty spaces and look at alternative heating systems such as solar heating. Put in place proper insulation and double glazed windows.

❑ Turn off appliances rather than putting them on standby. Up to 8% of domestic electricity is consumed by appliances such as TVs, DVDs, stereos and computers left on standby.

❑ Where available look at smart metres which allow customers to see energy use in real time.

Energy Star is a joint programme of the US Environmental Protection Agency and the US Department of Energy helping consumers and businesses save money and protect the environment through energy efficient products and practices (www.energystar.gov). The Green Power Market Development is run by the World Resource Institute and seeks to define the business case for the corporate purchase of green energy products to reduce market barriers faced by green power suppliers and for the buyer by providing independent information. Members include IKEA, General Motors, Tetra Pak, Unilever and Michelin (www.thegreenpowergroup.org).

Water

Water is not only vital for society but to business as well. Less than 3% of all water on Earth is fresh water, and many countries are facing shortages of fresh water. All organizations, directly or indirectly, need and use water for their operations. Water has many hidden costs including treatment, pumping, maintenance of pipe work, effluent treatment and discharge. Using water wisely can not only save you money, but a strategic approach to water management can also enhance the reputation of your company.

❑ Reduce water consumption to save money and reduce the environmental impact of your operation.

❑ Install water efficient fixtures, low flow appliances and devices to minimize wasting water.

- ❏ Check your systems for leaks and repair dripping taps.
- ❏ Collect rain water from the roof of your building to water the garden instead of using tap water.
- ❏ Reuse water in manufacturing and rinsing procedures, reuse waste water.
- ❏ Don't dump pollutants into the drains – dispose of them appropriately.
- ❏ Use biodegradable detergents.
- ❏ Install greywater systems.
- ❏ Water plants in the evening to avoid wasting water through evaporation.

> The UN Global Compact CEO water mandate is an initiative designed to assist companies in the development, implementation and disclosure of water sustainability policies and practices (www.unglobalcompact.org). GEMI Water Sustainability Tool (gemi.org/water) and the Water Footprint Network (www.waterfootprint.org) are also helpful resources. For more on water see the UN International Year of Freshwater which took place in 2003 (www.wateryear2003.org) and the decade which goes from 2005–2015 (www.un.org/waterforlifedecade). For more links see the 'What' section.

Waste and recycling

Gone are the days where your responsibility for the waste generated by your site ends when the waste contractor removes it from your site. Today, you must ensure they are disposing of your waste in a responsible and legal manner. Companies are finding that they can save money and reduce liabilities by reducing the amount of waste they generate in the first place. They are finding that they sometimes pay twice for products, for example paying to buy the product, and then paying to dispose of the product.

Reduce the amount of materials bought and used

- ❑ Buy durable products, rather than disposable ones. Examine in-house repair schedules, maintenance agreements and extended warranties as ways to extend product life.
- ❑ Stop multiple subscriptions of magazines for example when one copy can be shared.
- ❑ Coordinate product purchases and plan ahead to buy products in bulk to save time, money and transportation and packaging costs.
- ❑ Purchase products with less packaging.
- ❑ Purchase refillable products such as pens, pencils and tape dispensers.

Reuse

- ❑ Purchase products in reusable, refillable or returnable containers. For example, receive deliveries in reusable trays, totes or pallets that can be returned to the vendor for reuse.
- ❑ Set up a reuse system, or use an existing system, that makes unwanted items from one department available to other departments.
- ❑ Reuse file folders and binders.

Recycle

- ❑ Donate used materials to schools, NGOs or other businesses that could use them. Some charities collect used materials and make money from recycling them.
- ❑ Set up recycling bins next to wastebaskets and inform employees what is recyclable.
- ❑ Look at options to compost.
- ❑ Raise awareness in your office about what can and cannot be recycled.

Recycle Now is a UK website exploring how an office can recycle and has lots of information on how different items are recycled (www.recyclenow.com).

Paper

Offices use, and inevitably waste, a lot of paper in their regular operations. In fact around 70% of office waste is paper. This ends up costing too much money and puts unnecessary pressure on forests. Consider that the energy used in the manufacture of five sheets of paper is equivalent to the energy needed to run an 80 watt light bulb for one hour. Given that the US alone uses about 4 million tonnes of copy paper annually, that's a lot of energy which goes into the manufacturing of paper!

- ❑ Post information on bulletin boards or use e-mail rather than distributing paper memos.
- ❑ Use both sides of the paper where possible to minimize paper usage.
- ❑ Reuse paper printed on one side for drafts, fax cover sheets or notepads.
- ❑ Buy erasable boards as an alternative to paper flip charts.
- ❑ Set the photocopiers to print both sides as standard.
- ❑ Have reports easily available on a website so they can be viewed on screen.
- ❑ Don't send out catalogues and brochures to people who don't want them.
- ❑ Send bills by email rather than mail.
- ❑ Send cards by email or on recycled paper.
- ❑ Use print preview before you print so that you can see what you are about to print and whether it can be fitted onto less pages.
- ❑ Faxes can also be sent by email.
- ❑ Use paper that is certified as being from sustainable sources such as FSC.
- ❑ Buy paper that is post-consumer recycled content, unbleached and uncoloured.
- ❑ Minimize the amount of ink you use by setting the printer on draft.

Ecofont is a new font that uses up to 20% less ink. According to the ecofont website, 'After Dutch holey cheese, there now is a Dutch font with holes as well'. Ecofont is free to download and use at www.ecofont.eu. The Environmental Energy Technologies Division of the US government has more information on how to reduce your office paper usage (eetd.lbl.gov/).

Electronics

Modern offices are full of electronic equipment – it would be hard to imagine one without any. However, the electronics we rely on each day waste a lot of energy and generate a lot of waste – both e-waste at the end of their life and waste as a result of using them (i.e. printer cartridges). Many electronic products use between 1 and 20 watts just on standby, and are often in this mode for much of a day. According to the Energy Cost Saving Council, the average building owner can cut energy costs by up to 60% by replacing outdated, inefficient electrical equipment while Greenpeace has estimated that demand for new technology creates 4000 tonnes of e-waste per hour.

- ❏ Choose more energy efficient and durable products.
- ❏ Choose electronic equipment which minimizes the use of hazardous substances.
- ❏ Purchase computers that are easy to upgrade to maximize their useable life.
- ❏ Recycle computers properly by bringing them back to the manufactures or retailers where facilities exist or donate. Many manufactures such as IBM, Apple, Dell and HP have systems in place to recover these.
- ❏ Have computer settings on energy saving mode and turn off screen savers.
- ❏ Turn off computers when not in use including monitors. Monitors account for around 50% of a computer's energy use.
- ❏ Choose green data centres.

- ❏ Look at refilling inkjet cartridges instead of throwing them away for new ones.
- ❏ Ink cartridges can be recycled through office stores and manufactures.
- ❏ Buy solar-powered calculators and other devices to eliminate the need for batteries.
- ❏ Use rechargeable batteries.
- ❏ Rent, lease or contract for services, instead of buying infrequently used equipment.

The Global e-sustainability initiative was created in 2001 to further sustainability in the ICT sector (www.gesi.org). Also look at the Electronic Industry Code of Conduct (www. eicc.info, www.ewaste.ch). Other programmes of interest include the Greenpeace Guide to Greener Electronics, which is a scorecard that highlights electronic products and companies (www.greenpeace. org). For more news visit the website www.greenercomputing. com. EPEAT is an online tool that helps select and compare environmentally safe electronic products (www.epeat.net). European Union Waste Electrical and Electronic Equipment legislation allows customers to return their used equipment to manufacturers free of charge and also requires the substitution of various heavy metals and chemicals in new electronic equipment since 2006.

All those other little things

Sustainable procurement of supplies and services is the primary way to introduce green concepts in offices and facilities. According to UNEP, the best procurement processes address the following:

- Maximum value for money (price, quality, availability, functionality);
- Environmental aspects of goods over their entire life-cycle;
- Social aspects (issues such as poverty eradication, labour conditions, human rights).

Below are some tips that can help.

- ❏ Use cleaning products that are biodegradable and environ-mentally friendly. Hire cleaning services companies who use environmentally friendly products. Look at going back to basics by using white wine vinegar as a glass cleaner.
- ❏ Buy recycled, reusable, recyclable, biodegradable, energy efficient, water conserving, non toxic, locally available products (paper, glass, etc).
- ❏ Look at sustainable office furniture, for example using sustain-able forest certified wood.
- ❏ Buy reusable cafeteria dishware. Reusable dishes are often cost-effective over the long-term compared with disposables.
- ❏ Avoid using single-use cups. Buy mugs.
- ❏ Use beverage dispensers for milk, juice or soft drinks.
- ❏ Fill the dishwasher before you use it.
- ❏ Buy organic, fair trade, free range and local products for the kitchen such as coffee, tea, sugar, etc.
- ❏ Don't use bottled water, where possible drink tap water instead.

> UNEP Sustainable Procurement Program can be seen at www.uneptie.org/pc/sustain/policies/green-proc.htm. The Environmentally Preferable Purchasing Guide provides a reference tool for choosing more sustainable options (greenguardian.com/EPPG/). To see the growing range of options available for sustain-able office products check out different office supplier such as the Green Office (www.thegreenoffice.com).

Commuting to work

As cities around the world grow larger and traffic congestion gets worse, the daily commute can take hours out of each day for many employees. Have you ever noticed how many cars during the morning rush hour have just one person in them? Promote the use of car pool-ing, public transportation or other more sustainable forms of travel as much as possible. Consider commuting by motorbike or scooter – they cost less to purchase and run, take up less space and are easier to park. GlaxoSmithKline pharmaceutical company in the UK has a bike scheme where employees who bike to work get a voucher which can be used at a bike store or to buy new parts for the bike from Dr. Bike. Dr. Bike is a bike mechanic who is paid by the company to come in every two weeks to repair bikes. There are facilities for cyclists to change, shower and iron their clothes. Each cyclist costs the company approximately £400 pounds per year while a car space costs over £2000. Registered cyclists have increased from 50 to 350 and continue to rise.[116]

Below are some tips to make the daily commute less of a grind

By Public Transport

- Prepare a public transport information pack with prices and times of routes to work.
- Make a policy to use public transport for business purposes where practical.
- Arrange a taxi for staff using the bus for times when they may work late.
- Provide salary advances to pay for season tickets or provide them for free.
- When possible explore alternatives to travelling by plane such as trains and buses, especially for flights less than 2 hours.
- Explore telecommuting options for employees to work from home.

By Bike

- Give a free cycle helmet . . . or bike.
- Put up a cycling notice board for routes, bike repairers and organizations.
- Provide incentive schemes such as salary advances to buy bikes on instalments.
- Buy an office bike and link up with a local bike store for regular maintenance.
- Install shower and changing facilities for employees who choose to walk, run or bike to work.

- ❑ Provide a secure place at work to store bikes.
- ❑ Use cycle couriers for delivering small items within the town or city.
- ❑ Provide a roadside assistance programme for bikes that have mechanical failure (see for example the Royal Automobiles Club of Tasmania's Bike Assist programme).
- ❑ Promote the health benefits of cycling (or walking) to work.

By Foot

- ❑ Promote the benefits of walking to work for those who travel short distances by car.

By Car

- ❑ Promote good driving techniques. Simple techniques can reduce fuel consumption by as much as 25%.
- ❑ Ensure regular maintenance to maintain fuel efficiency and vehicle longevity.
- ❑ If you buy new, buy small, fuel-efficient models.
- ❑ Consider car pooling with other organizations or joining a local Car Club.
- ❑ Consider off peak commuting to help reduce traffic congestion and save time travelling.
- ❑ If you need to use a taxi look at green options, for example London's Go Green Car has a fleet of hybrid cars.
- ❑ Look at more sustainable ways to move packages from one location to another including bike couriers or using mail services that use sustainable transportation methods.
- ❑ If you are moving from one office to another look for moving companies that provide reusable plastic containers as opposed to cardboard boxes.

Some countries now have car pooling websites, like NZ (www.jayride.co.nz) and Australia (www.letscarpool.com.au). Some information on public transport can be found at greenlivingideas.com/public-transportation/greening-public-transportation. The UK has a tax-free scheme to provide a cost effective way to purchase bikes to ride to work (www.cyclescheme.co.uk/). Yahoo Green has some tips on commuting (green.yahoo.com/living-green/commuting.html).

Organizing green events and meetings

Most organizations host events, meetings, seminars, annual general meetings and other conferences on a regular basis. Regardless of whether these are big or small events, they all consume resources, cost money and produce waste. Planning green events is about incorporating sustainability elements in traditional meeting planning. Hosting a green event can help conserve energy and reduce waste which saves money and provides an opportunity to raise awareness of issues. One event organizer replaced bottled water with reusable containers and bulk water dispensers, saving $15 000 with this simple step. The IUCN, an international conservation NGO, produced a guide to help its 8000 delegates at its 2008 Congress to make environmentally-smart decisions at different stages of their trip to, and stay in, Barcelona. It was part of the IUCN's effort to practice what it preached at the event on sustainability and conservation. After reading the manual, for those who didn't want to print the whole manual, they could just print out the one page summary included at the back (www.iucn.org/congress_08/about/green).

> ❑ *Meeting or no meeting:* Explore alternatives to meeting in person such as teleconferencing, videoconferencing and webinars.
> ❑ *Make your intentions clear:* Set priorities and make sure all involved in the organization are aware and included.
> ❑ *Look at visible and non visible:* Look at visible issues (recycled material use for programme material) and non visible ones (energy and waste management plans).
> ❑ *Facilities:* Choose a location that is easily accessible, i.e. direct flights, public transportation, etc. Check for locations that have their own environmental and social priorities.

- ❑ *Food and beverage:* Serve food that is sourced locally, fair trade, organic. Also think about how the food and drinks are served, for example by using mugs instead of disposable cups and bottles.
- ❑ *Accommodation:* Support hotels that are part of different green accreditation programmes or that have their own environmental policies such as TheGreenKey or Green Leaf.
- ❑ *Transportation:* Inform participants of public transportation and walking routes. Organize shuttles instead of taxis (these can provide good network opportunities for participants).
- ❑ *Procurement:* Choose supplies and suppliers with sustainability policies, such as certified products. Look at options such as renting rather than purchasing.
- ❑ *Get people involved:* Seek sponsors to help provide sustainable products. Consider getting the community involved. Advise participants in advance of a green attitude. Tell attendees what your sustainability plans are during the conference and tell them what they can do to get involved (i.e. recycle, give back name tags, turn off lights).
- ❑ *During the event:* Limit distribution of paper during events by having USB ports for people to download handouts or use email. Provide a reusable registration package. Look for 'sustainable' promotional products. Conduct registration and confirmation online. Measure your progress (i.e. how much paper is used, waste generated).
- ❑ *Post meeting:* Publish proceedings online and report on lessons learned. Have an on site drop off for attendees returning material that can be reused for other events or donated to local community groups and schools.
- ❑ *Sustainable tourism:* If participants are coming from abroad, give advice on sustainable tourism options in the area.

There are lots of resources online to green meetings www.epa.gov/oppt/greenmeetings/ US EPA It's Easy Being Green! A Guide to Planning and conducting environmentally aware meetings and events Environment Canada's Green Meeting Guide (www.greeninggovernment.gc.ca).

Putting together a green team

Employees are often very interested in sustainability issues and want to become engaged in moving their company forward in this area. The response to this has been the creation of 'Green Teams'. These are either formal or informal teams of employees who are engaging in sustainability in the office.

Other than getting employees engaged, green teams can provide an important avenue for companies to identify opportunities on how to become more sustainable and implement these ideas. They can also prove a driving force in pushing the company's overall sustainability objectives forward. Two examples of Green teams:

- In 2007, forty eBay employees stepped up to help the company make greener decisions. Now there are more than 1000 eBay employees in 18 countries in the eBay Green team (www.ebaygreenteam.com).
- Deloitte's 'Greening the Dot' initiative involves offices choosing from among 37 different greening projects. A 'Greening Toolkit' that includes implementation instructions and communication tools were given to each office. The result was that over half of the workforce got engaged in implementing over a thousand greening projects across nearly a hundred offices in just the first six months, which led to reduced energy, water and paper use, reduced travel and increased recycling.

Below are some tips that can help:

- ❑ *Put together your team:* Green teams can be either formal groups or informal groups. Start by networking. See if there are other teams across the organization that you can join.
- ❑ *Survey members of staff:* Talk to members of the team and other employees to find out what issues they are most interested in to determine the focus of the team. You can also organize brainstorming sessions to gather a wide range of ideas to start with.
- ❑ *Get support:* Actively recruit employees that have the power to make real changes happen into the team. If you want to work

on greening the building make sure you have someone from facilities on the team.

❑ *Focus on action:* Green teams often take a double role of raising awareness and putting in place real goals and programmes. Look at ways to create value for the company by reducing costs and creating new business opportunities.

❑ *Find a sponsor:* Make sure you have the right people on your side, for example management.

❑ *Start an email list focused on sustainability:* See OneNorthWest's tips for facilitating an environmental email list before you get started (www.onenw.org/toolkit/email-list-facilitation).

❑ *Communicate with the group:* There are many tools out there to help communicate with the rest of the team and other employees including newsletters, wikis, posting blogs or starting an online group (for example through Google or Yahoo).

❑ *Organize lunch time meetings:* Organize meetings during lunch hours (with lunch included) focused on raising awareness or coordinating action. Invite guest speakers, share challenges. Keep these meetings light and fun but relevant to people's jobs.

❑ *Create a contest:* Green teams at eBay started a 'funky mug' contest where employees brought mugs from home to replace disposable cups in the office.

❑ *Share best practice and challenges:* Put in place mechanisms for employees to share success stories in implementing sustainability and get help with challenges they are facing. This is especially interesting in large companies that operate in several offices or across several countries.

❑ *Present case studies:* Present examples from across the company and your industry of projects that have worked that could be done in your office.

❑ *Keep track of your successes:* Keep track of how you do and celebrate your successes with the rest of the office.

❑ *Keep it relevant:* If people aren't attending meetings, or it is the same people showing up over and over again change the focus of the meetings to make sure they are more relevant and interesting to others in the office.

Performance Contracting

One of the main reasons that organizations give for not getting involved in sustainability programmes is cost. At the same time, increasing evidence clearly shows that many programmes may cost more in the short run, but will actually save money in the long run. So, in response to these cost concerns, many innovative pricing strategies are being developed to help pay for business sustainable activities. One such strategy is performance contracting, According to BSD Global, 'Performance contracting is a means of raising money for investments in energy efficiency that is based on future savings. It enables money that will be saved as a result of the introduction of a new energy-efficient technology to be used to offset the cost of financing, installing and operating that technology.' This means reduced risk to the lending organization as the contractor takes on the risk of not achieving savings. There are several ways to structure a performance contract.

- *First out or guaranteed savings:* All the contractor's costs are repaid annually out of the savings as they accrue. The length of the contract (typically four to eight years) is usually determined to ensure that all costs are paid out by the end of the contract period.
- *Shared savings:* The business and the contractor agree to share the savings over the contract period. The actual cost of the measures is not included in the contract, and the business has no obligation to pay off those costs. Shared savings contract terms are usually longer – up to 10 years.
- *Chauffage*: A performance contractor effectively takes over the operation of a customer's utility or production facilities upgrades to them, and often payment of the customer's utility bills. The customer pays the contractor a regular fee equal to the utility bills before the project, or some other negotiated fee.

Other innovative financing strategies include green building tax credits and leasing services instead of purchasing equipment. Some programmes are being developed that base repayment on 'green' savings, such as the Green Loan Initiative of the City of Toronto. The builders repay the loan through funds that would otherwise be spent on heating, cooling and electricity.[116]

PART 4

WRAPPING IT ALL UP

What Can I Do?
What Will the Future Bring?

17 What can I Do?

This book has introduced sustainability and a wide range of tools being used to implement it in organizations around the world. It has presented various tips and ideas on how employees and businesses can get more active and engaged in sustainability and how sustainability can be explored to positively influence a business in terms of both reducing costs and potentially increasing revenue, while also having a positive impact on the environment, and society as a whole.

However, individuals are not only playing a role in bringing sustainability forward through their jobs. People create both the supply and the demand for products and services, create the innovations and push for change. Individuals make decisions on a daily basis as employees, as consumers and as citizens that have a direct impact on sustainability. Many believe that one person cannot make a difference, yet all of the things that people do on a daily basis collectively add up do make a difference. If employees start exploring these ideas in their jobs, if consumers start asking companies to provide them with sustainable choices and if citizens actively engage in strengthening their communities, that is when things will really start happening.

As an employee—leading by example

As seen throughout this book, employees interested in sustainability have several choices when it comes to career paths and getting engaged in these issues. These include:

- ***In any company.*** The main way for employees to get involved is by driving social and environmental change from within any company and at any level. Regardless of whether your company is fully engaged in the sustainability debate, these are tools that can be used to strengthen the business.

- ***In a 'green' job.*** With increased greening among all industries is coming a wave of new careers, most of which are an environmental twist on old professions. Engineers are doing research on renewable energies, people in finance are getting involved in trading carbon credits or microfinance within mainstream institutions, while architects are designing green buildings. In fact most of the topics introduced in this book have careers attached to them.

- ***In a 'green' company or other organization.*** A company does not need to advertise 'green' jobs in order to attract diverse talent. According to Greenbiz.com, 'More often than not, the environmental aspects of these jobs are hidden. That is, the jobs aren't advertised as "environmental". Rather, companies with strong commitments to environmental responsibility are looking for job candidates who "get it" . . . and who can seamlessly integrate those goals into their everyday jobs'.[118]

- ***As an entrepreneur.*** Whatever kind of business you decide to start, whether it has a social or environmental mission or not, there are many ways you can run your business that support the principles of sustainability from responsible sourcing, to greening your products, offices and services.

For many more ideas take a look at the lists at the end of each of the chapters in the book. Also take a look at different professional networks aimed at managers, for example Net Impact (www.netimpact.org). Green Drinks is a social networking group in over 40 countries and 463 cities (www.greendrinks.org). Many sites advertise 'green' jobs including MonsterTRAK GreenCareers, Greenbiz (jobs.greenbiz.com) BSR (www.bsr.org/resources/jobs) and DevNetJobs (www.devnetjobs.org).

How to turn any job into a green job

1. *Get involved in office greening programmes:* Get involved in activities that are already happening in your office such as recycling and employee engagement programmes. If these don't exist, start them.
2. *Take a look at your job:* Explore ways to incorporate sustainability into what is already in your job description and the goals of your team.
3. *Stay informed:* Look at professional or other organizations to which you already belong to see what they are doing in this area. Sign up for daily updates to keep informed. Take a course or attend an event, a conference or speaker series to learn more.
4. *Volunteer your time or expertise:* Volunteer your time and expertise on sustainability initiatives happening in the company and outside in the community.
5. *Give feedback:* The people who do the jobs are in the best place to provide insights on how to do things better. If you see something that could be done better, in a more sustainable and efficient way, in the work place speak up about it.
6. *Support others in their activities:* Be supportive of the work that your employees or your colleagues are doing in this area. Give employees and members of your team time to explore sustainability in the work place or in the community.
7. *Share your experiences:* Write articles, speak at events and to others to share your experience in working on sustainability issues in the work place and the challenges you have faced and how you overcame these. Speak up on the areas you think need more work.
8. *Be positive, but constructively critical:* Rather than saying something won't work, look at contributing to the discussion and working through ideas to see if and how they could work.

As a consumer—putting your money where your mouth is

The most important sector of them all, and the one that everyone is a part of is the rapidly growing consumer sector. There are almost 7 billion of us on the planet, each making decisions on a daily basis that affect businesses and society. As a consumer you can look at:

- ***What you buy.*** Companies provide products because they believe there will be, or there is a demand for them. As a consumer, choosing to support the products that you believe are good sends a strong message to companies. Where you choose to buy those products from, like retail stores that support the same sustainability values as you do, is also important.
- ***What you choose not to buy.*** Just as important as what you buy is what you choose not to buy. Choosing not to buy brands that have unsustainable practices and letting them know will send a clear message to these companies that they need to change in order to gain loyal customers.
- ***By giving feedback.*** If you want to know what the companies you buy from are doing in this area, or want them to provide more information or safer products, contact them and give them feedback. Companies such as Dell have created social networks where customers can provide direct feedback through two-way channels (http://www.dellideastorm.com). The goal is for you, the customer, to tell Dell what new products or services you'd like to see them develop.

The Green Guide gives information on how to be greener everyday including buying guides (www.thegreenguide.com). Green Living Ideas (www.greenlivingideas.com), Ethical consumer's guide (www.ethiscore.org). Science in the box helps consumers know more about the products they are buying (www.scienceinthe-box.com). Consumers International (www.consumersinternational. org). There are countless excellent books on the topic, often with country specific information. *Ecoholic* by Adria Vasil (Canada) is an excellent resource regardless of where you live. Also read *The Consumer's Guide to Effective Environmental Choices* by Michael Brower and Warren Leon.

PLEASE think before you buy

A Simple Guide to Making Choices as a Consumer

When faced with a choice of products, think about:

P: **Packaging**→Look at the packaging. Is it over-packaged? Is it under-packaged? Can I reuse the packaging? Is it recyclable?

L: **Location**→Look at where the product is from. Is it produced locally or far away? Look at the store you are buying it from. Are you buying from a small independent store, a cooperative, a large store? What do you know about the sustainability policies of that store?

E: **Essential**→Do you really need the item? Can you live without it?

A: **Alternative**→Are there alternatives that are more sustainable? Can you buy the product in bulk or in refillable containers?

S: **Story**→What is the story of the product? What company produced it? What information is on the label about that company and what do these labels tell you about the product? What are the ingredients?

E: **End of Life**→Is the product durable? Is it disposable? Is it easy to recycle? Can I bring it back to the manufacturer? Can I donate it to charity when I am done or pass it on to someone else to use?

As a citizen—be active in your community

All individuals, apart from being consumers and employees are also citizens and members of a community. As part of their community they can have a significant influence on sustainable and unsustainable practices in this realm as well.

- *Lifestyle choice:* How one chooses to live one's life has a significant impact. Whether you choose to participate in community activities, bike to work or to have a second car all has an impact.
- *Increasing efficiency:* Many of the same tools and frameworks used to apply sustainability to the business can be applied at home.

UNDecadeofEducation for Sustainable Development 2005–2015 (www.unesco.org/education/desd).

This includes reducing water and energy usage, recycling and disposing of waste appropriately.

- *Participate:* Many individuals around the world have a choice in who runs their countries and their communities, but do not make their choice heard. Rather than complaining about how ineffective something is, whether it is government, regulations, infrastructure or education, voice your opinion either through voting or supporting the causes you believe in.

> *'Never doubt that a small band of caring and committed people can change the world. Indeed it is the only thing that ever has'*
>
> MARGARET MEAD

18   What will the Future Bring?

This book has aimed to introduce you as managers to all the things that are happening in the area of sustainability with the hope that some of these will be relevant to your business and will inspire action. No one knows exactly what the future will bring. Here is one take.

Sustainability becomes the norm: This book explores sustainability as the balancing of social, environmental and economic issues in a way that is beneficial to both business and to society. However, for others sustainable means the financial sustainability of a company, the ability of a company to continue to operate over the long-term. The two words will increasingly connect until one day soon, they will mean the same thing. There will be no sustainable tourism, it will just be tourism . . . no sustainable office furniture, it will just be furniture. The minimum standard will be products and services that are sustainable and best practice could be something altogether different, products that give back, that do more.

From perceived benefit to actual: It will increasingly be easier to know how a company is actually doing as opposed to how it is perceived to be doing. In the same way as you can easily understand how a company is doing financially by looking at the numbers, in the future there will be ways to know clearly how a company is doing in terms of sustainability.

Direct to indirect: Many companies are just starting to get involved in sustainability. Their activities usually involve either doing the bare minimum, or many small, separate activities that are unrelated and happen in relative isolation. Tomorrow will see these small activities coming together into larger, stronger and more integrated strategies that cover the whole organization and all their activities. Companies will look beyond the direct impacts they have on the environment and society, for example, through their energy use and the waste they create, to indirect impacts like the footprint of not just their suppliers but also the suppliers of those suppliers. This will lead to moving away from quick fixes on parts of the system, to a greater appreciation of how to strengthen the system as a whole.

Increased transparency: Today a company that is working in sustainability can prove it through different certification programmes and eco-labels while companies that are not sustainable, and even in some cases those that are doing harm and are not compliant, have no information on their labels to inform consumers of this. In the future this may be the other way around. The norm will be sustainability, and all companies who do not uphold these basic, sustainable standards will need to provide information as to why and how on their labels. Labels will clearly show the amount of waste a product generates throughout the process and inefficiencies both in production and use.

The elephants will start dancing: There are certain major players in the world, groups that because of their sheer size have power and can have an important influence in pushing the sustainability agenda forward. Although slow to change, once these groups start it brings with it a momentum that changes everything. Look out for big companies making and implementing ground breaking commitments to sustainability and asking more and more from their suppliers, their employees and their customers. Look out to see how emerging market countries get engaged in these issues. Look towards the world of the SME who have power in numbers and who, once they get engaged as well, can have a crucial collective impact. Look at the poor who, through the emerging world of micro everything are starting to not only be served, but play a significant role.

Creating enabling environments: Many sustainability activities that businesses are encouraged to take part in are not possible unless they are working in an environment that allows this. If the city they work in does not recycle, if it does not have bike lanes or proper public transportation, if it does not have rules and regulations to create level playing fields, if it does not have alternative energy options, a company and its employees will struggle to be truly sustainable. Look for cities to become smarter in terms of how they generate, distribute and use water and energy. Look out for cities that focus on people, on communities.

Embedding sustainability into education: How do you ensure change occurs relatively quickly? By educating the new generation of professionals. If you want accountants, analysts, architects, politicians and managers to change the way they work, then incorporate sustainability into the way that they learn their profession. This means embedding it into mainstream teaching programmes to reach the whole profession, not just those with a particular interest in it. Look for schools to embed sustainability in the way they teach at all levels, from primary school to high school, in professional training programmes and specializations.

Anything goes: Look out for completely new ways of doing business. Look out for sustainability innovations to come out regardless of whether times are good or times are bad. Ultimately the future will be whatever we make it.

> *'This is not the end. It is not even the beginning of the*
> *end. But it is, perhaps, the end of the beginning.'*
> SIR WINSTON CHURCHILL

Twenty-one wise words of advice

1. ***Sometimes it works, sometimes it doesn't:*** Pilot and execute as a way to move your ideas from theory to action. Freedom to make mistakes and learn from them. Be willing to take those chances. As Benjamin Franklin once said 'I haven't failed, I've had 10 000 ideas that didn't work'.

2. *Be patient:* It didn't take a week to develop wind farms or solar panels. Things take time and effort. Companies can be slow to change, but when they do they bring lots of weight.

3. *Keep an open mind:* Question assumptions, ask yourself why you do things the way you do and if you couldn't do things differently.

4. *Answers often lie within:* Organizations are made up of an incredible amount of ideas and wealth that they regularly fail to tap into: their employees and their customers.

5. *Don't just do it like everyone else:* Not all green initiatives are created equal, don't make promises that you can't, or won't deliver on. Be different.

6. *Keep it relevant:* Make sure it makes sense. Products need to solve a consumer problem and work. Get involved because it is something you value, not because it is the thing to do.

7. *There are no shortcuts:* There are many tools that have been created to help in your efforts but none will provide assurance against failure or of success. Use them as guidance and part of a larger strategy.

8. *There is no black or white:* Perhaps polluting maximizes shareholder value by saving money but the public response does not. Your actions have unintended consequences, both negative and positive.

9. *Work together:* There is an increasingly wide range of experience within organizations in different industries and different countries. Customers want to be more involved. Work with others.

10. *Be active, not defensive:* Sustainability strategies developed in a defensive manner lead people to miss opportunities.

11. *It is all about balance:* You don't have to do everything, but what you do decide to do should be done well.

12. *Everything is connected:* Just because you don't see it, it doesn't mean that it isn't there. Decisions you make have an effect far away. Don't see the world in silos, everything is connected.

13 *Focus on the problem, not the symptoms:* It is not about putting a filter on polluted water before it is released, it is about looking at why the water is polluted in the first place.

14. *It doesn't need to be perfect:* Be honest and open about your efforts and what you are trying to do. Be flexible.

15. *Do something different:* Get out of your comfort zone. Read something different to find inspiration, see what others in completely different industries and fields are doing in sustainability.

16. *Don't just complain; do something:* Complaining about something is fine, if it is constructive and helping to move things forward. Get involved.

17. *Unlikely events are common:* The fact is that unlikely events happen more often than one thinks. No one can predict the future.

18. *Not everything that looks green is green:* Just because something looks green, and sounds green it doesn't mean that it is green. Sustainability is not a PR exercise; it is a way of operating.

19. *Do it right the first time:* Rather than doing it wrong over and over again.

20. *It doesn't really matter how it starts, or why it starts:* What matters is how it continues.

21. *Enjoy it*

Additional Resources: Who, What, Where and How

Who: different groups

Although much of the information and resources in this book are aimed at the business sector, they are by far not the only ones that are active in this area. The business sector is increasingly working with, and building on, the initiatives already being undertaken by governments, international organizations, NGOs and other networks.

All these groups can use the tools in the book in their own operations and need to tweak them to fit their own unique situation in the same ways that individual businesses need to. There is no longer such a big difference between the different groups; NGOs are being encouraged to incorporate business principles such as efficiency in order to be more financially sustainable while companies are learning advocacy and different ways of seeing the world from NGOs.

There is also increasingly a blurring between the different actors. Universities and NGOs are providing consulting services; Consulting firms are becoming think tanks and providing not for profit services. There is also an increase in NGOs who are providing consulting services such as the WWF. Finally, the different groups are increasingly working together on projects. This in part means that more kinds of information and resources at different levels are available.

The following information is meant to introduce the reader to sustainability as it relates to these other actors and provide some links to organizations that are working on sustainability.

Educational institutions: Universities are getting involved in the sustainability debate in several ways. First, through their facilities in energy, water and waste management plans for new and existing buildings. Second, through their curriculum and teaching both in existing programmes and new specialty programmes. Third, through the development of new technologies and ideas. The Principles for Responsible Management Education, are endorsed by a growing number of universities around the world (www.unprme.org). The Talloires Declaration is a ten point action plan for incorporating sustainability into teaching and research (www.ulsf.org/programs_talloires.html). The Aspen Institute Centre for Business Education (www.aspencbe.org) has several programmes including Beyond Grey Pinstripes (www.beyondgrey pinstripes.org), which provides rankings of MBA programmes based on sustainability curriculum and research as well as an online database of case studies, syllabi and innovative teaching materials on business and sustainability (www.caseplace.org). Another resource is the World Resource Institute's BELL programme (www.wri.org/project/bell) which is also focused on business education. Most schools now have one or several student groups working in this area, some part of larger international networks such as Net Impact (www.netimpact.org), Oikos (www.oikos-international.org) and AIESEC (www.aiesec.org). Schools from preschool all the way up to continuing education are starting to provide training in these areas. The United Nations Decade for Education for Sustainable Development runs from 2005–2015 (www.unesco.org).

Government: Governments play a crucial role in sustainability. These large organizations are the world's biggest employers, landowners, energy users, and are a huge purchaser of goods and services. Governments also play a crucial role in developing and implementing international agreements, national policies, laws, regulations and incentives. They also put in place infrastructure and services (transport, recycling, etc.) that enable people to have more sustainable lifestyles and business practices. They provide guidance for business and consumers, monitoring how things are going, and providing enforcement where necessary. Finally, they play a key role in protecting the commons, society and the natural environment in their country. ICLEI is an international association of local, national and regional governments that have made a commitment to sustainable development (www.iclei. org). Some cities to take a look at include Curitiba in Brazil, Vancouver in Canada (www.vancouver.ca) and Malmo in Sweden (www.malmo. se), who are focused on sustainability. At the national level sustainability information is often found within the parts of the government responsible for the environment or for business, for example. Many governments also have departments which provide development advice and funds to certain other countries based on national interest and priorities, including in many cases work on private sector development and promoting responsible business practices. Examples include Canadian International Development Agency (www.acdi-cida. gc.ca), UK Department for International Development (www.dfid.gov. uk) and US Agency for International Development (www.usaid.gov). At the regional level governments also work together through organizations such as the OECD, which brings together the governments of 30 countries committed to democracy and the market economy (www. oecd.org) and the European Union (europa.eu/).

International organizations: Many of these were established just after World War II to promote international cooperation and stability. They are funded by member governments but are largely independent and most have budgets of several hundred million dollars. They tend to be bureaucratic relative to the private sector because of the consensus required to move forward, but they provide an important platform to move forward on these issues at an international level. A good example is the UN (www.un.org) which is made up of 30 affiliated organizations (www.unsystem.org) that work on everything including food and agriculture (www.fao.org), AIDS (www.unaids.org), the environment (www.unep.org) and even telecommunications (www.itu.int). Another group includes the International Financial Organizations including the World Bank (www.worldbank.org), the International Monetary Fund (www.imf.org), the African Development Bank (www.afdb.org) and the Asian Development Bank (www.adb.org). There is a lot of guidance for businesses on how to work with these international organizations, in particular with the UN, on the different websites. There are also links to many UN–business partnerships throughout this book. (WBCSD Guide to development actors and website has list of information on different development actors at www.wbcsd.org/web/devguide.htm.)

Non-Governmental Organization: It is estimated that NGOs represent over $1 trillion in assets and employ over 19 million people making them the world's eighth largest economy.[1] These several million organizations around the world range considerably by size, by issue, by funding, by scope, by affiliate but also by professionalism and how willing they are to work with business (as opposed to against it). Increasingly some of the large NGOs have business divisions working at partnerships with the business sector. NGOs receive funding from governments, grants, business and private donations. International NGOs shape and drive the CR and sustainability agendas. Their role is likely to grow in importance, and many of them are now working with business. As NGOs build major brands and move into the mainstream they face growing calls for greater transparency. CERES, GRI and IISD all are reporting now with GRI. Some examples of the major NGOs that are also working with business include the World Wildlife Federation (WWF) (www.wwf.org), Greenpeace (www.greenpeace.org), The World Conservation Union (also known as IUCN www.iucn.org) and Conservation International (www.conservation.org, www.celb.org). An interesting document on the subject is The Twenty-first Century NGO: In the market for change (www.sustainability.com/). For lists of NGOs by country visit www.csrwire.com/directory, www.iblf.org/csr/csrwebassist.nsf/content/e1.html, www.developmentgateway.org.

Think-tanks: These organizations focus on research. Some examples include the World Resource Institute (www.wri.org), the Aspen Institute (www.aspeninstitute.org/) and the International Institute for Sustainable Development (www.iisd.org). Many other organizations are also involved in think-tank related activities including a number of consulting firms for example SustainAbility (www.sustainability.com) and the Rocky Mountain Institute (www.rmi.org). Also look at the Earth Institute (www.earth.columbia.edu).

Working Together

The UN recognizes nine 'major groups' in society. These groups actively participate in all UN meetings and present internationally coordinated positions on the issues discussed.

- *Women* make up half of the global population and are key actors because of their role and influence in communities and families. For more see the work by the Women's Environment and Development Organization (www.wedo.org).
- *Children and youth* comprise nearly half of the world population and will inherit the responsibility of looking after the Earth. Take a look at International Youth Caucus (www.youthlink.org) and YouthXchange (www.youthxchange.org).
- *Indigenous people* comprise 5% of the world's population but embody 80% of the world's cultural diversity. It is estimated that they occupy 20% of the world's land surface but nurture 80% of the world's biodiversity on ancestral lands and territories.
- *NGOs* perform a variety of services including bringing citizens' concerns to government, monitor policy and programme implementation, and encouraging participation at the community level (www.un.org/dpi/ngosection).
- *Workers and trade unions* work at addressing industrial change, with a high priority given to protection of the work environment and the related natural environment and promotion of socially responsible and economic development. The International Confederation of Free Trade Unions (www.icftu.org).
- *Business and industry* have an important role in operating responsibly. See the International Chamber of Commerce (www.iccwbo.org) and the WBCSD (www.wbcsd.org).
- *Science and technology* are developing environmentally friendly technologies and making discoveries in health and disease eradication, just to name a few. International Council for Scientific Union (www.icsu.org).
- *Farmers* play an important role. Agriculture occupies one third of the land surface of the Earth and is the central activity for much of the world's population. Federation of Agricultural Producers (www.ifap.org).
- *Local authorities* which includes city mayors and local governments. International Council for Local Environmental Initiatives (www.iclei.org).

What: sustainability issues

Agriculture and Fish: Keeping pace with population growth and alleviating poverty over the next decades will require greater food production with less environmental impact. Problems include soil erosion; reduced rates of yield gains, less fertile land, contamination of water, desertification, pesticides, etc. Agriculture uses over 70% of water resources. There are many international organizations working on sustainable agriculture including the Food and Agriculture Organization (www.fao.org) and the European Conservation Agriculture Federation (www.ecaf.org). The Codex Alimentarius has information about food standards (www.codexalimentarius.net). The Sustainable Agriculture Initiative aims to foster more sustainable practices among farmers (www. saiplatform.org). Organic farming follows certain techniques including no synthetic chemical use, recycling of organic substances, crop rotation and biological control of pests and diseases. There are increasingly labels to educate consumers about the farming techniques used in different products including organic farming (www.fao.org/organicag). The Soil Association is one of many organizations working on certifying organic food and farming (www.soilassociation.org). The Marine Stewardship Council (MSC), based on the Food and Agriculture Organization's Code of Conduct for Responsible Fisheries, seeks to harness consumer purchasing power to generate change and promote environmentally responsible stewardship of the world's fisheries (www.msc.org).

Biodiversity: Biodiversity according to the Convention on Biodiversity refers to 'The variability among living organisms from all sources including terrestrial, marine and other aquatic ecosystems and the ecological complexes of which they are part. This includes diversity within species, between species and of ecosystems.' This also includes goods such as clear air, fresh water, food, medicines and shelter and also provides services and functions such as pollination, air, water and land purification, climate regulation, drought and flood control, habitats, etc. Threats to biodiversity include loss of forests, wetlands, mangroves, invasive species to name but a few. There are many international conventions on biodiversity which are relevant and affect business including the Convention on Wetlands (www.ramsar.org), Convention for the Protection of the Natural Heritage (www.unesco.org), Convention to Regulate International Trade in Endangered Species of Wild Flora and Fauna (www.cites.org) and UN Convention on Biological Diversity (www.biodiv.org). Biodiversity hotspots is a programme by Conservation International which focuses on the richest and most threatened reserves of plant and animal life on earth (www. biodiversityhotspots.org).The IFC produced a Guide to Biodiversity for the Private Sector available at ifc.org/ifcext/sustainability.nsf/ Content/BiodiversityGuide.The WRI has also produced a Business and Ecosystems Issue Brief which explores six challenges relating to ecosystems and their implications for business (www.wri.org).

Climate Change: Of all the issues that affect our environment and society today, climate change is the one that has benefited from unprecedented interest and an increasing business response.The United Nations Convention on Climate Change entered into force on 21st March 1994 and was ratified by virtually all countries. It is important as it instigated discussions on what could be done to reduce global warming. Above national measures, the treaty offers different market-based mechanisms to achieve these targets. One of the largest outcomes of the Kyoto Treaty is the development of carbon markets.The carbon emissions unit provides an economic tool to measure the climate change control activities of governments, institutions and individuals. Carbon emissions trading makes up the largest emissions trading mechanism in the world. The 2008 world carbon market worth was stated at $ 118 billion and it is expected to grow to $ 150 billion in 2009 despite poor economic conditions.[2]

The business sector is responding to the climate change challenge by actively trying to understand the impacts environmental issues have across business, and implementing strategies to address them. In addition to these internal efforts, businesses have also stepped up to advocate and drive governmental policy development. Businesses contribute to the solution in many ways.They create new business models, innovate technologies and implement different ways of operating.

Business managers can take a proactive approach to addressing climate change by understanding the potential impacts on business operations and by looking for opportunities to cut emissions across the supply chain. There are many resources now on climate change and business. A few examples include the Pew Centre on Global Climate Change, which has a series of Climate Change 101 reports outlining what climate change is and what is being done about it (www.pewclimate. org). Greenhouse Gas Protocol is the most widely used international accounting tool for government and business to understand, quantify and manage greenhouse gas emissions (www.ghgprotocol.org). Also look at the UN Framework Convention on Climate Change and the Kyoto Protocol (www.unfccc.int), and the Intergovernmental Panel on Climate Change (www.ipcc.ch).

Cultural Heritage: Cultural heritage refers to tangible forms such as property and sites, however, it also includes intangible forms of culture such as cultural knowledge, innovation and community practices. Companies should protect cultural and natural heritage from the adverse impacts of project activities and support its preservation. This applies to cultural heritage regardless of whether or not it has been legally protected or previously disturbed. (See The Convention Concerning the Protection of the World Cultural and Natural Heritage 1972 and UNESCO World Heritage, at whc.unesco.org.)

Energy: Energy use is rising worldwide. Fossil fuels dominate the world's energy supply, yet the resulting greenhouse gas emissions are causing climate change. Currently about 2 billion people live off the electrical generation grid representing huge markets for other energy systems such as wind, solar, natural gas, etc. The impacts of energy production and consumption are introducing risks to industries. In response to this, proactive businesses are conducting inventories of their operations to reduce energy intensity, use and emissions. International organizations such as the World Energy Council (www.worldenergy.org) and the International Energy Agency (www.iea.org) have resources and programmes in this area. Some international initiatives include WBCSD's Electricity Utilities Sector Project (www.wbcsd.org), Global

Network on Energy for Sustainable Development (www.gnesd.org) and International Renewable Energy Alliance (www.ren-alliance.org). For coal the World Coal Institute (www.worldcoal.org). International Petroleum Industry Environmental Conservation Association (www.ipieca.org).The Global Gas Flaring Reduction Initiative (www.worldbank.org/ggfr).

Forest: Forests cover 30% of the world's land area and support a wide variety of critical natural processes, including carbon absorption, biodiversity and air filtering, in addition to providing us with raw materials for various goods and services. Issues include the sustainable sourcing of products, the sustainable management of forests and the social aspects relating to local communities and indigenous peoples whose lives are intertwined with the forest. In terms of ratings and certification schemes the Forest Stewardship Council (FSC) is an international label that allows customers worldwide to recognize products that promote the responsible management of the world's forests (www.fsc.org). The WWF–World Bank Global Forest Alliance has published a tool for assessing the comprehensiveness of forest certification systems (www.worldwildlife.org). Environmental Paper Assessment Tool (epat.org) and the WWF Paper Scorecard and Tissue Scoring (panda.org). There are also many international initiatives in this area including the FAO Sustainable Forests (fao.org) and the UN Forum on Forests (un.org/esa/forests). The WBCSD has information on the Forest Products Industry Sector (wbcsd.org), while UNEP has resources on cleaner production in pulp and paper mills (uneptie.org).The World Resource Institute has information on the Sustainable Procurement of Wood and Paper-Based Products (sustainableforestprods.org) (credibleforestcertification.org).

The FSC criteria:

- Prohibit conversion of forests or any other natural habitat.
- Respect of international workers rights.
- Prohibition of use of hazardous chemicals.
- Respect of human rights with particular attention to indigenous peoples.

- No corruption – follow all applicable laws.
- Identification and appropriate management of areas that need special protection (e.g. cultural or sacred sites, habitat of endangered animals or plants).

Mining: The mining industry has come under pressure to improve its social and environmental performance, and transparency. Issues include the process of extraction, impact on the environment and communities, as well as labour issues. The ICMM is a CEO-led organization representing many of the world's leading mining and metals companies, committed to the responsible production of the minerals and metals society needs (www.icmm.org). The Extractive industries transparency initiative aims to strengthen governance by improving transparency and accountability in the extractives sector (www.eitransparency. org). There are also certain certification systems coming into effect, such as the Kimberley Process, which impose extensive requirements to enable suppliers to certify shipments of rough diamonds as 'conflict free' (www.kimberleyprocess.com). Good Practice is a joint initiative between several international organizations which provides access to a library of good practice guidelines, standards and case studies (www. goodpracticemining.com).

Textiles: The types of materials used to make textiles and fabric, how they're sourced as well as how and where they're made, all have an impact on many parts of society. Organizations such as the Ethical Trading Initiative (www.ethicaltrade.org), the clean clothes campaign (www.cleanclothes.org) and the Business Social Compliance Initiative (www.bsci-eu.com) are dedicated to proper work conditions in factories and suppliers. There is also increasing interest in the kinds of materials used as well as how they are grown, harvested and processed. Cotton for example, although it seems like the most natural of materials, uses large amounts of chemical fertilizers and water. The processes used then to turn these raw materials into products also need greening for example textile wet processing and leather tanning (www.uneptie. org). Work is also being done to explore natural dyes made from plants (www.pioneerthinking.com/naturaldyes.html).

Tourism: The tourism sector has over 300 different sustainable tourism standards. In an attempt to provide a unified standard, over 30 organizations from the industry came together in 2008 to create the Partnership for Global Sustainability Tourism Criteria which works to foster increased understanding of sustainable tourism practice and the adoption of universal sustainable tourism principles (sustainabletourismcriteria.org). There are several international initiatives such as UNEP's Sustainable Tourism Programme (www.uneptie.fr), the World Tourism Organization (www.unwto.org) and The World Travel and Tourism Council (www.wttc.org). For more information see the links section at the Centre for Sustainable Destinations (www.nationalgeographic.com/travel/sustainable). The Tour operators Initiative works to develop operate and market tourism in a sustainable manner (www.toinitiative.org). Destinations are also going sustainable, Costa Rica are building a reputation of being an eco-destination.

Where: around the world

Sustainability is happening all over the world, but the ways in which it is being approached and the kinds of issues that are important are vastly different. It is also an area that is changing, fast. For this reason this section aims to give you links to a few organizations in different

---

Want more? state of the world reports

Around the same time that companies are busy putting together their annual reports, the different NGOs and international organizations around the world are producing their annual state of the world reports. There are a growing number of these covering every possible topic imaginable. Here is a selection of popular examples:

- **The Living Planet Index** published by the World Wildlife Federation is a periodic update on the state of the world's ecosystems (www.panda.org).
- Worldwatch Institute's **State of the World Report** provides yearly information on issues that are important (www.worldwatch.org).

- The UN produces a wide range of yearly reports covering every topic imaginable in this area. **United Nations Commission on Sustainable Development** releases a report every few years with the latest trends in sustainable development (www.un.org/esa/sustdev). UNEP Global Outlook (www.unep.org/geo) and UNDP Human Development Report (hdr.undp.org/) both provide data on the state of the world. Other specialized agencies provide annual reports on a range of topics including the state of the world's children (www.unicef.org), agriculture (www.fao.org), forests and desertification, to name but a few.
- The **World Resource Institute** produced Tomorrow's Markets: global trends and their implication for business, which provides interesting background on the issues (pdf.wri.org/tm_tomorrows_markets.pdf) and Earth Trends (www.earthtrends.wri.org) as well as Environmental Stories to Watch, released every year.
- The **Encyclopedia of Earth** is an online reference about the Earth, its natural environments and their interaction with society (www.eoearth.org).

countries where you can start your research if you are interested in finding out what is happening in your country, or another country. Many of the organizations and NGOs presented in this book also have offices in countries around the world with more information (i.e. WWF, IUCN, Ashoka and different consulting firms).

Some links just to get you started.

Africa: African Institute of Corporate Citizenship (www.aiccafrica.com), Green Business Africa (www.greenbusinessafrica.com), NEPAD Business Foundation (www.nepadbusinessfoundation.org). **Algeria:** Association pour la Promotion de l'Efficacite et la Qualite des Entreprises (www.apeque.asso.dz). **Ethiopia:** Cleaner Production Centre (www.ecpc.org.et). **Kenya:** National Cleaner Production Centre (www.cpkenya.org). **Morocco:** Cleaner Production Centre (www.cmpp.ma). **Mozambique:** Forum Empresarial para o Meio Ambiente (FEMA) (www.fema.org.mz). **South Africa:** National Business Initiative (www.nbi.org.za), National Cleaner Production Centre (www.ncpc. co.za). **Tunisia:** Cleaner Production Centre (www.citet.nat.tn). **Uganda:** Cleaner Production Centre (www.ucpc.co.ug). **Zimbabwe:** Business Council for Sustainable Development Zimbabwe (www.bcsdz. co.zw), SIRDC Cleaner Production Center (www.sirdc.ac.zw).

Asia: Asia is Green (www.asiaisgreen.com). **China:** The Business Environment Council Hong Kong (www.bed.org.hk), China Business Council for Sustainable Development (www.cbcsd.org.cn), Ministry of Environmental Protection (www.zhb.gov.cn), Clean Development Mechanisms in China (cdm.ccchina.gov.cn), Cleaner Production Centre (www.cncpn.org.cn), China CSR (www.chinacsr.com), The Responsible Supply Chain Association (www.csc9000.org.cn). **India:** (www.terieurope.org/docs/csr_state.pdf) Confederation of Indian Industry (www.sustainabledevelopment.in), TERI-BCSD (www.bcsd. ter.res.in), Cleaner Production Centre (www.npcindia.org). **Japan:** Japan Business Federation (www.keidanren.or.jp). **Kazakhstan:** Kazakhstan Business Council for Sustainable Development (www.kap. kz).**Korea:** Business Council for Sustainable Development Korea (www. kbcsd.or.kr), National Cleaner Production Center (www.kitech. re.kr). **Malaysia:** Business Council for Sustainable Development (www.bcsdm.com.my). **Mongolia:** Business Council for Sustainable Development (www.mongolchamber.mn). **Pakistan:** Pakistan Council of Renewable Energy Technologies (www.pcret.gov.pk/). **Philippines:** Philippine Business for the Environment (www.pbe.org.ph). **Taiwan:** Business Council for Sustainable Development Taiwan (www.bcsd.org. tw). **Thailand:** Business Council for Sustainable Development Thailand (www.tei.or.th/tbcsd). **Turkey:** Business Council for Sustainable Development Turkey (www.tbcsd.org). **Uzbekistan:** National Cleaner Production Centre (www.ncpc.uz). **Vietnam:** National Cleaner Production Center (www.vncpc.org).

Europe: European Commission (ec.europe.eu/environment/eussd), European Environment Agency (www.eea.eu.int), CSR Europe (www. csreurope.org). **Austria:** Centre for Corporate Citizenship (www. ccc-austria.at), respACT Austrian Business council for sustainable development (www.respact.at). **Croatia:** Business Council for Sustainable Development Croatia (www.hrpsor.hr). **Czech Republic:** Cleaner Production Centre (www.cenia.cz). **Denmark:** Danish Council for Sustainable Business (www.rbenet.dk) The Danish Institute for Human Rights (www.humanrightsbusiness.org). **France:** Entreprises pour L'Environment (EpE) (www.epe-asso.org). **Germany:** Econsense is the Forum for Sustainable Development of German Business. Econsense provides information on the sustainable business practices of 23 German businesses(www.econsense.de/documents/praxisbeispiele_anim/index.html). **Hungary:** Business Council for Sustainable Development Hungary (www.bcsdh.hu), National Cleaner Production Centre (hcpc.uni-corvinus.hu). **Norway:** Confederation of Norwegian Enterprise (www.nho.no/csr). **Poland:** BI-NGO (www.bi-ngo.pl), Ecolabel EKO (www.pcbc.gov.pl), eFTE (www.efte.org) (www.fob.org.pl). **Portugal:** Business Council for Sustainable Development Portugal (www.bcsdportugal.org). **Romania:** Ministry for Small and Medium Enterprise Unit for Sustainable Enterprise Development (en.animmc.ro). **Russia:** Vernadsky Foundation (www.vernadsky.ru), National Environmental Management and Cleaner Production Center (www.ncpc.gubkin.ru and www.nwicpc.ru). **Serbia:** Cleaner Production Centre (www.cpc-serbia.org/csr.html). **Slovak Republic:** Cleaner Production Centre (www.scpc.sk). **Spain:** Fundacion Entorno (www.fundacionentorno.org), Fundacio Forum Ambiental (www.forumambiental.org). **Sweden:** Stockholm Environment Institute (www.sei.se). **UK:** Business Council for Sustainable Development UK (www.bcsd-uk.co.uk).

Middle East: Egypt: Association of Enterprises for Environmental Conservation (www.aeec.com.eg). **Israel:** Maala-Business for Social Responsibility founded in 1998 is a non-profit membership organization for business (www.maala.com.il). **Lebanon:** Cleaner Production Centre (www.lebanese-cpc.net). **United Arab Emirates:** Emirates Environmental Group (www.eeg-uae.org).

North America: United States: US Government and Sustainable Development (www.usda.gov/sustainable), US Business Council for Sustainable Development (www.usbcsd.org). **Canada:** (www.sdinfo.

gc.ca, www.ec.gc.ca/susdev_e.html, strategic.ic.gc.ca/sd), Environment Canada Economics and sustainability (www.ec.gc.ca/default. asp?lang=En&n=C07483BF-1), Canadian Government and Sustainable Development (www.sdinfo.gc.ca), (www.ec.gc.ca/susdev_e.html), (strategic.ic.gc.ca/sd).

South America: Argentina: (www.ceads.org.ar). **Bolivia:** (www. cedesbolivia.org). **Brazil:** CIVES (www.cives.org.br), FBDS www. fbds.org.br), Akatu Institute (www.akatu.net), CEBDS is the Brazilian Business Council for Sustainable Development (www.cebds.org.br), Ethos is an NGO which works with companies to manage their operations in a socially responsible manner (www.ethos.org.br), The Brazilian Institute of Corporate Governance (www.ibgc.org.br). **Chile:** Accion RSE (www.accionrse.cl). **Costa Rica:** (AED www.aedcr.com). **Columbia:** (www.cecodes.org.co). **Cuba:** Cleaner Production Centre (www.redpml.cu). **Dominican Republic:** (medioambienterd.org/category/industria/). **Ecuador:** (www.cemdes.org). **El Salvador:** (www. cedes.org.sv) Centro Nactional de Produccion mas Limpia (www.cnpml. org.sv). **Guatemala:** (www.centrarse.org) National Cleaner Production Centre (www.cgpl.org.gt). **Honduras:** (www.cehdes.org). **Nicaragua:** (www.unirse.org) Centro de Produccion Mas Limpia (www.cpminic. org.ni). **Mexico:** New Ventures Mexico (www.nvm.org.mx), The Mexican Cleaner Production Center/IPN (www.cmpl.com.mx). Ecobanca (www. ecobanca.org). CONIECO (www.conieco.com.mx) a league of environmentally concerned businesses. Certification: www.cemefi.org—the main CRS certifying entity www.pactomundialmexico.org.mx— the Global Compact in Mexico (www.bioagricoop.tripod.com.mx www.ceres-cert.com). **Panama:** IntegraRSE (www.integrarse.org.pa). **Paraguay:** Red de Empresa para el Desarrollo Sostenible (www.redes. org.py). **Peru:** Peru2021 (www.peru2021.org). **Uruguay:** DERES (www. deres.org.uy). **Venezuela:** CEVEDES Business Council for Sustainable Development Small island development network (www.sidsnet.org).

Oceania: Australia: Business Council of Australia (www.bca.com. au), Department of the Environment, Water, Heritage and the Arts (www.environment.gov.au). **New Zealand:** New Zealand Business

Council for Sustainable Development (www.nzcsd.org.nz), Sustainable Business Network (www.sustainable.org.nz), Zero Waste New Zealand Trust (www.zerowaste.co.nz), Ministry for the Environment (www. mfe.govt.nz).

How: keeping up to date

Getting up to date information from the web There are many different online news networks on sustainability issues. Each has its own flavour so take a look at all of them and find your favourite. All these have RSS, regular email newsletters and lots of interesting and fun information and cover business and non business issues. The boom of social networking sites online has also included many networks dedicated to social and environmental issues. Some such as Facebook, MySpace, LinkedIn, Responsible World Citizen and Ning allow you to connect with other people with the same interests as you or in some cases, create your own social network.

- *Hugg* is a collection of user submitted green news, articles and web sites (www.hugg.com/).
- *Grist* 'believe that news about green issues and sustainability living doesn't have to be predictable, demoralizing or dull'. They serve up the latest green news and trends as they say, with extra butter and salt (www.grist.org).
- *Treehugger* is dedicated to driving sustainability mainstream with green news, solutions and product information (www.treehugger. com/).
- *WorldChanging* is a solutions-based online magazine that brings together the tools, models and ideas for building a better future (www.worldchanging.com).
- *CSRWire* is a newswire for corporate social responsibility (www. csrwire.com).
- *Green Biz* is an online news and information resource on how to align environmental responsibility with business success (www. greenbiz.com).

- *PlanetArk* provides environmental world news courtesy of the Reuters news agency (www.planetark.com).
- *Green search engines* bring up both standard searches but some only bring up 'green' related topics. Check out Green maven (green-maven.com/), Green Planet search (www.greenplanetsearch.com), Green link central (www.greenlinkcentral.com), Gooef gooef.com/, Grenona www.greenona.com and Eco Seek www.ecoseek.net.
- *The Dictionary of Sustainable Management* is an open dictionary for business leaders and students of sustainability and business-related terms (www.sustainabilitydictionary.com/).
- *Wikia Green* is a resource being built online with information on everything green (green.wikia.com/wiki/Wikia_Green).
- *Springwise and Trendwatching* are networks of spotters around the world looking for smart new business ideas (www.springwise.com, www.trendwatching.com).
- *Google's green trends* allows you to compare the world's interest in your favourite topics. Enter up to five topics and see how often they've been searched on Google over time (www.google.com/trends).
- *Ecorazzi* provides the latest in green celebrity gossip (www.ecorazzi.com).

For up to date statistics and data

- *GlobeScan* has several global annual surveys including Corporate Social Responsibility Monitor, Survey of Sustainability Experts and its Climate Change Monitor (www.globescan.com/csrm_overview.htm).
- *The Cambridge Sustainability Research Digest* is a monthly briefing on a selection of the latest global research on leadership for sustainability, (www.cpi.cam.ac.uk/resources/publications/sustainability_research_digest.aspx).
- *Worldometers* provides world statistics updated in real time (www.worldometers.info).
- *The Little Green Data Book* has a succinct collection of information from the World Development Indicators report. Past yearly editions are available free online (www.worldbank.org).

- *International Futures* is a computer simulation of global systems for classroom and research purposes that can be used to understand demographics, economics, food, energy, the environment and international politics (www.ifsmodel.org).
- *GapMinder* is a non-profit venture promoting sustainable global development through the increased use and understanding of statistics (www.gapminder.org).
- *Show World* is a website where maps change their size. Instead of land mass, the size of each country will represent the data that you choose, social, environmental, etc. (show.mappingworlds.com/).

Reading list Below is a list of the books to read to get a better understanding of the general issues and to be inspired. There are also reading lists at the end of every chapter in the book.

- *Silent Spring* by Rachel Carson (1962) looks at the detrimental effects of pesticides on the environment. The book is often credited for helping launch the environmental movement.
- *The Ecology of Commerce* by Paul Hawken (1994) outlines the environmentally destructive aspects of many current business practices, but offers a vision of business adopting new practices to promote environmental restoration.
- *Guns, Germs and Steel: The Fates of Human Societies* by Diamond Jared (1997) argues that geographical and environmental factors shaped the modern world.
- *Cannibals with Forks* introduced the concept of the triple bottom line (1998) and *The Chrysalis Economic: How Citizen CEOS and Corporations can Fuse Values and Value Creation* (2001), both by John Elkington
- *Natural Capitalism* by Paul Hawken and Amory & Hunter Lovins (2000) explores the lucrative opportunities for business in an era of approaching environmental limits (available to download free of charge at www.natcap.org).
- *The Sustainability Advantage* (2002) and *The Next Sustainability Wave* (2005) by Bob Willard explore the business case for sustainability.

- *The Skeptical Environmentalist* by Bjorn Lomborg (2001) challenges widely held beliefs that the global environment is progressively getting worse using statistical information from internationally recognized research institutes.
- *The World Without Us* by Alan Weisman (2007) looks at how our planet would respond without the relentless pressures of human presence.

You Decide

- Some US hotels are reinventing the mini bar, well at least in certain luxury hotels. One green mini bar features coconut water, fermented tea, organic chocolate and water buffalo milk yogurt; another offers pure Tasmanian rain water, allegedly the purest in the world, coming all the way from Australia.
- Luxury items cost more to purchase, but are made from the highest quality material, often by hand. They are kept for generations and generations and do not get thrown out.
- A company has an advertising campaign about how they reduced their CO2 emissions by 10% this year. What they don't mention is that this was required by law.
- An electric can opener is labelled as being made of recycled material, recyclable and energy efficient. But can something that many consider to be fundamentally unnecessary (what is wrong with a hand held model?) really be called sustainable?
- If a company which says that their product is carbon neutral but it really is because the company paid money to a charity rather than doing any work to reduce their carbon, can they then really say they are carbon neutral, and use that as the basis of their advertising campaign?
- How do you choose over social or the environment? A company may be actively advertising that their product is fair trade and against animal testing, but is it good for your health? For the environment? Is it full of chemicals?

Endnotes

1. signature103.wordpress.com/2008/03/02/50-facts-that-should-change-the-world/.
2. sdgateway.net/introsd/definitions.htm.
3. www.greenbiz.com/podcast/2008/04/14/business-engine-creating-environmental-stewards.
4. On GE's website www.ge.com/files/usa/company/news/global_environmental_challenges.pdf, in a speech to the George Washington School of Business in 2005.
5. Jose Gergio Gabrielli de Azevedo, 'The Greening of Petrobras', *Harvard Business Review*, March 2009, pp. 43–47.
6. Grow, B., Hamm, S. and Lee L. (2005), 'The Debate Over Doing Good', *Business Week*, 15 August 2005, p. 76.
7. Bob Willard, *The Next Sustainability Wave*, Greenleaf Publishing, p. 21.
8. Michael E. Porter and Mark R. Kramer, 'Strategy and Society: The Link between Competitive Advantage and Corporate Social Responsibility', *Harvard Business Review*, December 2006.
9. www.accountancyage.com/accountancyage/features/2193566/accountinf-sustainability.
10. www.cdproject.net/cdp5-new-york-launch-bill-clinton-video.asp.
11. 'Industry as a partner for sustainable development', Accounting, Association of Chartered Certified Accountants (ACCA) and the United Nations Environment Programme, 2002, available online free of charge, quote taken from p. 7.
12. 'An Introduction to Environmental Accounting as a Business Management Tool: Key Concepts and Terms', US EPA.
13. This quote and the information in this section taken from Accountability reports, The Materiality Report and Redefining Materiality.
14. Accountability www.accountability21.net/uploadedFiles/publications/Redefining%20Materiality%20%20Full%20Report.pdf www.accountability21.net/materiality.
15. www.unglobalcompact.org/docs/news_events/8.1/un_rainforest_alliance.pdf.
16. www.projectsigma.co.uk/Toolkit/SIGMASustainabilityAccounting.pdf.

17. www.kpmg.com/SiteCollectionDocuments/International-corporate-responsibility-survey-2008.pdf.
18. Molly Finn, Gary M. Rahl and William Rowe Jr (Booz Allen Hamilton), 'Unrecognized Assets', *strategy=business* www.strategy-business.com/press/enewsarticle/enews113006?pg5+5.
19. Last four points from www.ifac.org/members/DownLoads/Scene_Setting_Article.pdf.
20. Herman Daly, 'On a road to disaster', p. 46–47, *New Scientist*, 18 October 2008.
21. eng.me.go.kr/docs/news/press_view.html?seq=282& page=8mcode.
22. ecosystemmarketplace.com/documents/cms_documents/PES_Matrix_Profiles_PROFOR.pdf.
23. 'A rising tide', *The Economist*, 20 September 2008, quote from Dan Flavey.
24. Herman Daly, 'On a road to disaster', *New Scientist* 18 October p. 47.
25. www.accenture.com/Global/Research_and_Insights/Policy_And_Corporate_Affairs/Multi-PolarWorld.htm.
26. A special report on globalization, *The Economist*, 20th September 2008.
27. From environmental economics blog.
28. www.wbcsd.org/plugins/DocSearch/details.asp?type5DocDet&ObjectId5MzE4Nzg.
29. Jason Scorse, 'What Environmentalists need to know about economics', pp. 33–37 http://policy.miis.edu/docs/IEP/books/Scorse_What_Environmentalists_Need_to_Know_entire.pdf.
30. www.wbcsd.org/plugins/DocSearch/details.asp?type5DocDet&ObjectId5MzI5MDM.
31. 'How much is an Ecosystem Worth? Assessing the Economic Value of Conservation', World Bank, IUCN and The Nature Conservancy, International Bank for Reconstruction and Development/World Bank, 2004.
32. Marlies Wierenga, 'A Brief Introduction to Environmental Ecomomics', ELAW August 2003 p. 2.
33. Marlies Wierenga, 'A Brief Introduction to Environmental Ecomomics', ELAW August 2003 p. 3, available at www.elaw.org/node/ 2475.
34. p. 2.
35. *EntreNews*, EFMD's Entrepreneurship Innovation and Small Business network Special Issue 1/2006 www.efmd.org/attachments/tmpl_1_art_050222usmw_att_060627bxsd.pdf.
36. www.skollfoundation.org/media/skoll_docs/2007SP_feature_martinosberg.pdf.
37. 'The Social Intrapreneur', A field guide for corporate changemakers based on interviews with 20 social intrapraneurs www.sustainability.com/consultingservices/entrepreneurshipandInnovation.asp.
38. blog.guykawasaki.com/2006/01/the_art_of_intr.html.

39. newsnet.byu.edu/story.cfm/68895. beyondgoodintentions.wordpress.com/2007/09/07/ssir-micro-franchise-against-malaria-for-profits-healing-and-enriching-the-rural-poor-in-kenya/.

40. Report of the Round Table on Fostering CSR among SMEs, EU ec.europa.eu/enterprise/csr/documents/smes_rt_final_report.pdf, www.iblf.org/docs/SocialEnterprise.pdf and IBLF Linkages are the sources for this section.

41. www.unep.fr/shared/publications/pdf/DTIx0763xPA-TalkWalk.pdf.

42. www.unssc.org/web/hrb Human Rights and Business Learning Tool.

43. www.fairtrade.net/figures.html.

44. Saul W. Gellerman, published in 'Why "Good" Managers Make Bad Ethical Choices', *Harvard Business Review*, July–August 1986.

45. www.ethics.org/resources/decision-making-process.asp.

46. www.unepfi.org/fileadmin/documents/materiality1/cg_deutsche_bank_2004.pdf.

47. 'Business Against Corruption: A framework for action', Transparency International, The Global Compact and IBLF.

48. www.unglobalcompact.org/docs/news_events/8.1/clean_business_is_good_business.pdf.

49. www.business-ethics.org/research.html the International Business Ethics Institute has a research project on 'Creating a non-retaliatory workplace' to address this issue.

50. Joseph L Badaracco Jr, Allen P. Webb, 'Business Ethics, A view from the trenches', *California Management Review* Vol. 37, No 2 Winter 1995 p. 2.

51. 'Banking on Sustainability', IFC p. 9.

52. p. 12 CFA.

53. www.ft.com/cms/s/0/0dbb3a24-e406-11dd-8274-0000779fd2ac.html?nclick_check=1.

54. www.fastcompany.com/magazine/110/next-reading-list.html.

55. 'The Prudent Investor', from Generation IM Foundation, p. 6.

56. www.cfapubs.org/doi/pdf/10.2469/ccb.v2008.n2.1.

57. 'How Green is the Deal? The Growing Role of Sustainability in M&A', Deloitte. 2008 available online free of charge at www.deloitte.com/dtt/cda/doc/content/US_M&A_How_Green_Is_the_Deal.pdf.

58. World Wealth Report 2008 by Capgemini and Merrill Lynch www.ml.com/media/100472.pdf. Also see the Eurosif study, www.eurosif.org/publications/HNWI_sustainable_investment_study.

59. www.greenbiz.com/news/2008/10/20/argentina.

60. www.uncdf.org/english/microfinance/pubs/newsletter/pages/2005_06/year_update.php#a2 Microfinance – Where we are now and where we are headed by Elizabeth Littlefield CGAP CEO, International Year of Microcredit 2005 Newsletter Issue 13 June 2005.

61. Anthony Kleanthous and Jules Peck, 'Let Them Eat Cake', WWF 2004 www.wwf.org.uk/filelibrary/pdf/let_them_eat_cake_abridged.pdf.

62. www.greenmarketing.com/index.php/articles/complete/power-of-green/.
63. United Nations Environment Programme/Wuppertal Institute Collaborating Centre on Sustainable Consumption and Production (UNEP CSCP).
64. One of the breakthrough ideas of 2007 in Harvard Business Reviews by the Fraser Consulting group
65. biggreenpurse.com.
66. blog.inc.com/the-eco-capitalist/2008/06/should_green_products_be_price.html accessed October 23, 2008.
67. Ken Peattie, 'Rethinking Marketing: Shifting to a greener paradigm' in *Greener Marketing* by Martin Charter, Greenleaf Publishing, p. 62.
68. www.giraerespira.legambiente.org/giraerespira/schede%20pdf/allegrini.pdf for a picture.
69. findarticles.com/p/articles/mi_m1310/is_1993_Sept/ai_14526975.
70. www.csrwire.com/News/14723.
71. www.globalecolabelling.net/pdf/pub_pdf01.pdf.
72. Philip Kotler, *Social Marketing*, Free Press, p. 9.
73. Quote from (Utopies). Taken from UNEP walk the talk.
74. foundationcenter.org/getstarted/faqs/html/cause_marketing.html.
75 www.innocentdrinks.co.uk/thebigknit/ to see all the fancy hat creations.
76. www.nytimes.com/2009/01/31/science/earth/31compete.html?_r=1.
77. www.neurosciencemarketing.com/blog/articles/green-marketing-work.htm.
78. Eric Phu, 'The little black squiggles that will change your marketing', by *Marketing*, September 2008 pp. 80–81 www.marketingmag.com.au.
79. greenormal.blogspot.com/2008/06/green-washing-vs-green-marketing-new.html accessed 27 October 2008.
80. Envirowise, 'Cleaner Product Design: an introduction to cleaner design', p. 6. Other three stats from Envirowise, 'GG296 Cleaner Product Design: a practical approach', both first published in September 2001 p. 8.
81. www.hp.com/hpinfo/globalcitizenship/environment/productdesign/design.html.
82. Based on the 12 Principles of Green Chemistry from Paul T. Anastas and John C. Warner, *Green Chemistry: Theory and Practice*. New York: Oxford University Press, 1998 and www.epa.gov/gcc/pubs/principles.html accessed 20 October 2008.
83. www.unep.fr/shared/publications/pdf/DTIx0585xPA-WhyLifeCycleEN.pdf.
84. EarthEnterprise Tool-kit, 1994 International Institute for Sustainable Development www.iisd.org/pdf/eetoolkit.pdf.
85. Forum for the Future, Clean Capital Financing clean technology firms in the UK.
86. Power from Kites www.wired.com/science/discoveries/news/2006/10/71908.

87. DHL press release on Eco-friendly sea transport from Bremen to Venezuela – first company to use ocean-going cargo vessel with wind propulsion system: www.us.danzas.com/frameset.cgi?winLocation=http:// www.us.danzas.com/whatsnew/pressreleases/2008/0118.html.

88. Bennett Daviss, 'Green sky thinking: eight ways to a cleaner flying future' *New Scientist*, www.newscientist.com/article/mg19325921.600-green-sky-thinking-eight-ways-to-a-cleaner-flying-future.html.

89. Ed Douglas, 'There's gold in them there landfills', *New Scientist*, 01 October 2008 www.newscientist.com/article/mg20026761.500-theres-gold-in-them-there-landfills.html.

90. Originally from 'Pedestrians to Generate Power', www.timesonline.co.uk, taken from IEMA 16 June 2008 p. 8.

91. www.unep.fr/shared/publications/pdf/DTIx0585xPA-WhyLife-cycleEN.pdf.

92. Quote taken from WBCSD HR Publication.

93. Boards must become better people managers, Doug Jukes, Global Head of People KPMG 2 November 2007 Australian Financial Review, accessed 1 Oct through LBS Portal Library.

94. Beth Holmes, 'Good to be green' *HourGlass* HR Issue 11 September 2008, PwC, p. 27.

95. Bob Doppelt, *Leading Change Towards Sustainability*, Greenleaf Publications, 2003, p. 181.

96. www.wbcsd.org/web/publications/case/sc_johnson_greenlist_full_case_final_web.pdf.

97. For a more complete list see p. 9 of WBCSD HR report taken from 'Helping People Learn', CIPD, 2004.

98. Example taken from p. 21 Corporate Citizenship – Employees and the Community, www.prnewswire.co.uk/cgi/news/release?id=104653.

99. www.Greatplacestowork.com/great/results.php.

100. www.kpmg.co.uk/news/detail.cfm?pr=3107.

101. Duncan Angwin, Stephen Cummings and Chris Smith, *The Strategy Pathfinders*, Blackwell Publishing, 2007, p. 7.

102. www.excelpartnership.ca/documents/Sustainability_Lens.pdf.

103. Bob Willard, *The Next Sustainability Wave*, New Society Publishers, April 2005, p. 90.

104. GE ecomagination Report 2007 www.ecomagination.com/report.

105. ecopreneurist.com/2009/01/11/is-greening-your-business-a-distraction/.

106. www.ssireview.org/articles/entry/lobbying_for_good/.

107. www.projectsigma.co.uk/Toolkit/SIGMASustainabilityAccounting.pdf.

108. Development Collaborations: None of Our Business? Non-Governmental Organization Transformation and the Evolution of Cross Sectoral Partnerships in the 21st century by Gib Bulloch, 2008, Accenture.

109. Example taken from www.sustainability.com/downloads_public/ insight_general/Successful_Stakeholder_Engagement.pdf.

110. www.uneptie.org/outreach/home/SE_%20Handbook(sm).pdf P1: Mapping your stakeholders p. 22 volume 2.

111. Michael E. Porter and Mark R. Kramer, 'Strategy and Society: The Link Between Competitive Advantage and Corporate Social Responsibility', *Harvard Business Review*, December 2006.

112. The Future of Corporate Responsibility Codes, Standards and Frameworks. by Ernst Ligteringen and Simon Zadek definition taken from p.1.

113. Business for Social Responsibility. Green Building Design Issue Brief www. bsr.org/research/issue-brief-details.cfm?DocumentID=49772.

114. www.rmi.org/images/other/GDS/D94-27_GBBL.pdf.

115. ert.rmi.org/files/documents/CGU.RMI.pdf.

116. www.cyclefriendlyemployers.org.uk/img/Conference_SK.pdf.

117. www.unepfi.org/fileadmin/documents/greenprods_01.pdf.

118. www.greenbiz.com/resources/resource/good-green-jobs.

119. www.wbcsd.org/DocRoot/o8WwB2HBJZBiv21xDqa7/sl-devactors.pdf p. 25.

120. 'Carbon market worth up to $118 bln in 2008-report', *Reuters*, 8 Jan 2009.

Index